ANCIENT MONUMENTS AND ARCHAEOLOGICAL AREAS ACT 1979 (UK)

Updated as of March 26, 2018

THE LAW LIBRARY

TABLE OF CONTENTS

Introductory Text	4
Part I Ancient Monuments	4
General provisions as to compensation for depreciation under Part I.	61
Disposal of land acquired under Part I.	61
Voluntary contributions towards expenditure under Part I.	62
Interpretation of Part I.	62
Part 1A Inventories of gardens and designed landscapes and of battlefields	63
Part II Archaeological Areas	65
Interpretation of Part II.	72
Part III Miscellaneous and Supplemental	72
Schedules	93
Schedule 1. Control of Works Affecting Scheduled Monuments	93
Schedule 2. DETERMINATION OF CERTAIN APPEALS BY PERSON APPOINTED BY THE SCOTTISH MINISTERS	102
Schedule 3. Designation Orders	104
Schedule 4. Transitional Provisions	107
Schedule 5. Consequential amendments	110
Schedule 6. Enactments Repealed	112
Open Government Licence v3.0	112

Introductory Text

Ancient Monuments and Archaeological Areas Act 1979

1979 CHAPTER 46

An Act to consolidate and amend the law relating to ancient monuments; to make provision for the investigation, preservation and recording of matters of archaeological or historical interest and (in connection therewith) for the regulation of operations or activities affecting such matters; to provide for the recovery of grants under section 10 of the Town and Country Planning (Amendment) Act 1972 or under section 4 of the Historic Buildings and Ancient Monuments Act 1953 in certain circumstances; and to provide for grants by the Secretary of State to the Architectural Heritage Fund.

[4th April 1979]

Modifications etc. (not altering text)

C1. Act extended by Gas Act 1986 (c.44, SIF 44:2), s. 67. (1)(3), Sch. 7 para. 2. (1)(xxxvii), Sch. 8 para. 33

C2. Act amended (E.W.) by Water Act 1989 (c.15, SIF 130), ss. 58. (7), 101. (1), 141. (6), 160. (1)(2)(4), 189. (4)–(10), 190, 193. (1), Sch. 25 para. 1. (2)(xxiii), Sch. 26 paras. 3. (1)(2), 17, 40. (4), 57. (6), 58

C3. Act extended by Electricity Act 1989 (c.29, SIF 44:1), s. 112. (1)(3), Sch. 16 para. 1. (1)(xxxiii), Sch. 17 paras. 33, 35. (1)

C4. Act modified (17.7.1992) by S.I. 1992/1732, arts. 1, 3. (1)

C5. Act amended (1.3.1996) by 1995 c. 45, s. 16. (1), Sch. 4 para. 2. (1)(xxvii); S.I. 1996/218, art.2

C6. Act restricted (18.12.1996) by 1996 c. 61, s. 12, Sch. 7 para. 4. (4)

Act except the Treasury function under s. 50: powers transferred (1.7.1999) by virtue of S.I. 1999/672, art. 2, Sch.1

Act modified (6.5.1999) by S.I. 1999/677, art. 3.

C7. Act (except Pt. II) extended (S.) (8.9.2000) by 2000 asp 10, s. 36, Sch. 5 para. 7 (with s. 32); S.I. 2000/312, art. 2

C8. Act modified (30.5.2007) by National Assembly for Wales Commission (Crown Status) (No.2) Order 2007 (S.I. 2007/1353), art. 3

C9. Act restricted (22.7.2008) by Crossrail Act 2008 (c. 18), Sch. 9 para. 4. (4)

C10. Act transfer of functions (2.7.2012) by The British Waterways Board (Transfer of Functions) Order 2012 (S.I. 2012/1659), art. 2, Sch. 1 (with arts. 4-6)

Commencement Information

I1. Act not in force at Royal Assent see s. 65. (3); Act wholly in force at 14.4.1982

Part I Ancient Monuments

Part I Ancient Monuments

Modifications etc. (not altering text)
C1. Pt. I (ss. 1-32) extended (E.W.) (19.9.1995) by 1995 c. 25, ss. 70, 125. (2), Sch. 9 para.10. (1) (with ss. 7. (6), 115, 117, Sch. 8 para. 7)

1 Schedule of monuments.

(1) [F1. The Secretary of State] [F1. Historic Environment Scotland] shall compile and maintain for the purposes of this Act (in such form as [F2he] [F2it] thinks fit) a schedule of monuments (referred to below in this Act as "the Schedule").
(2) The Secretary of State shall on first compiling the Schedule include therein—
   (a) any monument included in the list last published before the commencement of this Act under section 12 of the M1. Ancient Monuments Consolidation and Amendment Act 1913; and
   (b) any monument in respect of which the Secretary of State has before the commencement of this Act served notice on any person in accordance with section 6. (1) of the M2. Ancient Monuments Act 1931 of his intention to include it in a list to be published under section 12.
(3) Subject to subsection (4) below, [F3the Secretary of State] [F3. Historic Environment Scotland] may on first compiling the Schedule or at any time thereafter include therein any monument which appears to [F4him] [F4it] to be of national importance.
[F5 The Secretary of State shall consult the Historic Buildings and Monuments Commission for England (in this Act referred to as " the Commission ") before he includes in the Schedule a monument situated in England.]
(4) The power of [F6the Secretary of State] [F6. Historic Environment Scotland] under subsection (3) above to include any monument in the Schedule does not apply to any structure which is occupied as a dwelling house by any person other than a person employed as the caretaker thereof or his family.
(5) [F7. The Secretary of State] [F7. Historic Environment Scotland] may—
   (a) exclude any monument from the Schedule; or
   (b) amend the entry in the Schedule relating to any monument (whether by excluding anything previously included as part of the monument or adding anything not previously so included, or otherwise).
[F8. In the case of a monument situated in England, the Secretary of State shall consult with the Commission before he makes an exclusion or amendment.]
(6) [F9. As soon as may be after—
   (a) including any monument in the Schedule under subsection (3) above;
   (b) amending the entry in the Schedule relating to any monument; or
   (c) excluding any monument from the Schedule;
the Secretary of State shall [F10. (subject to subsection (6. A) below)] inform the owner and (if the owner is not the occupier) the occupier of the monument, and any local authority in whose area the monument is situated, of the action taken and, in a case falling within paragraph (a) or (b) above, shall also send to him or them a copy of the entry or (as the case may be) of the amended entry in the Schedule relating to that monument.]
[F9. Where Historic Environment Scotland—
   (a) includes a monument in the Schedule under subsection (3),
   (b) amends the entry in the Schedule relating to a monument, or
   (c) excludes a monument from the Schedule,
it must notify such persons as may be prescribed in such form and manner, and within such time, as may be prescribed of the action taken.]
[F11. (6. A) Subsection (6) above shall not apply as regards a monument situated in England but, as soon as may be after acting as mentioned in paragraph (a), (b) or (c) of that subsection as regards such a monument, the Secretary of State shall inform the Commision of the action taken and, in a case falling within paragraph (a) or (b) of that subsection, shall also send to the Commission a copy of the entry or (as the case may be) of the amended entry in the Schedule

relating to that monument.]
(7) [F12[F13. Subject to subsection (7. A) below] The Secretary of State shall from time to time publish a list of all the monuments which are for the time being included in the Schedule, whether as a single list or in sections containing the monuments situated in particular areas; but in the case of a list published in sections, all sections of the list need not be published simultaneously.]
[F14. (7. A)Subsection (7) above shall not apply as regards monuments situated in England, but the Secretary of State shall from time to time supply the Commission with a list of all the monuments which are so situated and are for the time being included in the Schedule, whether as a single list or in sections containing the monuments situated in particular areas; but in the case of a list supplied in sections, all sections of the list need not be supplied simultaneously.]
(8) [F12. The Secretary of State may from time to time publish amendments of any list published under subsection (7) above, and any such list (as amended) shall be evidence of the inclusion in the Schedule for the time being—

(a) of the monuments listed; and

(b) of any matters purporting to be reproduced in the list from the entries in the Schedule relating to the monuments listed.]

[F15. (8. A)The Secretary of State shall from time to time supply the Commission with amendments of any list supplied under subsection (7. A) above.]
(9) An entry in the Schedule recording the inclusion therein of a monument situated in England and Wales shall be a local land charge.
(10) It shall be competent to record in the Register of Sasines—

(a) a certified copy of the entry or (as the case may be) the amended entry in the Schedule relating to any monument in Scotland which is heritable; and

(b) where any such monument is excluded from the Schedule and a certified copy of the entry in the Schedule relating to it has previously been so recorded under paragraph (a) above, a certificate issued by or on behalf of [F16the Secretary of State] [F16. Historic Environment Scotland] stating that it has been so excluded.

(11) In this Act "scheduled monument" means any monument which is for the time being included in the Schedule.

Amendments (Textual)

F1. Words in s. 1. (1) substituted (S.) (27.2.2015 for specified purposes, 1.10.2015 in so far as not already in force) by Historic Environment Scotland Act 2014 (asp 19), s. 31. (2), sch. 2 para. 2. (a)(i) (with ss. 29, 30); S.S.I. 2015/31, art. 2, sch.; S.S.I. 2015/196, art. 2, sch.

F2. Word in s. 1. (1) substituted (S.) (27.2.2015 for specified purposes, 1.10.2015 in so far as not already in force) by Historic Environment Scotland Act 2014 (asp 19), s. 31. (2), sch. 2 para. 2. (a)(ii) (with ss. 29, 30); S.S.I. 2015/31, art. 2, sch.; S.S.I. 2015/196, art. 2, sch.

F3. Words in s. 1. (3) substituted (S.) (27.2.2015 for specified purposes, 1.10.2015 in so far as not already in force) by Historic Environment Scotland Act 2014 (asp 19), s. 31. (2), sch. 2 para. 2. (b)(i) (with ss. 29, 30); S.S.I. 2015/31, art. 2, sch.; S.S.I. 2015/196, art. 2, sch.

F4. Word in s. 1. (3) substituted (S.) (27.2.2015 for specified purposes, 1.10.2015 in so far as not already in force) by Historic Environment Scotland Act 2014 (asp 19), s. 31. (2), sch. 2 para. 2. (b)(ii) (with ss. 29, 30); S.S.I. 2015/31, art. 2, sch.; S.S.I. 2015/196, art. 2, sch.

F5. Words inserted by National Heritage Act 1983 (c. 47, SIF 78), s. 41, Sch. 4 para. 25. (2)

F6. Words in s. 1. (4) substituted (S.) (27.2.2015 for specified purposes, 1.10.2015 in so far as not already in force) by Historic Environment Scotland Act 2014 (asp 19), s. 31. (2), sch. 2 para. 2. (c) (with ss. 29, 30); S.S.I. 2015/31, art. 2, sch.; S.S.I. 2015/196, art. 2, sch.

F7. Words in s. 1. (5) substituted (S.) (27.2.2015 for specified purposes, 1.10.2015 in so far as not already in force) by Historic Environment Scotland Act 2014 (asp 19), s. 31. (2), sch. 2 para. 2. (d) (with ss. 29, 30); S.S.I. 2015/31, art. 2, sch.; S.S.I. 2015/196, art. 2, sch.

F8. Words inserted by National Heritage Act 1983 (c. 47, SIF 78), s. 41, Sch. 4 para. 25. (3)

F9. S. 1. (6) substituted (27.2.2015 for specified purposes, 1.10.2015 in so far as not already in force) by Historic Environment Scotland Act 2014 (asp 19), s. 31. (2), sch. 2 para. 2. (e) (with ss. 29, 30); S.S.I. 2015/31, art. 2, sch.; S.S.I. 2015/196, art. 2, sch.

F10. Words inserted by National Heritage Act 1983 (c. 47, SIF 78), s. 41, Sch. 4 para. 25. (4)
F11. S. 1. (6. A) inserted by National Heritage Act 1983 (c. 47, SIF 78), s. 41, Sch. 4 para. 25. (5)(9)
F12. S. 1. (7)(8) repealed (S.) (27.2.2015 for specified purposes, 1.10.2015 in so far as not already in force) by Historic Environment Scotland Act 2014 (asp 19), s. 31. (2), sch. 2 para. 2. (f) (with ss. 29, 30); S.S.I. 2015/31, art. 2, sch.; S.S.I. 2015/196, art. 2, sch.
F13. Words inserted by National Heritage Act 1983 (c. 47, SIF 78), s. 41, Sch. 4 para. 25. (6)
F14. S. 1. (7. A) inserted by National Heritage Act 1983 (c. 47, SIF 78), s. 41, Sch. 4 para. 25. (7)
F15. S. 1. (8. A) inserted by National Heritage Act 1983 (c. 47, SIF 78), s. 41, Sch. 4 para. 25. (8)
F16. Words in s. 1. (10)(b) substituted (S.) (27.2.2015 for specified purposes, 1.10.2015 in so far as not already in force) by Historic Environment Scotland Act 2014 (asp 19), s. 31. (2), sch. 2 para. 2. (g) (with ss. 29, 30); S.S.I. 2015/31, art. 2, sch.; S.S.I. 2015/196, art. 2, sch.
Modifications etc. (not altering text)
C2. S. 1. (6) savings for effects of 2014 asp 19, Sch. 2 para. 2. (e) (S.) (1.10.2015) by The Historic Environment Scotland Act 2014 (Saving, Transitional and Consequential Provisions) Order 2015 (S.S.I. 2015/239), arts. 1. (1), 2. (2)
C3. S. 1. (10)(b) savings for effects of 2014 asp 19, Sch. 2 para. 2. (g) (S.) (1.10.2015) by The Historic Environment Scotland Act 2014 (Saving, Transitional and Consequential Provisions) Order 2015 (S.S.I. 2015/239), arts. 1. (1), 3
Marginal Citations
M11913 c. 32.
M21931 c. 16.

[F171. A Commission's functions as to informing and publishing.

(1) As soon as may be after the Commission—
    (a) have been informed as mentioned in section 1. (6. A) of this Act, and
    (b) in a case falling within section 1. (6)(a) or (b) of this Act, have received a copy of the entry or (as the case may be) of the amended entry from the Secretary of State,
the Commission shall inform the owner and (if the owner is not the occupier) the occupier of the monument, and any local authority in whose area the monument is situated, of the inclusion, amendment or exclusion and, in a case falling within section 1. (6)(a) or (b), shall also send to him or them a copy of the entry or (as the case may be) of the amended entry in the Schedule relating to that monument.
(2) As soon as may be after the Commission receive a list or a section in pursuance of section 1. (7. A) of this Act, they shall publish the list or section (as the case may be).
(3) The Commission shall from time to time publish amendments of any list published under subsection (2) above, and any such list (as amended) shall be evidence of the inclusion in the Schedule for the time being—
    (a) of the monuments listed; and
    (b) of any matters purporting to be reproduced in the list from the entries in the Schedule relating to monuments listed.]
Amendments (Textual)
F17. S. 1. A inserted by National Heritage Act 1983 (c. 47, SIF 78), s. 41, Sch. 4 para. 26

[F181. BPublication of the ScheduleS

(1) Historic Environment Scotland must—
    (a) publish the Schedule compiled and maintained under section 1, and any amendments of the Schedule, and
    (b) make the Schedule available for public inspection,
in such manner as may be prescribed.

(2) The Scottish Ministers may by regulations make further provision for—
    (a) the publication of the Schedule,
    (b) the making of the Schedule available for public inspection,
    (c) the notification of the inclusion of a monument in, the amendment of an entry relating to a monument in or the exclusion of a monument from the Schedule.]
Amendments (Textual)
F18. S. 1. B inserted (27.2.2015 for specified purposes, 1.10.2015 in so far as not already in force) by Historic Environment Scotland Act 2014 (asp 19), s. 31. (2), sch. 2 para. 3 (with ss. 29, 30); S.S.I. 2015/31, art. 2, sch.; S.S.I. 2015/196, art. 2, sch.

[F191. CAppeal against inclusion etc. in Schedule of monumentsS

(1) This section applies where Historic Environment Scotland makes a decision—
    (a) to include a monument in the Schedule,
    (b) to amend an entry in the Schedule relating to a monument.
(2) A person mentioned in subsection (3) may appeal the decision to the Scottish Ministers.
(3) The person is—
    (a) the owner of the monument,
    (b) the tenant of the monument,
    (c) the occupier of the monument.
Amendments (Textual)
F19. Ss. 1. C-1. E inserted (27.2.2015 for specified purposes, 1.10.2015 in so far as not already in force) by Historic Environment Scotland Act 2014 (asp 19), s. 31. (2), sch. 2 para. 32 (with ss. 29, 30); S.S.I. 2015/31, art. 2, sch.; S.S.I. 2015/196, art. 2, sch.

1. DDetermination of appeals under section 1. CS

(1) The Scottish Ministers may—
    (a) dismiss an appeal under section 1. C,
    (b) allow such an appeal (in whole or in part).
(2) Where the Scottish Ministers allow an appeal, they may vary a part of the decision appealed against whether or not the appeal relates to that part of the decision.
(3) Where the Scottish Ministers allow an appeal, they may direct Historic Environment Scotland to exercise its power under section 1. (5) to modify the Schedule to give effect to their decision.
(4) Except as provided for by section 55, the decision of the Scottish Ministers on an appeal under section 1. C is final.
Amendments (Textual)
F19. Ss. 1. C-1. E inserted (27.2.2015 for specified purposes, 1.10.2015 in so far as not already in force) by Historic Environment Scotland Act 2014 (asp 19), s. 31. (2), sch. 2 para. 32 (with ss. 29, 30); S.S.I. 2015/31, art. 2, sch.; S.S.I. 2015/196, art. 2, sch.

1. EProcedure for appeals under section 1. CS

(1) The Scottish Ministers may by regulations make provision in connection with appeals under section 1. C, including provision about—
    (a) the grounds on which an appeal may be made,
    (b) the information that is to be provided to, or may be required by, the Scottish Ministers in connection with the appeal.
(2) Regulations under subsection (1) may also make provision about the procedure to be followed, including—
    (a) the form, manner and time for making an appeal,

(b) the notification of an appeal,
(c) the manner in which an appeal is to be conducted.
(3) Regulations made by virtue of subsection (2)(c) may also include provision that the manner in which an appeal, or any stage of an appeal, is to be conducted (as for example whether written submissions are to be presented or persons are to be heard) is to be at the discretion of the Scottish Ministers (or of a person appointed by them under this Act).
(4) Schedule 1. A (which makes provision about the determination of certain appeals by a person other than the Scottish Ministers) applies to appeals under section 1. C.]
Amendments (Textual)
F19. Ss. 1. C-1. E inserted (27.2.2015 for specified purposes, 1.10.2015 in so far as not already in force) by Historic Environment Scotland Act 2014 (asp 19), s. 31. (2), sch. 2 para. 32 (with ss. 29, 30); S.S.I. 2015/31, art. 2, sch.; S.S.I. 2015/196, art. 2, sch.

2 Control of works affecting scheduled monuments.

(1) If any person executes or causes or permits to be executed any works to which this section applies he shall be guilty of an offence unless the works are authorised under this Part of this Act [F20or by development consent].
(2) This section applies to any of the following works, that is to say—
(a) any works resulting in the demolition or destruction of or any damage to a scheduled monument;
(b) any works for the purpose of removing or repairing a scheduled monument or any part of it or of making any alterations or additions thereto; and
(c) any flooding or tipping operations on land in, on or under which there is a scheduled monument.
(3) Without prejudice to any other authority to execute works conferred under this Part of this Act, works to which this section applies are authorised under this Part of this Act if—
(a) the Secretary of State [F21or Historic Environment Scotland] has granted [F22written] consent (referred to below in this Act as "scheduled monument consent") for the execution of the works; and
(b) the works are executed in accordance with the terms of the consent and of any conditions attached to the consent.
[F23. (3. A)If—
(a) works to which this section applies have been executed without being authorised under this Part; and
(b) [F24the Scottish Ministers grant consent for the retention of the works,]
[F24consent for the retention of the works is granted by the Scottish Ministers or by Historic Environment Scotland,]
the works are authorised under this Part of this Act from the grant of the consent.
(3. B)References in this Act to scheduled monument consent include consent under subsection (3. A) above.]
(4) Scheduled monument consent may be granted either unconditionally or subject to conditions (whether with respect to the manner in which or the persons by whom the works or any of the works are to be executed or otherwise).
(5) Without prejudice to the generality of subsection (4) above, a condition attached to a scheduled monument consent may require that
[F25. (a)a person authorised by the Commission (in a case where the monument in question is situated in England), or
(b) [F26the Secretary of State] [F26. Historic Environment Scotland] or a person authorised by [F26the Secretary of State] [F26. Historic Environment Scotland] (in any other case)]
be afforded an opportunity, before any works to which the consent relates are begun, to examine the monument and its site and carry out such excavations therein as appear to [F27the Secretary of

State] [F27. Historic Environment Scotland] to be desirable for the purpose of archaeological investigation.

[F28. (5. A)The conditions that may be attached to scheduled monument consent under subsection (4) include a condition reserving specified details of the works (whether or not set out in the application for consent) for subsequent approval by Historic Environment Scotland.]

(6) Without prejudice to subsection (1) above, if a person executing or causing or permitting to be executed any works to which a scheduled monument consent relates fails to comply with any condition attached to the consent he shall be guilty of an offence, unless he proves that he took all reasonable precautions and exercised all due diligence to avoid contravening the condition.

(7) In any proceedings for an offence under this section in relation to works within subsection (2)(a) above it shall be a defence for the accused to prove that he took all reasonable precautions and exercised all due diligence to avoid or prevent damage to the monument.

(8) In any proceedings for an offence under this section in relation to works within subsection (2)(a) or (c) above it shall be a defence for the accused to [F29prove that] [F29show that, before executing, causing the execution of or, as the case may be, permitting the execution of the works—

(a) he had taken all reasonable steps to find out whether there was a scheduled monument within the area affected by the works, and]

he did not know and had no reason to believe that the monument was within the area affected by the works or (as the case may be) that it was a scheduled monument.

(9) In any proceedings for an offence under this section it shall be a defence to prove that the works were urgently necessary in the interests of safety or health and that notice in writing of the need for the works was given to [F30the Secretary of State] [F30. Historic Environment Scotland] as soon as reasonably practicable.

(10) A person guilty of an offence under this section shall be liable—

(a) on summary conviction or, in Scotland, on conviction before a court of summary jurisdiction, to a fine not exceeding [F31the statutory maximum] [F31£50,000]; or

(b) on conviction on indictment to a fine.

[F32. (10. A)In determining the amount of any fine to be imposed on a person under this section, the court shall in particular have regard to any financial benefit which has accrued or appears likely to accrue to the person in consequence of the offence.]

(11) Part I of Schedule 1 to this Act shall have effect with respect to applications for,[F33the manner of granting, and the form, content] and the effect of, scheduled monument consent.

Amendments (Textual)

F20. Words in s. 2. (1) inserted (1.3.2010) by Planning Act 2008 (c. 29), s. 241. (8), Sch. 2 para. 17 (with s. 226); S.I. 2010/101, art. 2 (with art. 6)

F21. Words in s. 2. (3)(a) inserted (S.) (27.2.2015 for specified purposes, 1.10.2015 in so far as not already in force) by Historic Environment Scotland Act 2014 (asp 19), s. 31. (2), sch. 2 para. 5. (a) (with ss. 29, 30); S.S.I. 2015/31, art. 2, sch.; S.S.I. 2015/196, art. 2, sch.

F22. Word in s. 2. (3)(a) repealed (S.) (1.12.2011) by Historic Environment (Amendment) (Scotland) Act 2011 (asp 3), ss. 2. (a), 33. (2); S.S.I. 2011/372, art. 2, Sch.

F23. S. 2. (3. A)(3. B) inserted (S.) (1.12.2011) by Historic Environment (Amendment) (Scotland) Act 2011 (asp 3), ss. 2. (b), 33. (2); S.S.I. 2011/372, art. 2, Sch.

F24. S. 2. (3. A)(b) substituted (27.2.2015 for specified purposes, 1.10.2015 in so far as not already in force) by Historic Environment Scotland Act 2014 (asp 19), s. 31. (2), sch. 2 para. 5. (b) (with ss. 29, 30); S.S.I. 2015/31, art. 2, sch.; S.S.I. 2015/196, art. 2, sch.

F25. Words substituted by National Heritage Act 1983 (c. 47, SIF 78), s. 41, Sch. 4 para. 27

F26. Words in s. 2. (5)(b) substituted (S.) (27.2.2015 for specified purposes, 1.10.2015 in so far as not already in force) by Historic Environment Scotland Act 2014 (asp 19), s. 31. (2), sch. 2 para. 5. (c) (with ss. 29, 30); S.S.I. 2015/31, art. 2, sch.; S.S.I. 2015/196, art. 2, sch.

F27. Words in s. 2. (5) substituted (S.) (27.2.2015 for specified purposes, 1.10.2015 in so far as not already in force) by Historic Environment Scotland Act 2014 (asp 19), s. 31. (2), sch. 2 para. 5. (c) (with ss. 29, 30); S.S.I. 2015/31, art. 2, sch.; S.S.I. 2015/196, art. 2, sch.

F28. S. 2. (5. A) inserted (27.2.2015 for specified purposes, 1.10.2015 in so far as not already in force) by Historic Environment Scotland Act 2014 (asp 19), s. 31. (2), sch. 2 para. 5. (d) (with ss. 29, 30); S.S.I. 2015/31, art. 2, sch.; S.S.I. 2015/196, art. 2, sch.

F29. Words in s. 2. (8) substituted (S.) (1.12.2011) by Historic Environment (Amendment) (Scotland) Act 2011 (asp 3), ss. 3. (2), 33. (2); S.S.I. 2011/372, art. 2, Sch.

F30. Words in s. 2. (9) substituted (S.) (27.2.2015 for specified purposes, 1.10.2015 in so far as not already in force) by Historic Environment Scotland Act 2014 (asp 19), s. 31. (2), sch. 2 para. 5. (e) (with ss. 29, 30); S.S.I. 2015/31, art. 2, sch.; S.S.I. 2015/196, art. 2, sch.

F31. Words in s. 2. (10) substituted (S.) (1.12.2011) by Historic Environment (Amendment) (Scotland) Act 2011 (asp 3), ss. 4. (2)(a), 33. (2); S.S.I. 2011/372, art. 2, Sch.

F32. S. 2. (10. A) inserted (S.) (1.12.2011) by Historic Environment (Amendment) (Scotland) Act 2011 (asp 3), ss. 4. (2)(b), 33. (2); S.S.I. 2011/372, art. 2, Sch.

F33. Words in s. 2. (11) inserted (S.) (30.6.2011 for specified purposes, 1.12.2011 in so far as not already in force) by Historic Environment (Amendment) (Scotland) Act 2011 (asp 3), ss. 15. (4), 33. (2); S.S.I. 2011/174, art. 2, Sch.; S.S.I. 2011/372, art. 2, Sch.

Modifications etc. (not altering text)

C4. S. 2 excluded (18.12.1996) by 1996 c. 61, s. 12, Sch. 7 para. 4. (2)

C5. S. 2 excluded (22.7.2008) by Crossrail Act 2008 (c. 18), Sch. 9 para. 4. (2)

C6. S. 2. (5)(b) savings for effects of 2014 asp 19, Sch. 2 para. 5. (c) (S.) (1.10.2015) by The Historic Environment Scotland Act 2014 (Saving, Transitional and Consequential Provisions) Order 2015 (S.S.I. 2015/239), arts. 1. (1), 4

C7. S. 2. (8) savings for effects of 2011 asp 3 s. 3. (2) (S.) (1.12.2011) by The Historic Environment (Amendment) (Scotland) Act 2011 (Saving, Transitional and Consequential Provisions) Order 2011 (S.S.I. 2011/377), arts. 1. (1), 2. (a)

C8. S. 2. (9) savings for effects of 2014 asp 19, Sch. 2 para. 5. (e) (S.) (1.10.2015) by The Historic Environment Scotland Act 2014 (Saving, Transitional and Consequential Provisions) Order 2015 (S.S.I. 2015/239), arts. 1. (1), 5

3 Grant of scheduled monument consent by order of the Secretary of State.

(1) The Secretary of State may by order grant scheduled monument consent for the execution of works of any class or description specified in the order, and any such consent may apply to scheduled monuments of any class or description so specified.

[F34. Before granting consent in relation to monuments of a class or description which includes monuments situated in England, the Secretary of State shall consult with the Commission in relation to the monuments so situated.]

(2) Any conditions attached by virtue of section 2 of this Act to a scheduled monument consent granted by an order under this section shall apply in such class or description of cases as may be specified in the order.

(3) The Secretary of State may direct that scheduled monument consent granted by an order under this section, shall not apply to any scheduled monument specified in the direction, and may withdraw any direction given under this subsection.

[F35. Before making a direction in relation to a monument situated in England, or withdrawing such a direction, the Secretary of State shall consult with the Commission.]

(4) A direction under subsection (3) above shall not take effect until notice of it has been served on the occupier or (if there is no occupier) on the owner of the monument in question.

(5) References below in this Act to a scheduled monument consent do not include references to a scheduled monument consent granted by an order under this section, unless the contrary intention is expressed.

Amendments (Textual)

F34. Words inserted by National Heritage Act 1983 (c. 47, SIF 78), s. 41, Sch. 4 para. 28. (2)

F35. Words inserted by National Heritage Act 1983 (c. 47, SIF 78), s. 41, Sch. 4 para. 28. (3)

[F363. AApplication for variation or discharge of conditionsS

(1) Any person interested in a scheduled monument in relation to which scheduled monument consent has been granted subject to conditions may apply to Historic Environment Scotland for the variation or discharge of the conditions.
(2) The application must indicate what variation or discharge of conditions is applied for and Part 1 of schedule 1 applies to such an application as it applies to an application for scheduled monument consent.
(3) Historic Environment Scotland or, as the case may be, the Scottish Ministers may, on such an application—
 (a) vary or discharge the conditions attached to the consent (whether or not the application relates to the condition varied or discharged),
 (b) add new conditions consequential upon the variation or discharge.]
Amendments (Textual)
F36. S. 3. A inserted (27.2.2015 for specified purposes, 1.10.2015 in so far as not already in force) by Historic Environment Scotland Act 2014 (asp 19), s. 31. (2), sch. 2 para. 6 (with ss. 29, 30); S.S.I. 2015/31, art. 2, sch.; S.S.I. 2015/196, art. 2, sch.

[F373. BReferral of certain applications to the Scottish MinistersS

(1) The Scottish Ministers may give directions requiring applications for—
 (a) scheduled monument consent,
 (b) variation or discharge of conditions to which scheduled monument consent is subject,
 (c) subsequent approval required by a condition to which scheduled monument consent is subject,
to be referred to them instead of being dealt with by Historic Environment Scotland.
(2) A direction under this section may relate either to a particular application or to applications of a class specified in the direction.
(3) A direction under this section may be withdrawn or modified by a subsequent direction.
(4) An application in respect of which a direction under this section has effect is to be referred to the Scottish Ministers accordingly.
(5) In determining an application under this section, the Scottish Ministers may deal with the application as if it had been made to them in the first instance.
(6) Except as provided for by section 55, the decision of the Scottish Ministers on any application referred to them under this section is final.
(7) The reference in subsection (1)(c) to scheduled monument consent includes a reference to consent granted by order under section 3.
Amendments (Textual)
F37. Ss. 3. B, 3. C inserted (27.2.2015 for specified purposes, 1.10.2015 in so far as not already in force) by Historic Environment Scotland Act 2014 (asp 19), s. 31. (2), sch. 2 para. 35 (with ss. 29, 30); S.S.I. 2015/31, art. 2, sch.; S.S.I. 2015/196, art. 2, sch.

3. CProcedure for referrals under section 3. BS

(1) The Scottish Ministers may by regulations make provision in connection with referrals under section 3. B, including provision about the information that is to be provided to, or may be required by, the Scottish Ministers in connection with the referral.
(2) Regulations under subsection (1) may also make provision about the procedure to be followed, including—

(a) the notification of a referral,
(b) the manner in which a referral is to be conducted.
(3) Regulations made by virtue of subsection (2)(b) may also include provision that the manner in which a referral, or any stage of a referral, is to be conducted (as for example whether written submissions are to be presented or persons are to be heard) is to be at the discretion of the Scottish Ministers (or of a person appointed by them under this Act).]
Amendments (Textual)
F37. Ss. 3. B, 3. C inserted (27.2.2015 for specified purposes, 1.10.2015 in so far as not already in force) by Historic Environment Scotland Act 2014 (asp 19), s. 31. (2), sch. 2 para. 35 (with ss. 29, 30); S.S.I. 2015/31, art. 2, sch.; S.S.I. 2015/196, art. 2, sch.

4 Duration, modification and revocation of scheduled monument consent.

(1) Subject to subsection (2) below, if no works to which a scheduled monument consent relates are executed or started within the period of five years beginning with the date on which the consent was granted, or such longer or shorter period as may be specified for the purposes of this subsection in the consent, the consent shall cease to have effect at the end of that period (unless previously revoked in accordance with the following provisions of this section).
(2) Subsection (1) above does not apply to a scheduled monument consent which provides that it shall cease to have effect at the end of a period specified therein.
(3) [F38. If it appears to the Secretary of State to be expedient to do so, he may by a direction given under this section modify or revoke a scheduled monument consent to any extent he considers expedient.
[F39. Where a direction would (if given) affect a monument situated in England, the Secretary of State shall consult with the Commission before he gives such a direction.]]
[F38. If it appears to Historic Environment Scotland that it is expedient to modify or revoke a scheduled monument consent, it may by order under this section modify or revoke the consent to such extent as it considers expedient.]
(4) [F38. Without prejudice to the generality of the power conferred by subsection (3) above to modify a scheduled monument consent, it extends to specifying a period, or altering any period specified, for the purposes of subsection (1) above, and to including a provision to the effect mentioned in subsection (2) above, or altering any period specified for the purposes of any such provision.]
[F38. The power conferred by subsection (3) to modify or revoke a scheduled monument consent in relation to any works may be exercised at any time before those works have been completed, but the modification or revocation does not affect so much of those works as has been previously carried out.]
(5) Part II of Schedule 1 to this Act shall have effect with respect to [F40directions] [F40orders] under this section modifying or revoking a scheduled monument consent.
Amendments (Textual)
F38. S. 4. (3)(4) substituted (27.2.2015 for specified purposes, 1.10.2015 in so far as not already in force) by Historic Environment Scotland Act 2014 (asp 19), s. 31. (2), sch. 2 para. 7. (a) (with ss. 29, 30); S.S.I. 2015/31, art. 2, sch.; S.S.I. 2015/196, art. 2, sch.
F39. Words inserted by National Heritage Act 1983 (c. 47, SIF 78), s. 41, Sch. 4 para. 29
F40. Word in s. 4. (5) substituted (S.) (27.2.2015 for specified purposes, 1.10.2015 in so far as not already in force) by Historic Environment Scotland Act 2014 (asp 19), s. 31. (2), sch. 2 para. 7. (b) (with ss. 29, 30); S.S.I. 2015/31, art. 2, sch.; S.S.I. 2015/196, art. 2, sch.
Modifications etc. (not altering text)
C9. S. 4 savings for effects of 2014 asp 19, Sch. 2 para. 7 (S.) (1.10.2015) by The Historic Environment Scotland Act 2014 (Saving, Transitional and Consequential Provisions) Order 2015 (S.S.I. 2015/239), arts. 1. (1), 7

[F41 4. A Modification and revocation of scheduled monument consent by Scottish Ministers S

(1) If it appears to the Scottish Ministers that it is expedient to modify or revoke a scheduled monument consent, they may by order under this section modify or revoke the consent to such extent as they consider expedient.
(2) The Scottish Ministers may not make an order under this section without consulting Historic Environment Scotland.
(3) Where the Scottish Ministers propose to make such an order, they must serve notice on—
    (a) the owner of the scheduled monument affected,
    (b) where the owner is not the occupier of the monument, the occupier, and
    (c) any other person who in their opinion will be affected by the order.
(4) The notice must specify the period (which must not be less than 28 days after its service) within which any person on whom it is served may require an opportunity of appearing before and being heard by a person appointed by the Scottish Ministers for the purpose.
(5) If within that period a person on whom the notice is served so requires, the Scottish Ministers must, before they make the order, give such an opportunity both to that person and to Historic Environment Scotland.
(6) The power conferred by this section to modify or revoke a scheduled monument consent in relation to any works may be exercised at any time before those works have been completed, but the modification or revocation does not affect so much of those works as has been previously carried out.
(7) An order under this section has effect as if it had been made by Historic Environment Scotland under section 4 and confirmed by the Scottish Ministers under paragraph 10 of Part 2 of schedule 1.]

Amendments (Textual)
F41. S. 4. A inserted (27.2.2015 for specified purposes, 1.10.2015 in so far as not already in force) by Historic Environment Scotland Act 2014 (asp 19), s. 31. (2), sch. 2 para. 8 (with ss. 29, 30); S.S.I. 2015/31, art. 2, sch.; S.S.I. 2015/196, art. 2, sch.

[F42 4. B Appeal in relation to scheduled monument consent S

(1) This section applies where Historic Environment Scotland makes a decision—
    (a) refusing an application for scheduled monument consent,
    (b) granting such an application subject to conditions,
    (c) refusing an application for variation or discharge of conditions to which a scheduled monument consent is subject,
    (d) granting such an application subject to conditions,
    (e) refusing an application for subsequent approval required by a condition to which a scheduled monument consent is subject.
(2) A person who made the application mentioned in subsection (1) may appeal the decision to the Scottish Ministers.
(3) A person may also appeal to the Scottish Ministers where Historic Environment Scotland has not given notice of its decision on an application mentioned in subsection (1)(a), (c) or (e) within the prescribed period or such other longer period as may be agreed between the applicant and Historic Environment Scotland.
(4) An appeal under this section may include the ground that—
    (a) the monument should not be included in the Schedule,
    (b) the entry in the Schedule relating to the monument should be amended.

Amendments (Textual)

F42. Ss. 4. B-4. D inserted (27.2.2015 for specified purposes, 1.10.2015 in so far as not already in force) by Historic Environment Scotland Act 2014 (asp 19), s. 31. (2), sch. 2 para. 33 (with ss. 29, 30); S.S.I. 2015/31, art. 2, sch.; S.S.I. 2015/196, art. 2, sch.

4. CDetermination of appeals under section 4. BS

(1) The Scottish Ministers may—
    (a) dismiss an appeal under section 4. B,
    (b) allow such an appeal (in whole or in part).
(2) In determining an appeal under section 4. B, the Scottish Ministers may deal with the application to which the appeal relates as if it had been made to them in the first instance.
(3) Where the Scottish Ministers allow an appeal, they may vary a part of the decision appealed against whether or not the appeal relates to that part of the decision.
(4) Subsection (5) applies where—
    (a) the grounds of appeal include the ground—
(i) that the monument should not be included in the Schedule, or
(ii) that the entry in the Schedule relating to the monument should be amended, and
    (b) the Scottish Ministers uphold that ground.
(5) The Scottish Ministers may direct Historic Environment Scotland to exercise its power under section 1. (5) to modify the Schedule to give effect to that decision.
(6) Except as provided for by section 55, the decision of the Scottish Ministers on an appeal under section 4. B is final.
Amendments (Textual)
F42. Ss. 4. B-4. D inserted (27.2.2015 for specified purposes, 1.10.2015 in so far as not already in force) by Historic Environment Scotland Act 2014 (asp 19), s. 31. (2), sch. 2 para. 33 (with ss. 29, 30); S.S.I. 2015/31, art. 2, sch.; S.S.I. 2015/196, art. 2, sch.

4. DProcedure for appeals under section 4. BS

(1) The Scottish Ministers may by regulations make provision in connection with appeals under section 4. B, including provision about—
    (a) subject to section 4. B(4), the grounds on which an appeal may be made,
    (b) the information that is to be provided to, or may be required by, the Scottish Ministers in connection with the appeal.
(2) Regulations under subsection (1) may also make provision about the procedure to be followed, including—
    (a) the form, manner and time for making an appeal,
    (b) the notification of an appeal,
    (c) the manner in which an appeal is to be conducted.
(3) Regulations made by virtue of subsection (2)(c) may also include provision that the manner in which an appeal, or any stage of an appeal, is to be conducted (as for example whether written submissions are to be presented or persons are to be heard) is to be at the discretion of the Scottish Ministers (or of a person appointed by them under this Act).
(4) Regulations under subsection (1) may also provide that an appeal in respect of an application—
    (a) for scheduled monument consent, or
    (b) for the variation or discharge of conditions to which such a consent is subject,
need not be entertained unless it is accompanied by a certificate in the prescribed form as to the interests in the monument to which the appeal relates.
(5) Sub-paragraphs (2) to (4) of paragraph 2 of schedule 1 apply to regulations imposing a requirement by virtue of subsection (4) as they apply to the requirement imposed by sub-paragraph (1) of that paragraph.

(6) Schedule 1. A (which makes provision about the determination of certain appeals by a person other than the Scottish Ministers) applies to appeals under section 4. B.]
Amendments (Textual)
F42. Ss. 4. B-4. D inserted (27.2.2015 for specified purposes, 1.10.2015 in so far as not already in force) by Historic Environment Scotland Act 2014 (asp 19), s. 31. (2), sch. 2 para. 33 (with ss. 29, 30); S.S.I. 2015/31, art. 2, sch.; S.S.I. 2015/196, art. 2, sch.

5 Execution of works for preservation of a scheduled monument by Secretary of State in cases of urgency.

(1) If it appears to [F43the Secretary of State] [F43. Historic Environment Scotland] that any works are urgently necessary for the preservation of a scheduled monument [F44he] [F44it] may enter the site of the monument and execute those works, after giving the owner and (if the owner is not the occupier) the occupier of the monument not less than seven days' notice in writing of [F45his] [F45its] intention to do so.
(2) Where the Secretary of State executes works under this section for repairing any damage to a scheduled monument—
    (a) any compensation order previously made in respect of that damage under [F46section 130 of the Powers of Criminal Courts (Sentencing) Act 2000] (compensation orders against convicted persons) in favour of any other person shall be enforceable (so far as not already complied with) as if it had been made in favour of the Secretary of State; and
    (b) any such order subsequently made in respect of that damage shall be made in favour of the Secretary of State.
[F47. (3)If it appears to the Secretary of State that any works are urgently necessary for the preservation of a scheduled monument situated in England, he may (instead of acting as mentioned in subsection (1) above) authorise the Commission to enter the site of the monument and execute the works as are specified in the authorisation.
(4) In that case, the Commission may enter the site and execute the works after giving the owner and (if the owner is not the occupier) the occupier of the monument not less than seven day's notice in writing of their intention to do so.
(5) Where the Secretary of State gives an authorisation under subsection (3) above, subsection (2) above shall have effect with the substitution of "Commission" for "Secretary of State" (in each place) and of "execute" for "executes".]
Amendments (Textual)
F43. Words in s. 5. (1) substituted (S.) (27.2.2015 for specified purposes, 1.10.2015 in so far as not already in force) by Historic Environment Scotland Act 2014 (asp 19), s. 31. (2), sch. 2 para. 9. (a) (with ss. 29, 30); S.S.I. 2015/31, art. 2, sch.; S.S.I. 2015/196, art. 2, sch.
F44. Word in s. 5. (1) substituted (S.) (27.2.2015 for specified purposes, 1.10.2015 in so far as not already in force) by Historic Environment Scotland Act 2014 (asp 19), s. 31. (2), sch. 2 para. 9. (b) (with ss. 29, 30); S.S.I. 2015/31, art. 2, sch.; S.S.I. 2015/196, art. 2, sch.
F45. Word in s. 5. (1) substituted (S.) (27.2.2015 for specified purposes, 1.10.2015 in so far as not already in force) by Historic Environment Scotland Act 2014 (asp 19), s. 31. (2), sch. 2 para. 9. (c) (with ss. 29, 30); S.S.I. 2015/31, art. 2, sch.; S.S.I. 2015/196, art. 2, sch.
F46. Words in s. 5. (2)(a) substituted (25.8.2000) by 2000 c. 6, ss. 165, 168. (1), Sch. 9 para. 58
F47. S. 5. (3)–(5) inserted by National Heritage Act 1983 (c. 47, SIF 78), s. 41, Sch. 4 para. 30

6 Powers of entry for inspection of scheduled monuments, etc.

(1) Any person duly authorised in writing by [F48the Secretary of State] [F48. Historic Environment Scotland] may at any reasonable time enter any land for the purpose of inspecting any scheduled monument in, on or under the land with a view to ascertaining its condition

[F49and[F49; and such power may, in particular, be exercised with a view to ascertaining—]]—

(a) whether any works affecting the monument are being carried out in contravention of section 2. (1) of this Act; or

(b) whether it has been or is likely to be damaged (by any such works or otherwise).

(2) Any person duly authorised in writing by the Secretary of State [F50or Historic Environment Scotland] may at any reasonable time enter any land for the purpose of inspecting any scheduled monument in, on or under the land in connection with—

(a) any application for scheduled monument consent for works affecting that monument; or

(b) any proposal by the Secretary of State [F50or Historic Environment Scotland] to modify or revoke a scheduled monument consent for any such works.

(3) Any person duly authorised in writing by the Secretary of State [F51or Historic Environment Scotland] may at any reasonable time enter any land for the purpose of—

(a) observing the execution on the land of any works to which a scheduled monument consent relates; and

(b) inspecting the condition of the land and the scheduled monument in question after the completion of any such works;

so as to ensure that the works in question are or have been executed in accordance with the terms of the consent and of any conditions attached to the consent.

[F52. (3. A)Any person duly authorised in writing by the Scottish Ministers [F53or Historic Environment Scotland] may at any reasonable time enter any land—

(a) to ascertain whether a scheduled monument enforcement notice, a stop notice or a temporary stop notice should be served in relation to a scheduled monument in, on or under that or any other land,

(b) for the purposes of displaying—

(i) a site notice,

(ii) a notice under section 9. G(7) in place of a site notice, or

(iii) a copy of a temporary stop notice, and a statement as to the effect of section 9. M, under section 9. K(4),

(c) to ascertain whether a scheduled monument enforcement notice, a stop notice or a temporary stop notice has been complied with,

(d) to ascertain whether any offence has been, or is being, committed with respect to any scheduled monument in, on or under that or any other land under section 2. (1) or (6), 9. E, 9. J or 9. M.]

(4) Any person duly authorised in writing by the Secretary of State [F54or Historic Environment Scotland] may at any reasonable time enter any land on which any works to which a scheduled monument consent relates are being carried out for the purpose of—

(a) inspecting the land (including any buildings or other structures on the land) with a view to recording any matters of archaeological or historical interest; and

(b) observing the execution of those works with a view to examining and recording any objects or other material of archaeological or historical interest, and recording any matters of archaeological or historical interest, discovered during the course of those works.

(5) Any person duly authorised in writing by the Secretary of State [F55or Historic Environment Scotland] may enter any land in, on or under which a scheduled monument is situated, with the consent of the owner and (if the owner is not the occupier) of the occupier of the land, for the purpose of erecting and maintaining on or near the site of the monument such notice boards and marker posts as appear to the Secretary of State [F55or Historic Environment Scotland] to be desirable with a view to preserving the monument from accidental or deliberate damage.

[F56. This subsection does not apply to land in England.]

(6) References in this section to scheduled monument consent include references to consent granted by order under section 3 of this Act.

Amendments (Textual)

F48. Words in s. 6. (1) substituted (27.2.2015 for specified purposes, 1.10.2015 in so far as not already in force) by Historic Environment Scotland Act 2014 (asp 19), s. 31. (2), sch. 2 para. 10.

(a) (with ss. 29, 30); S.S.I. 2015/31, art. 2, sch.; S.S.I. 2015/196, art. 2, sch.

F49. Words in s. 6. (1) substituted (S.) (30.6.2011) by Historic Environment (Amendment) (Scotland) Act 2011 (asp 3), ss. 5, 33. (2); S.S.I. 2011/174, art. 2, Sch.

F50. Words in s. 6. (2) inserted (S.) (27.2.2015 for specified purposes, 1.10.2015 in so far as not already in force) by Historic Environment Scotland Act 2014 (asp 19), s. 31. (2), sch. 2 para. 10. (b) (with ss. 29, 30); S.S.I. 2015/31, art. 2, sch.; S.S.I. 2015/196, art. 2, sch.

F51. Words in s. 6. (3) inserted (S.) (27.2.2015 for specified purposes, 1.10.2015 in so far as not already in force) by Historic Environment Scotland Act 2014 (asp 19), s. 31. (2), sch. 2 para. 10. (c) (with ss. 29, 30); S.S.I. 2015/31, art. 2, sch.; S.S.I. 2015/196, art. 2, sch.

F52. Words in s. 6. (3. A) inserted (S.) (30.6.2011 for specified purposes) by Historic Environment (Amendment) (Scotland) Act 2011 (asp 3), ss. 6. (2), 33. (2); S.S.I. 2011/174, art. 2, Sch.

F53. Words in s. 6. (3. A) inserted (S.) (27.2.2015 for specified purposes, 1.10.2015 in so far as not already in force) by Historic Environment Scotland Act 2014 (asp 19), s. 31. (2), sch. 2 para. 10. (d) (with ss. 29, 30); S.S.I. 2015/31, art. 2, sch.; S.S.I. 2015/196, art. 2, sch.

F54. Words in s. 6. (4) inserted (S.) (27.2.2015 for specified purposes, 1.10.2015 in so far as not already in force) by Historic Environment Scotland Act 2014 (asp 19), s. 31. (2), sch. 2 para. 10. (e) (with ss. 29, 30); S.S.I. 2015/31, art. 2, sch.; S.S.I. 2015/196, art. 2, sch.

F55. Words in s. 6. (5) inserted (S.) (27.2.2015 for specified purposes, 1.10.2015 in so far as not already in force) by Historic Environment Scotland Act 2014 (asp 19), s. 31. (2), sch. 2 para. 10. (f) (with ss. 29, 30); S.S.I. 2015/31, art. 2, sch.; S.S.I. 2015/196, art. 2, sch.

F56. Words inserted by National Heritage Act 1983 (c. 47, SIF 78), s. 41, Sch. 4 para. 31 Modifications etc. (not altering text)

C10. S. 6. (1) restricted (18.12.1996) by 1996 c. 61, s. 12, Sch. 7 para. 4. (3)

C11. S. 6. (1) restricted (22.7.2008) by Crossrail Act 2008 (c. 18), Sch. 9 para. 4. (3)

[F576. A Commission's powers of entry in relation to scheduled monuments.

(1)Any person duly authorised in writing by the Commission may at any reasonable time enter any land in England for the purpose of inspecting any scheduled monument in, on or under the land with a view to ascertaining whether any works affecting the monument have been or are being carried out in contravention of section 2. (1) of this Act and so to enabling the Commission to decide whether to institute proceedings in England for an offence under section 2. (1).

(2) Any person duly authorised in writing by the Commission may at any reasonable time enter any land in England for the purpose of—

(a) observing the execution on the land of any works to which a scheduled monument consent relates; and

(b) inspecting the condition of the land and the scheduled monument in question after the completion of any such works,

with a view to ascertaining whether the works in question are or have been executed in accordance with the terms of the consent and of any conditions attached to the consent, and so to enabling the Commission to decide whether to institute proceedings in England for an offence under section 2. (1) or (6) of this Act.

(3) Any person duly authorised in writing by the Commission may at any reasonable time enter any land in England for the purpose of inspecting any scheduled monument in, on or under the land in connection with any consultation made in respect of the monument under section 4. (3) of this Act or paragraph 3. (3)(c) of Schedule 1 to this Act.

(4) Any person duly authorised in writing by the Commission may enter any land which is in England and in, on or under which a scheduled monument is situated, with the consent of the owner and (if the owner is not the occupier) of the occupier of the land, for the purpose of erecting and maintaining on or near the site of the monument such notice boards and marker posts as

appear to the Commission to be desirable with a view to preserving the monument from accidental or deliberate damage.
(5) References in this section to scheduled monument consent include references to consent granted by order under section 3 of this Act.]
Amendments (Textual)
F57. S. 6. A inserted by National Heritage Act 1983 (c. 47, SIF 78), s. 41, Sch. 4 para. 32
Modifications etc. (not altering text)
C12. S. 6. A(1) restricted (22.7.2008) by Crossrail Act 2008 (c. 18), Sch. 9 para. 4. (3)
C13. S. 6. A(1) restricted (18.12.1996) by 1996 c. 61, s. 12, Sch. 7 para. 4. (3)

7 Compensation for refusal of scheduled monument consent.

(1) Subject to the following provisions of this section, where a person who has an interest in the whole or any part of a monument incurs expenditure or otherwise sustains any loss or damage in consequence of the refusal, or the granting subject to conditions, of a scheduled monument consent in relation to any works of a description mentioned in subsection (2) below, [F58the Secretary of State] [F58. Historic Environment Scotland or, where the Scottish Ministers refused the scheduled monument consent or granted it subject to conditions, Ministers] [F59or (where the monument in question is situated in England) the Commission] shall pay to that person compensation in respect of that expenditure, loss or damage.
References in this section and in section 8 of this Act to compensation being paid in respect of any works are references to compensation being paid in respect of any expenditure incurred or other loss or damage sustained in consequence of the refusal, or the granting subject to conditions, of a scheduled monument consent in relation to those works.
(2) The following are works in respect of which compensation is payable under this section—
    (a) works which are reasonably necessary for carrying out any development for which planning permission had been granted (otherwise than by a general development order) before the time when the monument in question became a scheduled monument and was still effective at the date of the application for scheduled monument consent;
    (b) works which do not constitute development, or constitute development such that planning permission is granted therefor by a general development order; and
    (c) works which are reasonably necessary for the continuation of any use of the monument for any purpose for which it was in use immediately before the date of the application for scheduled monument consent.
For the purposes of paragraph (c) above, any use in contravention of any legal restrictions for the time being applying to the use of the monument shall be disregarded.
(3) The compensation payable under this section in respect of any works within subsection (2)(a) above shall be limited to compensation in respect of any expenditure incurred or other loss or damage sustained by virtue of the fact that, in consequence of [F60the Secretary of State's] [F60. Historic Environment Scotland's or, as the case may be, the Scottish Ministers'] decision, any development for which the planning permission in question was granted could not be carried out without contravening section 2. (1) of this Act.
(4) A person shall not be entitled to compensation under this section by virtue of subsection (2)(b) above if the works in question or any of them would or might result in the total or partial demolition or destruction of the monument, unless those works consist solely of operations involved in or incidental to the use of the site of the monument for the purposes of agriculture or forestry (including afforestation).
(5) In a case where scheduled monument consent is granted subject to conditions, a person shall not be entitled to compensation under this section by virtue of subsection (2)(c) above unless compliance with those conditions would in effect make it impossible to use the monument for the purpose there mentioned.
(6) In calculating, for the purposes of this section, the amount of any loss or damage consisting of

depreciation of the value of an interest in land—

(a) it shall be assumed that any subsequent application for scheduled monument consent in relation to works of a like description would be determined in the same way; but

(b) if, in the case of a refusal of scheduled monument consent, [F61the Secretary of State] [F61. Historic Environment Scotland or, as the case may be, the Scottish Ministers] , on refusing that consent, undertook to grant such consent for some other works affecting the monument in the event of an application being made in that behalf, regard shall be had to that undertaking.

(7) References in this section to a general development order are references to a development order made as a general order applicable (subject to such exceptions as may be specified therein) to all land.

Amendments (Textual)

F58. Words in s. 7. (1) substituted (S.) (27.2.2015 for specified purposes, 1.10.2015 in so far as not already in force) by Historic Environment Scotland Act 2014 (asp 19), s. 31. (2), sch. 2 para. 11. (a) (with ss. 29, 30); S.S.I. 2015/31, art. 2, sch.; S.S.I. 2015/196, art. 2, sch.

F59. Words inserted by National Heritage Act 1983 (c. 47, SIF 78), s. 41, Sch. 4 para. 33

F60. Words in s. 7. (3) substituted (S.) (27.2.2015 for specified purposes, 1.10.2015 in so far as not already in force) by Historic Environment Scotland Act 2014 (asp 19), s. 31. (2), sch. 2 para. 11. (b) (with ss. 29, 30); S.S.I. 2015/31, art. 2, sch.; S.S.I. 2015/196, art. 2, sch.

F61. Words in s. 7. (6)(b) substituted (S.) (27.2.2015 for specified purposes, 1.10.2015 in so far as not already in force) by Historic Environment Scotland Act 2014 (asp 19), s. 31. (2), sch. 2 para. 11. (c) (with ss. 29, 30); S.S.I. 2015/31, art. 2, sch.; S.S.I. 2015/196, art. 2, sch.

8 Recovery of compensation under section 7 on subsequent grant of consent.

(1) Subject to the following provisions of this section, this section applies—

(a) in a case where compensation under section 7 of this Act was paid in consequence of the refusal of a scheduled monument consent, if the Secretary of State [F62or Historic Environment Scotland] subsequently grants scheduled monument consent for the execution of all or any of the works in respect of which the compensation was paid; and

(b) in a case where compensation under that section was paid in consequence of the granting of a scheduled monument consent subject to conditions, if the Secretary of State [F62or Historic Environment Scotland] subsequently so modifies that consent that those conditions, or any of them, cease to apply to the execution of all or any of the works in respect of which the compensation was paid or grants a new consent in respect of all or any of those works free from those conditions, or any of them.

(2) This section does not apply in any case unless—

(a) the compensation paid exceeded £20; and

[F63. (b)the requirement mentioned in subsection (2. A) below is fulfilled]

[F64. (2. A)The requirement is that—

(a) where the monument in question is situated in England, the Commission have caused notice of the payment of compensation to be deposited with the council of each district or London borough in which the monument is situated or (where it is situated in the City of London, the Inner Temple or the Middle Temple) with the Common Council of the City of London;

(b) where the monument in question is situated in Scotland, the Secretary of State [F65or Historic Environment Scotland] has caused such notice to be deposited with the local authority of each area in which the monument is situated;

(c) where the monument in question is situated in Wales, the Secretary of State has caused such notice to be deposited with the council of each [F66county or county borough] in which the monument is situated.]

(3) In granting or modifying a scheduled monument consent in a case to which this section applies the Secretary of State [F67or Historic Environment Scotland] may do so on terms that no works in

respect of which the compensation was paid are to be executed in pursuance of the consent until the recoverable amount has been repaid to the Secretary of State [F67or Historic Environment Scotland] or secured to his [F68or its] satisfaction [F69or (as the case may be) has been repaid to the Commission or secured to their satisfaction].

Subject to subsection (4) below, in this subsection "the recoverable amount" means such amount (being an amount representing the whole of the compensation previously paid or such part thereof as the Secretary of State [F67or Historic Environment Scotland] thinks fit) as the Secretary of State [F67or Historic Environment Scotland] may specify in giving notice of his [F68or its] decision on the application for scheduled monument consent or (as the case may be) in the direction modifying the consent.

(4) Where a person who has an interest in the whole or any part of a monument is aggrieved by the amount specified by the Secretary of State [F70or Historic Environment Scotland] as the recoverable amount for the purposes of subsection (3) above, he may require the determination of that amount to be referred to the [F71. Upper Tribunal or] (in the case of a monument situated in Scotland) to the Lands Tribunal for Scotland; and in any such case the recoverable amount for the purposes of that subsection shall be such amount (being an amount representing the whole or any part of the compensation previously paid) as that Tribunal may determine to be just in the circumstances of the case.

(5) A notice deposited under subsection (2)(b) above shall specify the decision which gave rise to the right to compensation, the monument affected by the decision, and the amount of the compensation.

(6) A notice so deposited in the case of a monument situated in England and Wales shall be a local land charge; and for the purposes of the M3. Local Land Charges Act 1975 the council with whom any such notice is deposited shall be treated as the originating authority as respects the charge thereby constituted.

(7) A notice so deposited in the case of any monument situated in Scotland which is heritable may be recorded in the Register of Sasines.

Amendments (Textual)

F62. Words in s. 8. (1) inserted (S.) (27.2.2015 for specified purposes, 1.10.2015 in so far as not already in force) by Historic Environment Scotland Act 2014 (asp 19), s. 31. (2), sch. 2 para. 12. (a) (with ss. 29, 30); S.S.I. 2015/31, art. 2, sch.; S.S.I. 2015/196, art. 2, sch.

F63. S. 8. (2)(b) substituted by National Heritage Act 1983 (c. 47, SIF 78), s. 41, Sch. 4 para. 34. (2)(5)

F64. S. 8. (2. A) inserted by National Heritage Act 1983 (c. 47, SIF 78), s. 41, Sch. 4 para. 34. (3)(5)

F65. Words in s. 8. (2. A) inserted (S.) (27.2.2015 for specified purposes, 1.10.2015 in so far as not already in force) by Historic Environment Scotland Act 2014 (asp 19), s. 31. (2), sch. 2 para. 12. (b) (with ss. 29, 30); S.S.I. 2015/31, art. 2, sch.; S.S.I. 2015/196, art. 2, sch.

F66. Words in s. 8. (2. A)(c) substituted (1.4.1996) by 1994 c. 19, s. 66. (6), Sch. 16 para. 56. (1) (with ss. 54. (5)(7), 55. (5), Sch. 17 paras. 22. (1), 23. (2)); S.I. 1996/396, art. 4, Sch.2

F67. Words in s. 8. (3) inserted (S.) (27.2.2015 for specified purposes, 1.10.2015 in so far as not already in force) by Historic Environment Scotland Act 2014 (asp 19), s. 31. (2), sch. 2 para. 12. (c)(i) (with ss. 29, 30); S.S.I. 2015/31, art. 2, sch.; S.S.I. 2015/196, art. 2, sch.

F68. Words in s. 8. (3) inserted (S.) (27.2.2015 for specified purposes, 1.10.2015 in so far as not already in force) by Historic Environment Scotland Act 2014 (asp 19), s. 31. (2), sch. 2 para. 12. (c)(ii) (with ss. 29, 30); S.S.I. 2015/31, art. 2, sch.; S.S.I. 2015/196, art. 2, sch.

F69. Words inserted by National Heritage Act 1983 (c. 47, SIF 78), s. 41, Sch. 4 para. 34. (4)(5)

F70. Words in s. 8. (4) inserted (S.) (27.2.2015 for specified purposes, 1.10.2015 in so far as not already in force) by Historic Environment Scotland Act 2014 (asp 19), s. 31. (2), sch. 2 para. 12. (d) (with ss. 29, 30); S.S.I. 2015/31, art. 2, sch.; S.S.I. 2015/196, art. 2, sch.

F71. Words in s. 8. (4) substituted (1.6.2009) by The Transfer of Tribunal Functions (Lands Tribunal and Miscellaneous Amendments) Order 2009 (S.I. 2009/1307), art. 1, Sch. 1 para. 127 (with Sch. 5)

Marginal Citations
M31975 c. 76.

9 Compensation where works affecting a scheduled monument cease to be authorised.

(1) Subject to the following provisions of this section, where any works affecting a scheduled monument which were previously authorised under this Part of this Act cease to be so, then, if any person who has an interest in the whole or any part of the monument—
    (a) has incurred expenditure in carrying out works which are rendered abortive by the fact that any further works have ceased to be so authorised; or
    (b) has otherwise sustained loss or damage which is directly attributable to that fact;
the Secretary of State [F72or Historic Environment Scotland] [F73or (where the monument in question is situated in England) the Commission] shall pay to that person compensation in respect of that expenditure, loss or damage.
(2) Subsection (1) above only applies where the works cease to be authorised under this Part of this Act—
    (a) by virtue of the fact that a scheduled monument consent granted by order under section 3 of this Act ceases to apply to any scheduled monument (whether by virtue of variation or revocation of the order or by virtue of a direction under subsection (3) of that section); or
    (b) by virtue of the modification or revocation of a scheduled monument consent by a direction given under section 4 of this Act; or
    (c) in accordance with paragraph 8 of Schedule 1 to this Act, by virtue of the service of a notice of proposed modification or revocation of a scheduled monument consent under paragraph 5 of that Schedule.
(3) A person shall not be entitled to compensation under this section in a case falling within subsection (2)(a) above unless, on an application for scheduled monument consent for the works in question, consent is refused, or is granted subject to conditions other than those which previously applied under the order.
(4) For the purposes of this section, any expenditure incurred in the preparation of plans for the purposes of any works, or upon other similar matters preparatory thereto, shall be taken to be included in the expenditure incurred in carrying out those works.
(5) Subject to subsection (4) above, no compensation shall be paid under this section in respect of any works carried out before the grant of the scheduled monument consent in question, or in respect of any other loss or damage (not being loss or damage consisting of depreciation of the value of an interest in land) arising out of anything done or omitted to be done before the grant of that consent.
Amendments (Textual)
F72. Words in s. 9. (1) inserted (S.) (27.2.2015 for specified purposes, 1.10.2015 in so far as not already in force) by Historic Environment Scotland Act 2014 (asp 19), s. 31. (2), sch. 2 para. 13 (with ss. 29, 30); S.S.I. 2015/31, art. 2, sch.; S.S.I. 2015/196, art. 2, sch.
F73. Words inserted by National Heritage Act 1983 (c. 47, SIF 78), s. 41, Sch. 4 para. 35

[F74. Scheduled monument enforcement noticesS

Amendments (Textual)
F74. Ss. 9. A-9. O and cross-heading inserted (S.) (30.6.2011 for specified purposes, 1.12.2011 in so far as not already in force) by Historic Environment (Amendment) (Scotland) Act 2011 (asp 3), ss. 6. (1), 33. (2); S.S.I. 2011/174, art. 2, Sch.; S.S.I. 2011/372, art. 2, Sch.

9. APower to issue scheduled monument enforcement noticeS

(1) Where it appears to [F75. Historic Environment Scotland] that—
(a) any works have been, or are being, executed to a scheduled monument or to land in, on or under which there is a scheduled monument, and
(b) the works are such as to involve a contravention of section 2. (1) or (6),
[F76it may, if it considers] it expedient having regard to the effect of the works on the character of the monument as one of national importance, serve a notice under this section (in this Act referred to as a "scheduled monument enforcement notice").
(2) A scheduled monument enforcement notice must specify the alleged contravention and must (either or both)—
(a) specify any works falling within subsection (1) which [F77. Historic Environment Scotland requires] to cease,
(b) require steps falling within subsection (3) and specified in the notice to be taken.
(3) Those steps are—
(a) for restoring the monument or land to its former state,
(b) if [F78. Historic Environment Scotland considers] that restoration to its former state would not be reasonably practicable or would be undesirable, for executing such further works specified in the notice as [F79it considers] are required to alleviate in a manner acceptable to [F80it] the effect of the works which were carried out without scheduled monument consent, or
(c) for bringing the monument or land to the state it would have been in if the conditions of any scheduled monument consent for the works had been complied with.
(4) In considering whether restoration is undesirable under subsection (3)(b), [F81. Historic Environment Scotland is] to have regard to the desirability of preserving—
(a) the national importance of the monument,
(b) its features of historical, architectural, traditional, artistic or archaeological interest.
(5) Where further works of a kind mentioned in subsection (3)(b) have been carried out on a monument or land, scheduled monument consent is treated as having been granted in respect of the works carried out on that monument or land.
Amendments (Textual)
F75. Words in s. 9. A(1) substituted (27.2.2015 for specified purposes, 1.10.2015 in so far as not already in force) by Historic Environment Scotland Act 2014 (asp 19), s. 31. (2), sch. 2 para. 17. (a)(i) (with ss. 29, 30); S.S.I. 2015/31, art. 2, sch.; S.S.I. 2015/196, art. 2, sch.
F76. Words in s. 9. A(1)(b) substituted (27.2.2015 for specified purposes, 1.10.2015 in so far as not already in force) by Historic Environment Scotland Act 2014 (asp 19), s. 31. (2), sch. 2 para. 17. (a)(ii) (with ss. 29, 30); S.S.I. 2015/31, art. 2, sch.; S.S.I. 2015/196, art. 2, sch.
F77. Words in s. 9. A(2)(a) substituted (27.2.2015 for specified purposes, 1.10.2015 in so far as not already in force) by Historic Environment Scotland Act 2014 (asp 19), s. 31. (2), sch. 2 para. 17. (b) (with ss. 29, 30); S.S.I. 2015/31, art. 2, sch.; S.S.I. 2015/196, art. 2, sch.
F78. Words in s. 9. A(3)(b) substituted (27.2.2015 for specified purposes, 1.10.2015 in so far as not already in force) by Historic Environment Scotland Act 2014 (asp 19), s. 31. (2), sch. 2 para. 17. (c)(i) (with ss. 29, 30); S.S.I. 2015/31, art. 2, sch.; S.S.I. 2015/196, art. 2, sch.
F79. Words in s. 9. A(3)(b) substituted (27.2.2015 for specified purposes, 1.10.2015 in so far as not already in force) by Historic Environment Scotland Act 2014 (asp 19), s. 31. (2), sch. 2 para. 17. (c)(ii) (with ss. 29, 30); S.S.I. 2015/31, art. 2, sch.; S.S.I. 2015/196, art. 2, sch.
F80. Word in s. 9. A(3)(b) substituted (27.2.2015 for specified purposes, 1.10.2015 in so far as not already in force) by Historic Environment Scotland Act 2014 (asp 19), s. 31. (2), sch. 2 para. 17. (c)(iii) (with ss. 29, 30); S.S.I. 2015/31, art. 2, sch.; S.S.I. 2015/196, art. 2, sch.
F81. Words in s. 9. A(4) substituted (27.2.2015 for specified purposes, 1.10.2015 in so far as not already in force) by Historic Environment Scotland Act 2014 (asp 19), s. 31. (2), sch. 2 para. 17. (d) (with ss. 29, 30); S.S.I. 2015/31, art. 2, sch.; S.S.I. 2015/196, art. 2, sch.
Modifications etc. (not altering text)
C14. S. 9. A savings for effects of 2014 asp 19, Sch. 2 para. 17 (1.10.2015) by The Historic Environment Scotland Act 2014 (Saving, Transitional and Consequential Provisions) Order 2015

(S.S.I. 2015/239), arts. 1. (1), 8

9. BScheduled monument enforcement notices: further provisionsS

(1) A scheduled monument enforcement notice—
  (a) must specify the date on which it is to take effect and, subject to section 9. C(3), takes effect on that date, and
  (b) must specify the period (the "period for compliance") within which—
(i) any works required to cease must cease,
(ii) any steps required to be taken must be taken,
and may specify different periods for different works or steps.
(2) Where different periods apply to different works or steps, references in this Act to the period for compliance with a scheduled monument enforcement notice, in relation to any works or step, are to the period within which the works are required to cease or the step is required to be taken.
(3) The date specified in the notice under subsection (1)(a) must be at least 28 days after the date on which the notice is served.
(4) A copy of a scheduled monument enforcement notice must be served—
  (a) on the owner, the lessee and the occupier of the monument to which it relates and of the land in, on or under which the monument is situated,
  (b) on any other person having an interest in the monument or land, being an interest which in the opinion of [F82. Historic Environment Scotland] is materially affected by the notice.
(5) [F83. Historic Environment Scotland] may, at any time—
  (a) withdraw a scheduled monument enforcement notice (without prejudice to [F84its] power to issue another), or
  (b) waive or relax any requirement of such a notice and, in particular, extend the period for compliance.
(6) [F85. Historic Environment Scotland] must, immediately after exercising the powers conferred by subsection (5), give notice of the exercise to every person who has been served with a copy of the scheduled monument enforcement notice or would, if the notice were reissued, be served with a copy of it.
(7) [F86. Historic Environment Scotland] must—
  (a) publish by electronic means (as for example by means of the internet) a list containing particulars of any monument in respect of which a scheduled monument enforcement notice has been served, and
  (b) on request, provide a copy of a scheduled monument enforcement notice.
Amendments (Textual)
F82. Words in s. 9. B(4)(b) substituted (27.2.2015 for specified purposes, 1.10.2015 in so far as not already in force) by Historic Environment Scotland Act 2014 (asp 19), s. 31. (2), sch. 2 para. 18. (a) (with ss. 29, 30); S.S.I. 2015/31, art. 2, sch.; S.S.I. 2015/196, art. 2, sch.
F83. Words in s. 9. B(5) substituted (27.2.2015 for specified purposes, 1.10.2015 in so far as not already in force) by Historic Environment Scotland Act 2014 (asp 19), s. 31. (2), sch. 2 para. 18. (b)(i) (with ss. 29, 30); S.S.I. 2015/31, art. 2, sch.; S.S.I. 2015/196, art. 2, sch.
F84. Word in s. 9. B(5)(a) substituted (27.2.2015 for specified purposes, 1.10.2015 in so far as not already in force) by Historic Environment Scotland Act 2014 (asp 19), s. 31. (2), sch. 2 para. 18. (b)(ii) (with ss. 29, 30); S.S.I. 2015/31, art. 2, sch.; S.S.I. 2015/196, art. 2, sch.
F85. Words in s. 9. B(6) substituted (27.2.2015 for specified purposes, 1.10.2015 in so far as not already in force) by Historic Environment Scotland Act 2014 (asp 19), s. 31. (2), sch. 2 para. 18. (c) (with ss. 29, 30); S.S.I. 2015/31, art. 2, sch.; S.S.I. 2015/196, art. 2, sch.
F86. Words in s. 9. B(7) substituted (27.2.2015 for specified purposes, 1.10.2015 in so far as not already in force) by Historic Environment Scotland Act 2014 (asp 19), s. 31. (2), sch. 2 para. 18. (d) (with ss. 29, 30); S.S.I. 2015/31, art. 2, sch.; S.S.I. 2015/196, art. 2, sch.

Modifications etc. (not altering text)
C15. S. 9. B savings for effects of 2014 asp 19, Sch. 2 para. 18 (1.10.2015) by The Historic Environment Scotland Act 2014 (Saving, Transitional and Consequential Provisions) Order 2015 (S.S.I. 2015/239), arts. 1. (1), 8

9. CAppeal against scheduled monument enforcement noticeS

(1) A person on whom a scheduled monument enforcement notice is served or any other person having an interest in the monument to which it relates or the land in, on or under which it is situated may, at any time before the date specified in the notice as the date on which it is to take effect, [F87appeal to the Scottish Ministers] on any of the grounds in subsection (2).

(2) Those grounds are—

[F88. (za)that the monument is not of national importance,]

(a) that the matters alleged to constitute a contravention of section 2. (1) or (6) have not occurred,

(b) that those matters (if they occurred) do not constitute such a contravention,

(c) that—

(i) works to the monument or land were urgently necessary in the interests of safety or health,
(ii) it was not practicable to secure safety or health by works of repair or works for affording temporary support or shelter, and
(iii) the works carried out were limited to the minimum measures immediately necessary,

[F89. (ca)that scheduled monument consent ought to be granted for the works, or that any relevant condition of such consent which has been granted ought to be discharged, or different conditions substituted,]

(d) that copies of the notice were not served as required by section 9. B(4),

[F90. (da)except in relation to such a requirement as is mentioned in section 9. A(3)(b) or (c), that the requirements of the notice exceed what is necessary for restoring the monument or land to its condition before the works were carried out,]

(e) that the period for compliance for any works or step falls short of what should reasonably be allowed.

[F91. (f)that the steps required by the notice for the purpose of restoring the character of the monument or land to its former state would not serve that purpose,

(g) that the cessation of any works required by the notice exceeds what is necessary to remedy the contravention of section 2. (1) or (6),

(h) that steps required to be taken by virtue of section 9. A(3)(b) exceed what is necessary to alleviate the effect of the works executed to the monument or land,

(i) that steps required to be taken by virtue of section 9. A(3)(c) exceed what may reasonably be required to bring the monument or land to the state in which it would have been if the scheduled monument consent had been complied with.]

[F92. (2. A)An appeal under this section is to be made by giving written notice of the appeal to the Scottish Ministers before the date specified in the scheduled monument enforcement notice as the date on which it is to take effect.]

(3) Where an appeal is brought under this section the notice is of no effect until the appeal is withdrawn or finally determined.

[F93. (3. A)A person who gives notice of appeal under this section must submit to the Scottish Ministers, either when giving the notice or within such time as may be prescribed, a statement in writing—

(a) specifying the grounds on which the appeal is made,

(b) giving such further information as may be prescribed.]

F94. (4)..............................
F95. (5)..............................

Amendments (Textual)

F87. Words in s. 9. C(1) substituted (27.2.2015 for specified purposes, 1.10.2015 in so far as not already in force) by Historic Environment Scotland Act 2014 (asp 19), s. 31. (2), sch. 2 para. 19. (a) (with ss. 29, 30); S.S.I. 2015/31, art. 2, sch.; S.S.I. 2015/196, art. 2, sch.

F88. S. 9. C(2)(za) inserted (27.2.2015 for specified purposes, 1.10.2015 in so far as not already in force) by Historic Environment Scotland Act 2014 (asp 19), s. 31. (2), sch. 2 para. 19. (b)(i) (with ss. 29, 30); S.S.I. 2015/31, art. 2, sch.; S.S.I. 2015/196, art. 2, sch.

F89. S. 9. C(2)(ca) inserted (27.2.2015 for specified purposes, 1.10.2015 in so far as not already in force) by Historic Environment Scotland Act 2014 (asp 19), s. 31. (2), sch. 2 para. 19. (b)(ii) (with ss. 29, 30); S.S.I. 2015/31, art. 2, sch.; S.S.I. 2015/196, art. 2, sch.

F90. S. 9. C(2)(da) inserted (27.2.2015 for specified purposes, 1.10.2015 in so far as not already in force) by Historic Environment Scotland Act 2014 (asp 19), s. 31. (2), sch. 2 para. 19. (b)(iii) (with ss. 29, 30); S.S.I. 2015/31, art. 2, sch.; S.S.I. 2015/196, art. 2, sch.

F91. Ss. 9. C(2)(f)-(i) inserted (27.2.2015 for specified purposes, 1.10.2015 in so far as not already in force) by Historic Environment Scotland Act 2014 (asp 19), s. 31. (2), sch. 2 para. 19. (b)(iv) (with ss. 29, 30); S.S.I. 2015/31, art. 2, sch.; S.S.I. 2015/196, art. 2, sch.

F92. S. 9. C(2. A) inserted (27.2.2015 for specified purposes, 1.10.2015 in so far as not already in force) by Historic Environment Scotland Act 2014 (asp 19), s. 31. (2), sch. 2 para. 19. (c) (with ss. 29, 30); S.S.I. 2015/31, art. 2, sch.; S.S.I. 2015/196, art. 2, sch.

F93. S. 9. C(3. A) inserted (27.2.2015 for specified purposes, 1.10.2015 in so far as not already in force) by Historic Environment Scotland Act 2014 (asp 19), s. 31. (2), sch. 2 para. 19. (d) (with ss. 29, 30); S.S.I. 2015/31, art. 2, sch.; S.S.I. 2015/196, art. 2, sch.

F94. S. 9. C(4) repealed (27.2.2015 for specified purposes, 1.10.2015 in so far as not already in force) by Historic Environment Scotland Act 2014 (asp 19), s. 31. (2), sch. 2 para. 19. (e) (with ss. 29, 30); S.S.I. 2015/31, art. 2, sch.; S.S.I. 2015/196, art. 2, sch.

F95. S. 9. C(5) repealed (27.2.2015 for specified purposes, 1.10.2015 in so far as not already in force) by Historic Environment Scotland Act 2014 (asp 19), s. 31. (2), sch. 2 para. 19. (e) (with ss. 29, 30); S.S.I. 2015/31, art. 2, sch.; S.S.I. 2015/196, art. 2, sch.

Modifications etc. (not altering text)

C16. S. 9. C savings for effects of 2014 asp 19, Sch. 2 para. 19 (1.10.2015) by The Historic Environment Scotland Act 2014 (Saving, Transitional and Consequential Provisions) Order 2015 (S.S.I. 2015/239), arts. 1. (1), 8

[F969. CADetermination of appeals under section 9. CS

(1) On determining an appeal under section 9. C, the Scottish Ministers may give directions for giving effect to the determination, including where appropriate directions for quashing the scheduled monument enforcement notice.

(2) On such an appeal the Scottish Ministers may if they are satisfied that the correction or variation will not cause injustice to the appellant or to Historic Environment Scotland—

(a) correct any defect, error or misdescription in the scheduled monument enforcement notice, or

(b) vary the terms of the notice.

(3) In a case where it would otherwise be a ground for determining the appeal in favour of the appellant that a person required by section 9. B(4) to be served with a copy of the notice was not served, the Scottish Ministers may disregard that fact if they are satisfied that the person has not been substantially prejudiced by the failure.

(4) The Scottish Ministers may—

(a) dismiss such an appeal if the appellant fails to comply with section 9. C(3. A) within the prescribed time,

(b) allow such an appeal or quash the scheduled monument enforcement notice if Historic Environment Scotland fails to comply within the prescribed period with any requirement imposed by regulations made by virtue of section 9. CB(1).

(5) On the determination of an appeal under section 9. C the Scottish Ministers may—
(a) grant scheduled monument consent for the works to which the scheduled monument enforcement notice relates,
(b) discharge any condition subject to which such consent was granted and substitute any other condition, whether more or less onerous, or
(c) direct Historic Environment Scotland to exercise its power under section 1. (5) to modify the Schedule to give effect to that determination.
(6) Any scheduled monument consent granted by the Scottish Ministers under subsection (5)(a) is to be treated as granted under section 2. (3).
(7) Except as provided for by section 55, the decision of the Scottish Ministers on an appeal under section 9. C is final.
Amendments (Textual)
F96. Ss. 9. CA, 9. CB inserted (27.2.2015 for specified purposes, 1.10.2015 in so far as not already in force) by Historic Environment Scotland Act 2014 (asp 19), s. 31. (2), sch. 2 para. 20 (with ss. 29, 30); S.S.I. 2015/31, art. 2, sch.; S.S.I. 2015/196, art. 2, sch.
Modifications etc. (not altering text)
C17. S. 9. CA savings for effects of 2014 asp 19, Sch. 2 para. 20 (1.10.2015) by The Historic Environment Scotland Act 2014 (Saving, Transitional and Consequential Provisions) Order 2015 (S.S.I. 2015/239), arts. 1. (1), 8

9. CBProcedure for appeals under section 9. CS

(1) The Scottish Ministers may by regulations make provision in connection with appeals under section 9. C, including provision about the information that is to be provided to, or may be required by, the Scottish Ministers in connection with the appeal.
(2) Regulations under subsection (1) may also make provision about the procedure to be followed, including—
(a) the form, manner and time for making an appeal,
(b) the notification of an appeal,
(c) the manner in which an appeal is to be conducted.
(3) Regulations made by virtue of subsection (2)(c) may also include provision that the manner in which an appeal, or any stage of an appeal, is to be conducted (as for example whether written submissions are to be presented or persons are to be heard) is to be at the discretion of the Scottish Ministers (or of a person appointed by them under this Act).
(4) Schedule 1. A (which makes provision about the determination of certain appeals by a person other than the Scottish Ministers) applies to appeals under section 9. C.]
Modifications etc. (not altering text)
C18. S. 9. CB savings for effects of 2014 asp 19, Sch. 2 para. 20 (1.10.2015) by The Historic Environment Scotland Act 2014 (Saving, Transitional and Consequential Provisions) Order 2015 (S.S.I. 2015/239), arts. 1. (1), 8

9. DExecution of works required by scheduled monument enforcement noticeS

(1) If any steps specified in the scheduled monument enforcement notice have not been taken within the period for compliance with the notice, [F97. Historic Environment Scotland] may—
(a) enter on the land in, on or under which the scheduled monument is situated and take those steps, and
(b) recover from the person who is then the owner or lessee of the monument or land any expenses reasonably incurred by [F98it] in doing so.
(2) Where a scheduled monument enforcement notice has been served in respect of a monument—

(a) any expenses incurred by the owner, lessee or occupier of a monument or the land in, on or under which it is situated for the purpose of complying with it, and

(b) any sums paid by the owner or lessee of a monument or land under subsection (1) in respect of expenses incurred by [F99. Historic Environment Scotland in taking steps required by the notice] ,

are to be treated as incurred or paid for the use and at the request of the person who carried out the works to which the notice relates.

(3) If on a complaint by the owner of any scheduled monument or land it appears to the sheriff that the occupier of the monument or land is preventing the owner from carrying out work required to be carried out by a scheduled monument enforcement notice, the sheriff may by warrant authorise the owner to enter the land and carry out the work.

(4) If [F100. Historic Environment Scotland takes] steps under subsection (1) [F101it] may sell any materials removed by [F102it] from the monument or land unless those materials are claimed by the owner within 3 days of their removal.

(5) After selling the materials [F103. Historic Environment Scotland] must pay the proceeds to the owner less the expenses recoverable by [F104it] from the owner.

(6) Where [F105. Historic Environment Scotland seeks] , under subsection (1), to recover any expenses from a person on the basis that the person is the owner of the scheduled monument or land, and the person proves that—

(a) the person is receiving the rent in respect of the monument or land merely as trustee, tutor, curator, factor or agent of some other person, and

(b) the person has not, and since the date of the service of the demand for payment has not had, in the person's hands on behalf of that other person sufficient money to discharge the whole demand of [F106. Historic Environment Scotland] ,

the person's liability is limited to the total amount of the money which the person has or has had in the person's hands on behalf of that other person.

(7) If by reason of subsection (6) [F107. Historic Environment Scotland has] not recovered the whole of any such expenses from a trustee, tutor, curator, factor or agent [F108it] may recover any unpaid balance from the person on whose behalf the rent is received.

(8) Any person who wilfully obstructs a person acting in the exercise of powers under subsection (1) is guilty of an offence and liable on summary conviction to a fine not exceeding level 3 on the standard scale.

Amendments (Textual)

F97. Words in s. 9. D(1) substituted (27.2.2015 for specified purposes, 1.10.2015 in so far as not already in force) by Historic Environment Scotland Act 2014 (asp 19), s. 31. (2), sch. 2 para. 21. (a)(i) (with ss. 29, 30); S.S.I. 2015/31, art. 2, sch.; S.S.I. 2015/196, art. 2, sch.

F98. Word in s. 9. D(1)(b) substituted (27.2.2015 for specified purposes, 1.10.2015 in so far as not already in force) by Historic Environment Scotland Act 2014 (asp 19), s. 31. (2), sch. 2 para. 21. (a)(ii) (with ss. 29, 30); S.S.I. 2015/31, art. 2, sch.; S.S.I. 2015/196, art. 2, sch.

F99. Words in s. 9. D(2)(b) substituted (27.2.2015 for specified purposes, 1.10.2015 in so far as not already in force) by Historic Environment Scotland Act 2014 (asp 19), s. 31. (2), sch. 2 para. 21. (b) (with ss. 29, 30); S.S.I. 2015/31, art. 2, sch.; S.S.I. 2015/196, art. 2, sch.

F100. Words in s. 9. D(4) substituted (27.2.2015 for specified purposes, 1.10.2015 in so far as not already in force) by Historic Environment Scotland Act 2014 (asp 19), s. 31. (2), sch. 2 para. 21. (c)(i) (with ss. 29, 30); S.S.I. 2015/31, art. 2, sch.; S.S.I. 2015/196, art. 2, sch.

F101. Word in s. 9. D(4) substituted (27.2.2015 for specified purposes, 1.10.2015 in so far as not already in force) by Historic Environment Scotland Act 2014 (asp 19), s. 31. (2), sch. 2 para. 21. (c)(ii) (with ss. 29, 30); S.S.I. 2015/31, art. 2, sch.; S.S.I. 2015/196, art. 2, sch.

F102. Word in s. 9. D(4) substituted (27.2.2015 for specified purposes, 1.10.2015 in so far as not already in force) by Historic Environment Scotland Act 2014 (asp 19), s. 31. (2), sch. 2 para. 21. (c)(iii) (with ss. 29, 30); S.S.I. 2015/31, art. 2, sch.; S.S.I. 2015/196, art. 2, sch.

F103. Words in s. 9. D(5) substituted (27.2.2015 for specified purposes, 1.10.2015 in so far as not already in force) by Historic Environment Scotland Act 2014 (asp 19), s. 31. (2), sch. 2 para. 21.

(d)(i) (with ss. 29, 30); S.S.I. 2015/31, art. 2, sch.; S.S.I. 2015/196, art. 2, sch.
F104. Word in s. 9. D(5) substituted (27.2.2015 for specified purposes, 1.10.2015 in so far as not already in force) by Historic Environment Scotland Act 2014 (asp 19), s. 31. (2), sch. 2 para. 21. (d)(ii) (with ss. 29, 30); S.S.I. 2015/31, art. 2, sch.; S.S.I. 2015/196, art. 2, sch.
F105. Words in s. 9. D(6) substituted (27.2.2015 for specified purposes, 1.10.2015 in so far as not already in force) by Historic Environment Scotland Act 2014 (asp 19), s. 31. (2), sch. 2 para. 21. (e)(i) (with ss. 29, 30); S.S.I. 2015/31, art. 2, sch.; S.S.I. 2015/196, art. 2, sch.
F106. Words in s. 9. D(6)(b) substituted (27.2.2015 for specified purposes, 1.10.2015 in so far as not already in force) by Historic Environment Scotland Act 2014 (asp 19), s. 31. (2), sch. 2 para. 21. (e)(ii) (with ss. 29, 30); S.S.I. 2015/31, art. 2, sch.; S.S.I. 2015/196, art. 2, sch.
F107. Words in s. 9. D(7) substituted (27.2.2015 for specified purposes, 1.10.2015 in so far as not already in force) by Historic Environment Scotland Act 2014 (asp 19), s. 31. (2), sch. 2 para. 21. (f)(i) (with ss. 29, 30); S.S.I. 2015/31, art. 2, sch.; S.S.I. 2015/196, art. 2, sch.
F108. Word in s. 9. D(7) substituted (27.2.2015 for specified purposes, 1.10.2015 in so far as not already in force) by Historic Environment Scotland Act 2014 (asp 19), s. 31. (2), sch. 2 para. 21. (f)(ii) (with ss. 29, 30); S.S.I. 2015/31, art. 2, sch.; S.S.I. 2015/196, art. 2, sch.
Modifications etc. (not altering text)
C19. S. 9. D savings for effects of 2014 asp 19, Sch. 2 para. 21 (1.10.2015) by The Historic Environment Scotland Act 2014 (Saving, Transitional and Consequential Provisions) Order 2015 (S.S.I. 2015/239), arts. 1. (1), 8

9. EOffence where scheduled monument enforcement notice not complied withS

(1) Where, after the end of the period for compliance with a scheduled monument enforcement notice, any works required by the notice to cease have not ceased or any step required by the notice has not been taken, the person who is for the time being owner of the scheduled monument or of the land in, on or under which it is situated is in breach of the notice.
(2) If at any time the owner of the monument or land is in breach of a scheduled monument enforcement notice the owner is guilty of an offence.
(3) An offence under this section may be charged by reference to any day or longer period of time.
(4) A person may, in relation to the same scheduled monument enforcement notice, be convicted of more than one offence under this section by reference to different days or different periods.
(5) In proceedings against any person for an offence under this section, it is a defence for the person to show that—
　(a) the person did everything the person could be expected to do to secure that all works required by the notice to cease were ceased or that all the steps required by the notice were taken, or
　(b) the person was not served with a copy of the notice and was not aware of its existence.
(6) A person guilty of an offence under this section is liable—
　(a) on summary conviction, to a fine not exceeding £20,000, and
　(b) on conviction on indictment, to a fine.
(7) In determining the amount of any fine to be imposed, the court is in particular to have regard to any financial benefit which has accrued or appears likely to accrue to the person in consequence of the offence.

9. FEffect of scheduled monument consent on scheduled monument enforcement noticeS

(1) If, after the issue of a scheduled monument enforcement notice, consent is granted under section 2. (3. A)—

(a) for the retention of any work to which the notice relates, or

(b) permitting the retention of works without complying with some condition subject to which a previous scheduled monument consent was granted,

the notice ceases to have effect in so far as such work is or such works are required by the notice to cease, or in so far as it requires steps to be taken involving the works not being retained or, as the case may be, for complying with that condition.

(2) The fact that a scheduled monument enforcement notice has wholly or partly ceased to have effect under subsection (1) does not affect the liability of any person for an offence in respect of a previous failure to comply with it. Stop notices

[F1099. FAEnforcement by the Scottish MinistersS

(1) If it appears to the Scottish Ministers that it is expedient that a scheduled monument enforcement notice should be served in respect of any monument or land in, on or under which there is a scheduled monument, they may serve such a notice under section 9. A.

(2) A scheduled monument enforcement notice served by the Scottish Ministers has the same effect as if it had been served by Historic Environment Scotland.

(3) The Scottish Ministers must not serve such a notice without consulting Historic Environment Scotland.

(4) The provisions of this Act relating to scheduled monument enforcement notices apply, so far as relevant, to a scheduled monument enforcement notice served by the Scottish Ministers as they apply to a scheduled monument enforcement notice served by Historic Environment Scotland, but with the substitution for any reference to Historic Environment Scotland of a reference to the Scottish Ministers, and any other necessary modifications.]

Amendments (Textual)

F109. S. 9. FA inserted (27.2.2015 for specified purposes, 1.10.2015 in so far as not already in force) by Historic Environment Scotland Act 2014 (asp 19), s. 31. (2), sch. 2 para. 22 (with ss. 29, 30); S.S.I. 2015/31, art. 2, sch.; S.S.I. 2015/196, art. 2, sch.

9. GStop noticesS

(1) Subsection (2) applies where [F110. Historic Environment Scotland considers] it expedient that any relevant works should cease before the expiry of the period for compliance with a scheduled monument enforcement notice.

(2) [F111. Historic Environment Scotland] may, when [F112it serves] the copy of the scheduled monument enforcement notice or afterwards, serve a notice (in this Act referred to as a "stop notice") prohibiting the execution of the relevant works to the scheduled monument to which the enforcement notice relates, or to land in, on or under which the monument is situated, or to any part of the monument or land specified in the stop notice.

(3) In this section and sections 9. H and 9. I, "relevant works" means any works specified in the scheduled monument enforcement notice as works which [F113. Historic Environment Scotland requires] to cease and any works carried out as part of, or associated with, such works.

(4) A stop notice may not be served if the scheduled monument enforcement notice has taken effect.

(5) A stop notice must specify the date when it is to come into effect, and that date—

(a) must not be earlier than 3 days after the date when the notice is served, unless [F114. Historic Environment Scotland considers] that there are special reasons for specifying an earlier date and a statement of those reasons is served with the stop notice, and

(b) must not be later than 28 days from the date when the notice is first served on any person.

(6) A stop notice may be served by [F115. Historic Environment Scotland] on any person who appears to [F116it] to have an interest in the monument or the land in, on or under which it is situated or who is executing, or causing to be executed, the relevant works specified in the

scheduled monument enforcement notice.
(7) [F117. Historic Environment Scotland] may at any time withdraw a stop notice (without prejudice to [F118its] power to serve another) by notice which must be—
　　(a) served on all persons who were served with the stop notice, and
　　(b) publicised by displaying it for 7 days in place of all or any site notices (within the meaning of section 9. H(3)).
Amendments (Textual)
F110. Words in s. 9. G(1) substituted (27.2.2015 for specified purposes, 1.10.2015 in so far as not already in force) by Historic Environment Scotland Act 2014 (asp 19), s. 31. (2), sch. 2 para. 24. (a) (with ss. 29, 30); S.S.I. 2015/31, art. 2, sch.; S.S.I. 2015/196, art. 2, sch.
F111. Words in s. 9. G(2) substituted (27.2.2015 for specified purposes, 1.10.2015 in so far as not already in force) by Historic Environment Scotland Act 2014 (asp 19), s. 31. (2), sch. 2 para. 24. (b)(i) (with ss. 29, 30); S.S.I. 2015/31, art. 2, sch.; S.S.I. 2015/196, art. 2, sch.
F112. Words in s. 9. G(2) substituted (27.2.2015 for specified purposes, 1.10.2015 in so far as not already in force) by Historic Environment Scotland Act 2014 (asp 19), s. 31. (2), sch. 2 para. 24. (b)(ii) (with ss. 29, 30); S.S.I. 2015/31, art. 2, sch.; S.S.I. 2015/196, art. 2, sch.
F113. Words in s. 9. G(3) substituted (27.2.2015 for specified purposes, 1.10.2015 in so far as not already in force) by Historic Environment Scotland Act 2014 (asp 19), s. 31. (2), sch. 2 para. 24. (c) (with ss. 29, 30); S.S.I. 2015/31, art. 2, sch.; S.S.I. 2015/196, art. 2, sch.
F114. Words in s. 9. G(5)(a) substituted (27.2.2015 for specified purposes, 1.10.2015 in so far as not already in force) by Historic Environment Scotland Act 2014 (asp 19), s. 31. (2), sch. 2 para. 24. (d) (with ss. 29, 30); S.S.I. 2015/31, art. 2, sch.; S.S.I. 2015/196, art. 2, sch.
F115. Words in s. 9. G(6) substituted (27.2.2015 for specified purposes, 1.10.2015 in so far as not already in force) by Historic Environment Scotland Act 2014 (asp 19), s. 31. (2), sch. 2 para. 24. (e)(i) (with ss. 29, 30); S.S.I. 2015/31, art. 2, sch.; S.S.I. 2015/196, art. 2, sch.
F116. Word in s. 9. G(6) substituted (27.2.2015 for specified purposes, 1.10.2015 in so far as not already in force) by Historic Environment Scotland Act 2014 (asp 19), s. 31. (2), sch. 2 para. 24. (e)(ii) (with ss. 29, 30); S.S.I. 2015/31, art. 2, sch.; S.S.I. 2015/196, art. 2, sch.
F117. Words in s. 9. G(7) substituted (27.2.2015 for specified purposes, 1.10.2015 in so far as not already in force) by Historic Environment Scotland Act 2014 (asp 19), s. 31. (2), sch. 2 para. 24. (f)(i) (with ss. 29, 30); S.S.I. 2015/31, art. 2, sch.; S.S.I. 2015/196, art. 2, sch.
F118. Word in s. 9. G(7) substituted (27.2.2015 for specified purposes, 1.10.2015 in so far as not already in force) by Historic Environment Scotland Act 2014 (asp 19), s. 31. (2), sch. 2 para. 24. (f)(ii) (with ss. 29, 30); S.S.I. 2015/31, art. 2, sch.; S.S.I. 2015/196, art. 2, sch.
Modifications etc. (not altering text)
C20. S. 9. G savings for effects of 2014 asp 19, Sch. 2 para. 24 (1.10.2015) by The Historic Environment Scotland Act 2014 (Saving, Transitional and Consequential Provisions) Order 2015 (S.S.I. 2015/239), arts. 1. (1), 8

9. HStop notices: supplementary provisionsS

(1) A stop notice ceases to have effect when—
　　(a) the scheduled monument enforcement notice to which it relates is withdrawn or quashed,
　　(b) the period for compliance expires, or
　　(c) notice of the withdrawal of the stop notice is served under section 9. G(7),
whichever occurs first.
(2) Where a requirement of the scheduled monument enforcement notice to which a stop notice relates is waived or relaxed by virtue of section 9. B(5) so that the scheduled monument enforcement notice no longer relates to any relevant works, the stop notice ceases to have effect in relation to those works.
(3) Where a stop notice has been served in respect of a scheduled monument [F119. Historic Environment Scotland] may publicise it by displaying on the land in, on or under which the

monument is situated or on the monument (except where doing so might damage it) a notice (in this section and in sections 6 and 9. J referred to as a "site notice")—
(a) stating that a stop notice has been served on a particular person or persons,
(b) indicating its requirements, and
(c) stating that any person contravening it may be prosecuted for an offence under section 9. J.
(4) A stop notice is not invalid by reason that a copy of the scheduled monument enforcement notice to which it relates was not served as required by section 9. B if it is shown that [F120. Historic Environment Scotland] took all such steps as were reasonably practicable to effect proper service.

Amendments (Textual)
F119. Words in s. 9. H(3) substituted (27.2.2015 for specified purposes, 1.10.2015 in so far as not already in force) by Historic Environment Scotland Act 2014 (asp 19), s. 31. (2), sch. 2 para. 25. (a) (with ss. 29, 30); S.S.I. 2015/31, art. 2, sch.; S.S.I. 2015/196, art. 2, sch.
F120. Words in s. 9. H(4) substituted (27.2.2015 for specified purposes, 1.10.2015 in so far as not already in force) by Historic Environment Scotland Act 2014 (asp 19), s. 31. (2), sch. 2 para. 25. (b) (with ss. 29, 30); S.S.I. 2015/31, art. 2, sch.; S.S.I. 2015/196, art. 2, sch.

Modifications etc. (not altering text)
C21. S. 9. H savings for effects of 2014 asp 19, Sch. 2 para. 25 (1.10.2015) by The Historic Environment Scotland Act 2014 (Saving, Transitional and Consequential Provisions) Order 2015 (S.S.I. 2015/239), arts. 1. (1), 8

[F1219. HAPower of the Scottish Ministers to serve stop noticeS

(1) If it appears to the Scottish Ministers that it is expedient that a stop notice should be served in respect of any monument or land in, on or under which there is a scheduled monument, they may serve such a notice under section 9. G.
(2) A stop notice served by the Scottish Ministers has the same effect as if it had been served by Historic Environment Scotland.
(3) The Scottish Ministers must not serve such a notice without consulting Historic Environment Scotland.
(4) The provisions of this Act relating to stop notices apply, so far as relevant, to a stop notice served by the Scottish Ministers as they apply to a stop notice served by Historic Environment Scotland, but with the substitution for any reference to Historic Environment Scotland of a reference to the Scottish Ministers, and any other necessary modifications.]

Amendments (Textual)
F121. S. 9. HA inserted (27.2.2015 for specified purposes, 1.10.2015 in so far as not already in force) by Historic Environment Scotland Act 2014 (asp 19), s. 31. (2), sch. 2 para. 26 (with ss. 29, 30); S.S.I. 2015/31, art. 2, sch.; S.S.I. 2015/196, art. 2, sch.

9. ICompensation for loss due to stop noticeS

(1) Where a stop notice ceases to have effect a person who, when the notice is first served, has an interest (whether as owner or occupier or otherwise) in the scheduled monument to which the notice relates or the land in, on or under which the monument is situated is entitled to be compensated by [F122. Historic Environment Scotland] in respect of any loss or damage falling within subsection (2).
(2) That is loss or damage directly attributable to—
(a) the prohibition contained in the stop notice, or
(b) in a case within subsection (3)(b), the prohibition of such of the works prohibited by the stop notice as cease to be relevant works.
(3) For the purposes of this section, a stop notice ceases to have effect when—
(a) the scheduled monument enforcement notice is quashed,

(b) a requirement of the scheduled monument enforcement notice is waived or relaxed by virtue of section 9. B(5) so that any works the execution of which are prohibited by the stop notice cease to be relevant works,

(c) the scheduled monument enforcement notice is withdrawn by [F123. Historic Environment Scotland] otherwise than in consequence of the grant by [F124it] of scheduled monument consent for the works to which the notice relates, or

(d) the stop notice is withdrawn.

(4) The loss or damage in respect of which compensation is payable under this section in respect of a prohibition includes any sum payable in respect of a breach of contract caused by the taking of action necessary to comply with the prohibition.

(5) No compensation is payable under this section—

(a) in respect of the prohibition in a stop notice of any works which, at any time when the notice is in force, are such as to involve a contravention of section 2. (1) or (6), or

(b) in the case of a claimant who was required to provide information under section 57 (power to require information as to interests in land) in respect of any loss or damage suffered by the claimant which could have been avoided if the claimant had provided the information or had otherwise co-operated with [F125. Historic Environment Scotland] when responding to the notice.

Amendments (Textual)

F122. Words in s. 9. I(1) substituted (27.2.2015 for specified purposes, 1.10.2015 in so far as not already in force) by Historic Environment Scotland Act 2014 (asp 19), s. 31. (2), sch. 2 para. 27. (a) (with ss. 29, 30); S.S.I. 2015/31, art. 2, sch.; S.S.I. 2015/196, art. 2, sch.

F123. Words in s. 9. I(3)(c) substituted (27.2.2015 for specified purposes, 1.10.2015 in so far as not already in force) by Historic Environment Scotland Act 2014 (asp 19), s. 31. (2), sch. 2 para. 27. (b)(i) (with ss. 29, 30); S.S.I. 2015/31, art. 2, sch.; S.S.I. 2015/196, art. 2, sch.

F124. Word in s. 9. I(3)(c) substituted (27.2.2015 for specified purposes, 1.10.2015 in so far as not already in force) by Historic Environment Scotland Act 2014 (asp 19), s. 31. (2), sch. 2 para. 27. (b)(ii) (with ss. 29, 30); S.S.I. 2015/31, art. 2, sch.; S.S.I. 2015/196, art. 2, sch.

F125. Words in s. 9. I(5)(b) substituted (27.2.2015 for specified purposes, 1.10.2015 in so far as not already in force) by Historic Environment Scotland Act 2014 (asp 19), s. 31. (2), sch. 2 para. 27. (c) (with ss. 29, 30); S.S.I. 2015/31, art. 2, sch.; S.S.I. 2015/196, art. 2, sch.

Modifications etc. (not altering text)

C22. S. 9. I savings for effects of 2014 asp 19, Sch. 2 para. 27 (1.10.2015) by The Historic Environment Scotland Act 2014 (Saving, Transitional and Consequential Provisions) Order 2015 (S.S.I. 2015/239), arts. 1. (1), 8

9. JPenalties for contravention of stop noticeS

(1) A person who contravenes a stop notice after a site notice has been displayed, or after the stop notice has been served on the person, is guilty of an offence.

(2) Contravention of a stop notice includes causing or permitting its contravention.

(3) An offence under this section may be charged by reference to any day or longer period of time.

(4) A person may, in relation to the same stop notice, be convicted of more than one offence under this section by reference to different days or different periods.

(5) It is a defence in any proceedings under this section that—

(a) the stop notice was not served on the accused, and

(b) the accused had no reasonable cause to believe that the works were prohibited by the stop notice.

(6) A person guilty of an offence under this section is liable—

(a) on summary conviction, to a fine not exceeding £20,000, and

(b) on conviction on indictment, to a fine.

(7) In determining the amount of the fine, the court is in particular to have regard to any financial benefit which has accrued or appears likely to accrue to the person in consequence of the offence.]

[F74. Temporary stop noticesS

9. KTemporary stop noticesS

(1) Where it appears to [F126. Historic Environment Scotland] that—
    (a) any works have been, or are being, executed to a scheduled monument or to land in, on or under which there is a scheduled monument,
    (b) the works are such as to involve a contravention of section 2. (1) or (6), and
    (c) it is expedient that the works are (or any part of the works is) stopped immediately,
[F127it may, if it considers] it expedient to do so having regard to the effect of the works on the character of the monument as one of national importance, issue a temporary stop notice.
(2) The notice must be given in writing and must—
    (a) specify the works in question,
    (b) prohibit execution of the works (or so much of the works as is specified in the notice), and
    (c) set out [F128. Historic Environment Scotland's] reasons for issuing the notice.
(3) A temporary stop notice may be served on any of the following—
    (a) a person who appears to [F129. Historic Environment Scotland] to be executing, or causing to be executed, the works,
    (b) a person who appears to [F129. Historic Environment Scotland] to have an interest in the scheduled monument or the land in, on or under which the monument is situated (whether as owner or occupier or otherwise).
(4) [F130. Historic Environment Scotland] must display on the land in, on or under which the monument is situated or on the monument (except where doing so might damage it)—
    (a) a copy of the notice, and
    (b) a statement as to the effect of section 9. M.
(5) A temporary stop notice has effect from the time a copy of it is first displayed in pursuance of subsection (4).
(6) A temporary stop notice ceases to have effect at the end of the period of 28 days starting on the day the copy notice is so displayed.
(7) But if a shorter period starting on that day is specified in the notice, the notice instead ceases to have effect at the end of that shorter period.
(8) And if the notice is withdrawn by [F131. Historic Environment Scotland] before that period of 28 days (or, as the case may be, that shorter period) expires, the notice ceases to have effect on being so withdrawn.

Amendments (Textual)
F126. Words in s. 9. K(1) substituted (27.2.2015 for specified purposes, 1.10.2015 in so far as not already in force) by Historic Environment Scotland Act 2014 (asp 19), s. 31. (2), sch. 2 para. 28. (a)(i) (with ss. 29, 30); S.S.I. 2015/31, art. 2, sch.; S.S.I. 2015/196, art. 2, sch.
F127. Words in s. 9. K(1) substituted (27.2.2015 for specified purposes, 1.10.2015 in so far as not already in force) by Historic Environment Scotland Act 2014 (asp 19), s. 31. (2), sch. 2 para. 28. (a)(ii) (with ss. 29, 30); S.S.I. 2015/31, art. 2, sch.; S.S.I. 2015/196, art. 2, sch.
F128. Words in s. 9. K(2)(c) substituted (27.2.2015 for specified purposes, 1.10.2015 in so far as not already in force) by Historic Environment Scotland Act 2014 (asp 19), s. 31. (2), sch. 2 para. 28. (b) (with ss. 29, 30); S.S.I. 2015/31, art. 2, sch.; S.S.I. 2015/196, art. 2, sch.
F129. Words in s. 9. K(3) substituted (27.2.2015 for specified purposes, 1.10.2015 in so far as not already in force) by Historic Environment Scotland Act 2014 (asp 19), s. 31. (2), sch. 2 para. 28. (c) (with ss. 29, 30); S.S.I. 2015/31, art. 2, sch.; S.S.I. 2015/196, art. 2, sch.
F130. Words in s. 9. K(4) substituted (27.2.2015 for specified purposes, 1.10.2015 in so far as not already in force) by Historic Environment Scotland Act 2014 (asp 19), s. 31. (2), sch. 2 para. 28. (d) (with ss. 29, 30); S.S.I. 2015/31, art. 2, sch.; S.S.I. 2015/196, art. 2, sch.

F131. Words in s. 9. K(8) substituted (27.2.2015 for specified purposes, 1.10.2015 in so far as not already in force) by Historic Environment Scotland Act 2014 (asp 19), s. 31. (2), sch. 2 para. 28. (e) (with ss. 29, 30); S.S.I. 2015/31, art. 2, sch.; S.S.I. 2015/196, art. 2, sch.
Modifications etc. (not altering text)
C23. S. 9. K savings for effects of 2014 asp 19, Sch. 2 para. 28 (1.10.2015) by The Historic Environment Scotland Act 2014 (Saving, Transitional and Consequential Provisions) Order 2015 (S.S.I. 2015/239), arts. 1. (1), 9

9. LTemporary stop notices: restrictionsS

(1) A second or subsequent temporary stop notice must not be issued in respect of the same works unless [F132. Historic Environment Scotland has] in the meantime taken some other enforcement action in relation to the contravention of section 2. (1) or (6) which is constituted by the works.
(2) In subsection (1), "enforcement action" includes obtaining the grant of an interdict under section 9. O.
Amendments (Textual)
F132. Words in s. 9. L(1) substituted (27.2.2015 for specified purposes, 1.10.2015 in so far as not already in force) by Historic Environment Scotland Act 2014 (asp 19), s. 31. (2), sch. 2 para. 29 (with ss. 29, 30); S.S.I. 2015/31, art. 2, sch.; S.S.I. 2015/196, art. 2, sch.

9. MTemporary stop notices: offencesS

(1) A person who contravenes a temporary stop notice—
   (a) which has been served on the person, or
   (b) a copy of which has been displayed in pursuance of section 9. K(4),
is guilty of an offence.
(2) Contravention of a temporary stop notice includes causing or permitting its contravention.
(3) An offence under this section may be charged by reference to a day or to a longer period of time.
(4) A person may, in relation to the same temporary stop notice, be convicted of more than one offence under this section by reference to different days or different periods.
(5) It is a defence in any proceedings under this section that—
   (a) the temporary stop notice was not served on the accused, and
   (b) the accused did not know, and could not reasonably have been expected to know, of its existence.
(6) A person guilty of an offence under this section is liable—
   (a) on summary conviction, to a fine not exceeding £20,000,
   (b) on conviction on indictment, to a fine.
(7) In determining the amount of the fine, the court is in particular to have regard to any financial benefit which has accrued or appears likely to accrue to the convicted person in consequence of the execution of the works which constituted the offence.

9. NTemporary stop notices: compensationS

(1) A person who, at the date on which a temporary stop notice is first displayed in pursuance of section 9. K(4), has an interest (whether as owner or occupier or otherwise) in the scheduled monument to which the notice relates or the land in, on or under which the monument is situated is entitled to be compensated by [F133. Historic Environment Scotland] in respect of any loss or damage directly attributable to the prohibition effected by that notice.
(2) But subsection (1) applies only if the circumstances are as set out in one or both of the following paragraphs—

(a) the works specified in the notice are authorised by scheduled monument consent granted on or before the date mentioned in that subsection,

(b) [F134. Historic Environment Scotland withdraws] the notice other than following such grant of scheduled monument consent as is mentioned in paragraph (a).

(3) Subsections (4) and (5) of section 9. I apply to compensation payable under this section as they apply to compensation payable under that section; and for the purpose of that application references in subsection (5) of that section to a stop notice are to be taken to be references to a temporary stop notice.]

Amendments (Textual)

F133. Words in s. 9. N(1) substituted (27.2.2015 for specified purposes, 1.10.2015 in so far as not already in force) by Historic Environment Scotland Act 2014 (asp 19), s. 31. (2), sch. 2 para. 30. (a) (with ss. 29, 30); S.S.I. 2015/31, art. 2, sch.; S.S.I. 2015/196, art. 2, sch.

F134. Words in s. 9. N(2)(b) substituted (27.2.2015 for specified purposes, 1.10.2015 in so far as not already in force) by Historic Environment Scotland Act 2014 (asp 19), s. 31. (2), sch. 2 para. 30. (b) (with ss. 29, 30); S.S.I. 2015/31, art. 2, sch.; S.S.I. 2015/196, art. 2, sch.

Modifications etc. (not altering text)

C24. S. 9. N savings for effects of 2014 asp 19, Sch. 2 para. 30 (1.10.2015) by The Historic Environment Scotland Act 2014 (Saving, Transitional and Consequential Provisions) Order 2015 (S.S.I. 2015/239), arts. 1. (1), 9

[F74. InterdictsS

9. OInterdicts restraining unauthorised works on scheduled monumentsS

(1) Whether or not [F135. Historic Environment Scotland has exercised or proposes to exercise any of its] other powers under this Act, [F136it] may seek to restrain or prevent any actual or apprehended breach of any of the controls provided by or under this Act on the execution of works affecting scheduled monuments by means of an application for interdict.

[F137. (1. A)Whether or not the Scottish Ministers have exercised or propose to exercise any of their powers under this Act, they may seek to restrain or prevent any actual or apprehended breach of any of the controls provided by or under this Act on the execution of works affecting scheduled monuments by means of an application for interdict.]

(2) On an application under [F138subsection (1) or (1. A)] the court may grant such interdict as it thinks appropriate for the purpose of restraining or preventing the breach.

(3) In this section "the court" means the Court of Session or the sheriff.]

Amendments (Textual)

F135. Words in s. 9. O(1) substituted (27.2.2015 for specified purposes, 1.10.2015 in so far as not already in force) by Historic Environment Scotland Act 2014 (asp 19), s. 31. (2), sch. 2 para. 40. (a)(i) (with ss. 29, 30); S.S.I. 2015/31, art. 2, sch.; S.S.I. 2015/196, art. 2, sch.

F136. Word in s. 9. O(1) substituted (27.2.2015 for specified purposes, 1.10.2015 in so far as not already in force) by Historic Environment Scotland Act 2014 (asp 19), s. 31. (2), sch. 2 para. 40. (a)(i) (with ss. 29, 30); S.S.I. 2015/31, art. 2, sch.; S.S.I. 2015/196, art. 2, sch.

F137. S. 9. O(1. A) inserted (27.2.2015 for specified purposes, 1.10.2015 in so far as not already in force) by Historic Environment Scotland Act 2014 (asp 19), s. 31. (2), sch. 2 para. 40. (b) (with ss. 29, 30); S.S.I. 2015/31, art. 2, sch.; S.S.I. 2015/196, art. 2, sch.

F138. Words in s. 9. O(2) substituted (27.2.2015 for specified purposes, 1.10.2015 in so far as not already in force) by Historic Environment Scotland Act 2014 (asp 19), s. 31. (2), sch. 2 para. 40. (c) (with ss. 29, 30); S.S.I. 2015/31, art. 2, sch.; S.S.I. 2015/196, art. 2, sch.

Acquisition of ancient monuments

10 Compulsory acquisition of ancient monuments.

(1) The Secretary of State may acquire compulsorily any ancient monument for the purpose of securing its preservation [F139; but, where the monument in question is situated in England, he shall consult with the Commission before making a compulsory purchase order.]
(2) The M4[F140. Acquisition of Land Act 1981] shall apply to any compulsory acquisition by the Secretary of State under this section of an ancient monument situated in England and Wales . . . F141
(3) The M5. Acquisition of Land (Authorisation Procedure) (Scotland) Act 1947 shall apply to any compulsory acquisition by the Secretary of State under this section of an ancient monument situated in Scotland as it applies to a compulsory acquisition by another Minister or by the Secretary of State under section 58 of the M6. National Health Service (Scotland) Act 1972 in a case falling within section 1. (1) of the said Act of 1947.
(4) For the purpose of assessing compensation in respect of any compulsory acquisition under this section of a monument which, immediately before the date of the compulsory purchase order, was scheduled, it shall be assumed that scheduled monument consent would not be granted for any works which would or might result in the demolition, destruction or removal of the monument or any part of it.
Amendments (Textual)
F139. Words inserted by National Heritage Act 1983 (c. 47, SIF 78), s. 41, Sch. 4 para. 36
F140. Words substituted by Acquisition of Land Act 1981 (c. 67), Sch. 4 para. 1 Table
F141. Words repealed by Acquisition of Land Act 1981 (c. 67), Sch. 6 Pt. I
Marginal Citations
M41981 c. 67.
M51947 c. 42.
M61972 c. 58.

11 Acquisition by agreement or gift of ancient monuments.

(1) The Secretary of State may acquire by agreement any ancient monument [F142but, where the monument in question is situated in England, he shall consult with the Commission before doing so.]
[F143. (1. A)With the consent of the Secretary of State, the Commission may acquire by agreement any ancient monument situated in England.]
(2) Any local authority may acquire by agreement any ancient monument situated in or in the vicinity of their area.
(3) The Secretary of State or any local authority may accept a gift (whether by deed or will) of any ancient monument [F144; but, where the monument in question is situated in England, the Secretary of State shall consult with the Commission before accepting]
[F145. (3. A)With the consent of the Secretary of State, the Commission may accept a gift (whether by deed or will) of any ancient monument situated in England.]
(4) The provisions of Part I of the M7. Compulsory Purchase Act 1965 (so far as applicable) other than sections 4 to 8, section 10 and section 31, shall apply in relation to any acquisition under subsection (1) or (2) above of an ancient monument situated in England and Wales.
(5) For the purpose of any acquisition under subsection (1) or (2) above of any ancient monument situated in Scotland which is heritable—
   (a) the Lands Clauses Acts (with the exception of the provisions excluded by subsection (6) below) and sections 6 and 70 to 78 of the M8. Railways Clauses Consolidation (Scotland) Act

1845 (as originally enacted and not as amended by section 15 of the M9. Mines (Working Facilities and Support) Act 1923) shall be incorporated with this section; and

(b) in construing those Acts for the purposes of this section, this section shall be deemed to be the special Act and the Secretary of State or the local authority acquiring the monument shall be deemed to be the promoter of the undertaking or company (as the case may require).

(6) The provisions of the Lands Clauses Acts excluded from being incorporated with this section are—

(a) those which relate to the acquisition of land otherwise than by agreement;

(b) those which relate to access to the special Act; and

(c) sections 120 to 125 of the M10. Lands Clauses Consolidation (Scotland) Act 1845.

Amendments (Textual)
F142. Words inserted by National Heritage Act 1983 (c. 47, SIF 78), s. 41, Sch. 4 para. 37. (2)
F143. S. 11. (1. A) inserted by National Heritage Act 1983 (c. 47, SIF 78), s. 41, Sch. 4 para. 37. (3)
F144. Words inserted by National Heritage Act 1983 (c. 47, SIF 78), s. 41, Sch. 4 para. 37. (4)
F145. S. 11. (3. A) inserted by National Heritage Act 1983 (c. 47, SIF 78), s. 41, Sch. 4 para. 37. (5)

Modifications etc. (not altering text)
C25. S. 11 functions made exercisable concurrently (E.W.) (with effect in accordance with art. 25. (1) of the amending S.I.) by The Cotswolds Area of Outstanding Natural Beauty (Establishment of Conservation Board) Order 2004 (S.I. 2004/1777), arts. 1, 25. (2)(xxv) (with art. 35)
C26. S. 11 functions made exercisable concurrently (E.W.) (with effect in accordance with art. 25. (1) of the amending S.I.) by The Chilterns Area of Outstanding Natural Beauty (Establishment of Conservation Board) Order 2004 (S.I. 2004/1778), arts. 2, 25. (1), 25. (1), 25. (2)(xxv) (with art. 35)

Marginal Citations
M71965 c. 56.
M81845 c. 33.
M91923 c. 20.
M101845 c. 19.

Guardianship of ancient monuments

12 Power to place ancient monument under guardianship.

(1) Subject to subsection (4) below, a person who has—

(a) an interest of any description mentioned in subsection (3) below in an ancient monument situated in England and Wales; or

(b) any heritable interest in an ancient monument situated in Scotland;

may, with the consent of the Secretary of State, constitute him by deed guardian of the monument.

[F146. Where the monument in question is situated in England, the Secretary of State shall consult with the Commission before he so consents.]

[F147. (1. A)Subject to subsection (4) below, a person who has an interest of any description mentioned in subsection (3) below in an ancient monument situated in England may, with the consent of the Commission, given after obtaining the consent of the Secretary of State, constitute the Commission by deed guardian of the Monument.]

(2) Subject to subsection (4) below, a person who has any such interest in an ancient monument may with the consent of any local authority in or in the vicinity of whose area the monument is situated constitute that authority by deed guardians of the monument.

(3) The interests in an ancient monument situated in England and Wales which qualify a person to establish guardianship of the monument under subsection (1) [F148or (1. A)] or (2) above are the

following—

(a) an estate in fee simple absolute in possession;

(b) a leasehold estate or interest in possession, being an estate or interest for a term of years of which not less than forty-five are unexpired or (as the case may be) renewable for a term of not less than forty-five years; and

(c) an interest in possession for his own life or the life of another, or for lives (whether or not including his own), under any existing or future [F149trust of land] under which the estate or interest for the time being subject to the trust falls within paragraph (a) or (b) above.

(4) A person who is not the occupier of an ancient monument may not establish guardianship of the monument under this section unless the occupier is also a party to the deed executed for the purposes of subsection (1) [F148. (1. A)] or (2) above.

(5) Any person who has an interest in an ancient monument may be a party to any such deed in addition to the person establishing the guardianship of the monument and (where the latter is not the occupier) the occupier.

(6) In relation to any monument of which the Secretary of State [F150or the Commission] or any local authority have been constituted the guardians under this Act, references below in this Act to the guardianship deed are references to the deed executed for the purposes of subsection (1) or [F151. (1. A) or (2) above (as the case may be)]

(7) A guardianship deed relating to any ancient monument situated in England and Wales shall be a local land charge.

(8) A guardianship deed relating to any ancient monument situated in Scotland may be recorded in the Register of Sasines.

(9) Every person deriving title to any ancient monument from, through or under any person who has executed a guardianship deed shall be bound by the guardianship deed unless—

(a) in the case of a monument in England and Wales, he derives title by virtue of any disposition made by the person who executed the deed before the date of the deed; or

(b) in the case of a monument in Scotland, he is a person who in good faith and for value acquired right (whether completed by infeftment or not) to his interest in the monument before the date of the deed.

(10) The Secretary of State [F152or the Commission] or a local authority shall not consent to become guardians of any structure which is occupied as a dwelling house by any person other than a person employed as the caretaker thereof or his family.

(11) Except as provided by this Act, any person who has any estate or interest in a monument under guardianship shall have the same right and title to, and estate or interest in, the monument in all respects as if the Secretary of State or [F153the Commission or the local authority in question (as the case may be)] had not become guardians of the monument.

Extent Information

E1. This version of this provision extends to England and Wales only; a separate version has been created for Scotland only

Amendments (Textual)

F146. Words inserted by National Heritage Act 1983 (c. 47, SIF 78), s. 41, Sch. 4 para. 38. (2)

F147. S. 12. (1. A) inserted by National Heritage Act 1983 (c. 47, SIF 78), s. 41, Sch. 4 para. 38. (3)

F148. Words inserted by National Heritage Act 1983 (c. 47, SIF 78), s. 41, Sch. 4 para. 38. (4)

F149. Words in s. 12. (3) substituted (E.W.) (1.1.1997) by 1996 c. 47, s. 25. (1), Sch. 3 para. 17. (a) (with s. 24. (2), 25. (4)); S.I. 1996/2974, art.2

F150. Words inserted by National Heritage Act 1983 (c. 47, SIF 78), s. 41, Sch. 4 para. 38. (5)

F151. Words substituted by National Heritage Act 1983 (c. 47, SIF 78), s. 41, Sch. 4 para. 38. (5)

F152. Words inserted by National Heritage Act 1983 (c. 47, SIF 78), s. 41, Sch. 4 para. 38. (6)

F153. Words substituted by National Heritage Act 1983 (c. 47, SIF 78), s. 41, Sch. 4 para. 38. (7)

Modifications etc. (not altering text)

C27. Ss. 12-17 functions made exercisable concurrently (E.W.) (with effect in accordance with art. 25. (1) of the amending S.I.) by The Cotswolds Area of Outstanding Natural Beauty

(Establishment of Conservation Board) Order 2004 (S.I. 2004/1777), arts. 1, 25. (2)(xxvi) (with art. 35)
C28. Ss. 12-17 functions made exercisable concurrently (E.W.) (with effect in accordance with art. 25. (1) of the amending S.I.) by The Chilterns Area of Outstanding Natural Beauty (Establishment of Conservation Board) Order 2004 (S.I. 2004/1778), arts. 2, 25. (1), 25. (1), 25. (2)(xxvi) (with art. 35)

12 Power to place ancient monument under guardianship.S

(1) Subject to subsection (4) below, a person who has—
    (a) an interest of any description mentioned in subsection (3) below in an ancient monument situated in England and Wales; or
    (b) any heritable interest in an ancient monument situated in Scotland;
may, with the consent of the Secretary of State, constitute him by deed guardian of the monument.
[F252. Where the monument in question is situated in England, the Secretary of State shall consult with the Commission before he so consents.]
[F253. (1. A)Subject to subsection (4) below, a person who has an interest of any description mentioned in subsection (3) below in an ancient monument situated in England may, with the consent of the Commission, given after obtaining the consent of the Secretary of State, constitute the Commission by deed guardian of the Monument.]
(2) Subject to subsection (4) below, a person who has any such interest in an ancient monument may with the consent of any local authority in or in the vicinity of whose area the monument is situated constitute that authority by deed guardians of the monument.
(3) The interests in an ancient monument situated in England and Wales which qualify a person to establish guardianship of the monument under subsection (1) [F254or (1. A)] or (2) above are the following—
    (a) an estate in fee simple absolute in possession;
    (b) a leasehold estate or interest in possession, being an estate or interest for a term of years of which not less than forty-five are unexpired or (as the case may be) renewable for a term of not less than forty-five years; and
    (c) an interest in possession for his own life or the life of another, or for lives (whether or not including his own), under any existing or future trust for sale under which the estate or interest for the time being subject to the trust falls within paragraph (a) or (b) above.
(4) A person who is not the occupier of an ancient monument may not establish guardianship of the monument under this section unless the occupier is also a party to the deed executed for the purposes of subsection (1) [F254. (1. A)] or (2) above.
(5) Any person who has an interest in an ancient monument may be a party to any such deed in addition to the person establishing the guardianship of the monument and (where the latter is not the occupier) the occupier.
(6) In relation to any monument of which the Secretary of State [F255or the Commission] or any local authority have been constituted the guardians under this Act, references below in this Act to the guardianship deed are references to the deed executed for the purposes of subsection (1) or [F256. (1. A) or (2) above (as the case may be)]
(7) A guardianship deed relating to any ancient monument situated in England and Wales shall be a local land charge.
(8) A guardianship deed relating to any ancient monument situated in Scotland may be recorded in the Register of Sasines.
(9) Every person deriving title to any ancient monument from, through or under any person who has executed a guardianship deed shall be bound by the guardianship deed unless—
    (a) in the case of a monument in England and Wales, he derives title by virtue of any disposition made by the person who executed the deed before the date of the deed; or
    (b) in the case of a monument in Scotland, he is a person who in good faith and for value

acquired right (whether [F257title has been completed] or not) to his interest in the monument before the date of the deed.

(10) The Secretary of State [F258or the Commission] or a local authority shall not consent to become guardians of any structure which is occupied as a dwelling house by any person other than a person employed as the caretaker thereof or his family.

(11) Except as provided by this Act, any person who has any estate or interest in a monument under guardianship shall have the same right and title to, and estate or interest in, the monument in all respects as if the Secretary of State or [F259the Commission or the local authority in question (as the case may be)] had not become guardians of the monument.

Extent Information

E3. This version of this provision extends to Scotland only; a separate version has been created for England and Wales only.

Amendments (Textual)

F252. Words inserted by National Heritage Act 1983 (c. 47, SIF 78), s. 41, Sch. 4 para. 38. (2)
F253. S. 12. (1. A) inserted by National Heritage Act 1983 (c. 47, SIF 78), s. 41, Sch. 4 para. 38. (3)
F254. Words inserted by National Heritage Act 1983 (c. 47, SIF 78), s. 41, Sch. 4 para. 38. (4)
F255. Words inserted by National Heritage Act 1983 (c. 47, SIF 78), s. 41, Sch. 4 para. 38. (5)
F256. Words substituted by National Heritage Act 1983 (c. 47, SIF 78), s. 41, Sch. 4 para. 38. (5)
F257. Words in s. 12. (9)(b) substituted (28.11.2004) by Abolition of Feudal Tenure etc. (Scotland) Act 2000 (asp 5), ss. 71, 77. (2), Sch. 12 para. 40. (2) (with ss. 58, 62, 75); S.S.I. 2003/456, art. 2
F258. Words inserted by National Heritage Act 1983 (c. 47, SIF 78), s. 41, Sch. 4 para. 38. (6)
F259. Words substituted by National Heritage Act 1983 (c. 47, SIF 78), s. 41, Sch. 4 para. 38. (7)

Modifications etc. (not altering text)

C27. Ss. 12-17 functions made exercisable concurrently (E.W.) (with effect in accordance with art. 25. (1) of the amending S.I.) by The Cotswolds Area of Outstanding Natural Beauty (Establishment of Conservation Board) Order 2004 (S.I. 2004/1777), arts. 1, 25. (2)(xxvi) (with art. 35)

C28. Ss. 12-17 functions made exercisable concurrently (E.W.) (with effect in accordance with art. 25. (1) of the amending S.I.) by The Chilterns Area of Outstanding Natural Beauty (Establishment of Conservation Board) Order 2004 (S.I. 2004/1778), arts. 2, 25. (1), 25. (1), 25. (2)(xxvi) (with art. 35)

13 Effect of guardianship.

(1) The Secretary of State [F154and the Commission] and any local authority shall be under a duty to maintain any monument which is under their guardianship by virtue of this Act.

(2) The Secretary of State [F154and the Commission] and any local authority shall have full control and management of any monument which is under their guardianship by virtue of this Act.

[F155. (2. A)The power conferred by subsection (2) above includes power—
   (a) to control the holding of events in or on the monument;
   (b) to control and manage such events;
   (c) to require payment of a charge in respect of the holding of such events;
   (d) to exclude, restrict or otherwise control public access to the monument in connection with such events.]

(3) With a view to fulfilling their duty under subsection (1) above to maintain a monument of which they are the guardians, the Secretary of State [F156or the Commission] or any local authority shall have power to do all such things as may be necessary for the maintenance of the monument and for the exercise by them of proper control and management with respect to the monument.

(4) Without prejudice to the generality of the preceding provisions of this section, the Secretary of

State [F156or the Commission] or any local authority shall have power—

(a) to make any examination of a monument which is under their guardianship by virtue of this Act;

(b) to open up any such monument or make excavations therein for the purpose of examination or otherwise; and

(c) to remove the whole or any part of any such monument to another place for the purpose of preserving it.

(5) The Secretary of State [F156or the Commission] or any local authority may at any reasonable time enter the site of a monument which is under their guardianship by virtue of this Act for the purpose of exercising any of their powers under this section in relation to the monument (and may authorise any other person to exercise any of those powers on their behalf).

(6) Subsections (2) to (4) above are subject to any provision to the contrary in the guardianship deed.

(7) In this Part of this Act "maintenance" includes fencing, repairing, and covering in, of a monument and the doing of any other act or thing which may be required for the purpose of repairing the monument or protecting it from decay or injury, and "maintain" shall be construed accordingly.

[F157. (8)In subsection (2. A) above—

(a) "events" includes functions and any other organised activities;

(b) references to the holding of events, in relation to organised activities, are to be construed as references to the carrying out of such activities.]

Amendments (Textual)

F154. Words inserted by National Heritage Act 1983 (c. 47, SIF 78), s. 41, Sch. 4 para. 39. (2)

F155. S. 13. (2. A) inserted (S.) (30.6.2011) by Historic Environment (Amendment) (Scotland) Act 2011 (asp 3), ss. 7. (2)(a), 33. (2); S.S.I. 2011/174, art. 2, Sch.

F156. Words inserted by National Heritage Act 1983 (c. 47, SIF 78), s. 41, Sch. 4 para. 39. (3)

F157. S. 13. (8) added (S.) (30.6.2011) by Historic Environment (Amendment) (Scotland) Act 2011 (asp 3), ss. 7. (2)(b), 33. (2); S.S.I. 2011/174, art. 2, Sch.

Modifications etc. (not altering text)

C27. Ss. 12-17 functions made exercisable concurrently (E.W.) (with effect in accordance with art. 25. (1) of the amending S.I.) by The Cotswolds Area of Outstanding Natural Beauty (Establishment of Conservation Board) Order 2004 (S.I. 2004/1777), arts. 1, 25. (2)(xxvi) (with art. 35)

C28. Ss. 12-17 functions made exercisable concurrently (E.W.) (with effect in accordance with art. 25. (1) of the amending S.I.) by The Chilterns Area of Outstanding Natural Beauty (Establishment of Conservation Board) Order 2004 (S.I. 2004/1778), arts. 2, 25. (1), 25. (1), 25. (2)(xxvi) (with art. 35)

14 Termination of guardianship.

(1) Subject to the following provisions of this section, where the Secretary of State [F158or the Commission] or a local authority have become guardians of any monument under this Act, they may by agreement made with the persons who are for the time being immediately affected by the operation of the guardianship deed—

(a) exclude any part of the monument from guardianship; or

(b) renounce guardianship of the monument;

but except as provided above the monument shall remain under guardianship (unless it is acquired by its guardians) until an occupier of the monument who is entitled to terminate the guardianship gives notice in writing to that effect to the guardians of the monument.

An occupier of a monument is entitled to terminate the guardianship of the monument if—

(a) he has any interest in the monument which would qualify him to establish guardianship of the monument under section 12 of this Act; and

(b) he is not bound by the guardianship deed.

(2) A local authority shall consult with the Secretary of State before entering into any agreement under this section.

[F159. Where the monument in question is situated in England, the Secretary of State shall consult with the Commission before entering into any such agreement.

The Commission shall consult with the Secretary of State before entering into any such agreement.]

(3) Neither the Secretary of State [F160nor the Commission] nor a local authority may enter into any such agreement unless he or they are satisfied with respect to the part of the monument or (as the case may be) with respect to the whole of the monument in question—

(a) that satisfactory arrangements have been made for ensuring its preservation after termination of the guardianship; or

(b) that it is no longer practicable to preserve it (whether because of the cost of preserving it or otherwise).

(4) An agreement under this section must be made under seal in the case of a monument situated in England and Wales.

(5) Where in the case of a monument situated in Scotland the guardianship deed has been recorded in the Register of Sasines in accordance with section 12 of this Act an agreement under this section relating to that monument may also be so recorded.

Amendments (Textual)
F158. Words inserted by National Heritage Act 1983 (c. 47, SIF 78), s. 41, Sch. 4 para. 40. (2)
F159. Words inserted by National Heritage Act 1983 (c. 47, SIF 78), s. 41, Sch. 4 para. 40. (3)
F160. Words inserted by National Heritage Act 1983 (c. 47, SIF 78), s. 41, Sch. 4 para. 40. (4)
Modifications etc. (not altering text)
C27. Ss. 12-17 functions made exercisable concurrently (E.W.) (with effect in accordance with art. 25. (1) of the amending S.I.) by The Cotswolds Area of Outstanding Natural Beauty (Establishment of Conservation Board) Order 2004 (S.I. 2004/1777), arts. 1, 25. (2)(xxvi) (with art. 35)
C28. Ss. 12-17 functions made exercisable concurrently (E.W.) (with effect in accordance with art. 25. (1) of the amending S.I.) by The Chilterns Area of Outstanding Natural Beauty (Establishment of Conservation Board) Order 2004 (S.I. 2004/1778), arts. 2, 25. (1), 25. (1), 25. (2)(xxvi) (with art. 35)

Acquisition and guardianship of land in the vicinity of an ancient monument, etc.

15 Acquisition and guardianship of land in the vicinity of an ancient monument.

(1) References in sections 10 to 12 of this Act to an ancient monument shall include references to any land adjoining or in the vicinity of an ancient monument which appears to the Secretary of State [F161or the Commission] or a local authority to be reasonably required for any of the following purposes, that is to say—

(a) the maintenance of the monument or its amenities;
(b) providing or facilitating access to the monument;
(c) the exercise of proper control or management with respect to the monument;
(d) the storage of equipment or materials for the purpose mentioned in paragraph (a) above; and
(e) the provision of facilities and services for the public for or in connection with affording public access to the monument;

(and one of those purposes shall accordingly be sufficient to support the compulsory acquisition of

any such land under section 10. (1) of this Act, instead of the purpose there mentioned).
[F162. Land may be acquired, or taken into guardianship, by the Commission by virtue of this section only if the land is situated in England.]
(2) Land may be acquired or taken into guardianship by virtue of this section for any of the purposes relating to an ancient monument mentioned in subsection (1) above either at the same time as the monument or subsequently.
(3) The Secretary of State [F163and the Commission] and any local authority shall have full control and management of any land which is under their guardianship by virtue of this Act after being taken into guardianship by virtue of this section for a purpose relating to any ancient monument, and[F164without prejudice to that generality] shall have power to do all such things as may be necessary—
    (a) for the exercise by them of proper control and management with respect to the land; and
    (b) for the use of the land for any of the purposes relating to the monument mentioned in subsection (1) above.
[F165. (3. A)The power of full control and management of land under guardianship conferred by subsection (3) above includes power—
    (a) to control the holding of events on associated land;
    (b) to control and manage such events;
    (c) to require payment of a charge in respect of the holding of such events;
    (d) to exclude, restrict or otherwise control public access to associated land in connection with such events.]
(4) The Secretary of State [F163and the Commission] and any local authority may at any reasonable time enter any land which is under their guardianship by virtue of this Act for the purpose of exercising their power under subsection (3) above (and may authorise any other person to do so, and to exercise that power, on their behalf).
[F166. (4. A)Subsections (3), (3. A) and (4) are subject to any provision to the contrary in the guardianship deed.]
(5) Section 14. (1) and (2) of this Act shall apply in relation to any land taken into guardianship by virtue of this section for any purpose relating to an ancient monument as they apply in relation to a monument, but, apart from any termination of guardianship by virtue of that section, any such land shall also cease to be under guardianship if the monument in question ceases to be under guardianship otherwise than by virtue of being acquired by its guardians or ceases to exist.
(6) References below in this Act, in relation to any monument of which the Secretary of State [F167or the Commission] or a local authority are the owners or guardians by virtue of this Act, to land associated with that monument (or to associated land) are references to any land acquired or taken into guardianship by virtue of this section for a purpose relating to that monument, or appropriated for any such purpose under a power conferred by any other enactment.
[F168. (7)In subsection (3. A) above—
    (a) "events" includes functions and any other organised activities;
    (b) references to the holding of events, in relation to organised activities, are to be construed as references to the carrying out of such activities.]
Amendments (Textual)
F161. Words inserted by National Heritage Act 1983 (c. 47, SIF 78), s. 41, Sch. 4 para. 41. (2)
F162. Words inserted by National Heritage Act 1983 (c. 47, SIF 78), s. 41, Sch. 4 para. 41. (2)
F163. Words inserted by National Heritage Act 1983 (c. 47, SIF 78), s. 41, Sch. 4 para. 41. (3)
F164. Words in s. 15. (3) inserted (S.) (30.6.2011) by Historic Environment (Amendment) (Scotland) Act 2011 (asp 3), ss. 7. (3)(a), 33. (2); S.S.I. 2011/174, art. 2, Sch.
F165. S. 15. (3. A) inserted (S.) (30.6.2011) by Historic Environment (Amendment) (Scotland) Act 2011 (asp 3), ss. 7. (3)(b), 33. (2); S.S.I. 2011/174, art. 2, Sch.
F166. S. 15. (4. A) inserted (S.) (30.6.2011) by Historic Environment (Amendment) (Scotland) Act 2011 (asp 3), ss. 7. (3)(c), 33. (2); S.S.I. 2011/174, art. 2, Sch.
F167. Words inserted by National Heritage Act 1983 (c. 47, SIF 78), s. 41, Sch. 4 para. 41. (4)
F168. S. 15. (7) added (S.) (30.6.2011) by Historic Environment (Amendment) (Scotland) Act

2011 (asp 3), ss. 7. (3)(d), 33. (2); S.S.I. 2011/174, art. 2, Sch.
Modifications etc. (not altering text)
C27. Ss. 12-17 functions made exercisable concurrently (E.W.) (with effect in accordance with art. 25. (1) of the amending S.I.) by The Cotswolds Area of Outstanding Natural Beauty (Establishment of Conservation Board) Order 2004 (S.I. 2004/1777), arts. 1, 25. (2)(xxvi) (with art. 35)
C28. Ss. 12-17 functions made exercisable concurrently (E.W.) (with effect in accordance with art. 25. (1) of the amending S.I.) by The Chilterns Area of Outstanding Natural Beauty (Establishment of Conservation Board) Order 2004 (S.I. 2004/1778), arts. 2, 25. (1), 25. (1), 25. (2)(xxvi) (with art. 35)

16 Acquisition of easements and other similar rights over land in the vicinity of an ancient monument.

(1) The Secretary of State may acquire, by agreement or compulsorily, over land adjoining or in the vicinity of any monument which is under his ownership by virtue of this Act, any easement which appears to him to be necessary—
  (a) for any of the purposes relating to that monument mentioned in section 15. (1) of this Act; or
  (b) for the use of any land associated with that monument for any of those purposes.
[F169. Where the land in question is situated in England, the Secretary of State shall consult with the Commission before entering into the agreement or making the compulsory purchase order (as the case may be).]
[F170. (1. A)The Commission may by agreement acquire over land adjoining or in the vicinity of any monument which is under their ownership by virtue of this Act, any such easement as the Secretary of State may acquire by virtue of subsection (1) above.]
(2) A local authority may by agreement acquire over land adjoining or in the vicinity of any monument which is under their ownership by virtue of this Act any such easement as the Secretary of State may acquire by virtue of subsection (1) above.
(3) The power of acquiring an easement under subsection (1) [F171or (1. A)] or (2) above shall include power to acquire any such easement by the grant of a new right.
(4) The Secretary of State [F172or the Commission] or any local authority may acquire, for the benefit of any monument or land under his or their guardianship by virtue of this Act, a right of any description which he or they would be authorised to acquire under any of the preceding provisions of this section if the monument or land was under his or their ownership by virtue of this Act, and those provisions shall apply accordingly in any such case.
(5) Any right to which subsection (4) above applies—
  (a) shall be treated for the purposes of its acquisition under this section and in all other respects as if it were a legal easement; and
  (b) may be enforced by the guardians for the time being of the monument or land for whose benefit it was acquired as if they were the absolute owner in possession of that monument or land.
(6) Any right to which subsection (4) above applies which is acquired by agreement under this section for a purpose relating to any monument under guardianship, or for the use of any land associated with any such monument for any purpose relating to that monument—
  (a) subject to any provision to the contrary in the agreement under which it was acquired, may be revoked by the grantor; and
  (b) may be revoked by any successor in title of the grantor as respects any of the land over which it is exercisable in which he has an interest;
if the monument ceases to be under guardianship otherwise than by virtue of being acquired by its guardians or ceases to exist.
(7) References above in this section to an easement or (as the case may be) to a legal easement shall be construed in relation to land in Scotland as references to a servitude.
(8) Any right to which subsection (4) above applies—

(a) shall be a local land charge, if it relates to land in England and Wales; and

(b) may be recorded in the Register of Sasines, if it relates to land in Scotland.

(9) The M11[F173. Acquisition of Land Act 1981] shall apply to any compulsory acquisition by the Secretary of State under this section of any easement over land in England and Wales . . . F174

(10) The M12. Acquisition of Land (Authorisation Procedure) (Scotland) Act 1947 shall apply to any compulsory acquisition by the Secretary of State under this section of any servitude over land in Scotland as it applies to a compulsory acquisition by another Minister or by the Secretary of State under section 58 of the M13. National Health Service (Scotland) Act 1972 in a case falling within section 1. (1) of the said Act of 1947.

(11) The provisions of Part I of the M14. Compulsory Purchase Act 1965 (so far as applicable) other than sections 4 to 8, section 10 and section 31, shall apply in relation to any acquisition by agreement under this section of any easement over land in England and Wales.

(12) For the purposes of any acquisition by agreement under this section of any servitude over land in Scotland—

(a) the Lands Clauses Acts (with the exception of the provisions excluded by subsection (13) below) and sections 6 and 70 to 78 of the M15. Railways Clauses Consolidation (Scotland) Act 1845 (as originally enacted and not as amended by section 15 of the M16. Mines (Working Facilities and Support) Act 1923) shall be incorporated with this section; and

(b) in construing those Acts for the purposes of this section, this section shall be deemed to be the special Act and the Secretary of State or the local authority acquiring the servitude shall be deemed to be the promoter of the undertaking or company (as the case may require).

(13) The provisions of the Lands Clauses Acts excluded from being incorporated with this section are—

(a) those which relate to the acquisition of land otherwise than by agreement;

(b) those which relate to access to the special Act; and

(c) sections 120 to 125 of the M17. Lands Clauses Consolidation (Scotland) Act 1845.

Amendments (Textual)

F169. Words inserted by National Heritage Act 1983 (c. 47, SIF 78), s. 41, Sch. 4 para. 42. (2)

F170. S. 16. (1. A) inserted by National Heritage Act 1983 (c. 47, SIF 78), s. 41, Sch. 4 para. 42. (3)

F171. Words inserted by National Heritage Act 1983 (c. 47, SIF 78), s. 41, Sch. 4 para. 42. (4)

F172. Words inserted by National Heritage Act 1983 (c. 47, SIF 78), s. 41, Sch. 4 para. 42. (5)

F173. Words substituted by Acquisition of Land Act 1981 (c. 67), Sch. 4 para. 1 Table

F174. Words repealed by Acquisition of Land Act 1981 (c. 67), Sch. 6 Pt. I

Modifications etc. (not altering text)

C27. Ss. 12-17 functions made exercisable concurrently (E.W.) (with effect in accordance with art. 25. (1) of the amending S.I.) by The Cotswolds Area of Outstanding Natural Beauty (Establishment of Conservation Board) Order 2004 (S.I. 2004/1777), arts. 1, 25. (2)(xxvi) (with art. 35)

C28. Ss. 12-17 functions made exercisable concurrently (E.W.) (with effect in accordance with art. 25. (1) of the amending S.I.) by The Chilterns Area of Outstanding Natural Beauty (Establishment of Conservation Board) Order 2004 (S.I. 2004/1778), arts. 2, 25. (1), 25. (1), 25. (2)(xxvi) (with art. 35)

Marginal Citations

M111981 c. 67.

M121947 c. 42.

M131972 c. 58.

M141965 c. 56.

M151845 c. 33.

M161923 c. 20.

M171845 c. 19.

Agreements concerning ancient monuments, etc.

17 Agreements concerning ancient monuments and land in their vicinity.

(1) The Secretary of State may enter into an agreement under this section with the occupier of an ancient monument or of any land adjoining or in the vicinity of an ancient monument.
[F175. (1. A)The Commission may enter into an agreement under this section with the occupier of an ancient monument situated in England or of any land so situated which adjoins or is in the vicinity of an ancient monument so situated.]
(2) A local authority may enter into an agreement under this section with the occupier of any ancient monument situated in or in the vicinity of their area or with the occupier of any land adjoining or in the vicinity of any such ancient monument.
[F176. (2. A)Historic Environment Scotland may enter into an agreement under this section with the occupier of an ancient monument situated in Scotland or of any land so situated which adjoins or is in the vicinity of an ancient monument so situated.]
(3) Any person who has an interest in an ancient monument or in any land adjoining or in the vicinity of an ancient monument may be a party to an agreement under this section in addition to the occupier.
(4) An agreement under this section may make provision for all or any of the following matters with respect to the monument or land in question, that is to say—
    (a) the maintenance and preservation of the monument and its amenities;
    (b) the carrying out of any such work, or the doing of any such other thing, in relation to the monument or land as may be specified in the agreement;
    (c) public access to the monument or land and the provision of facilities and information or other services for the use of the public in that connection;
    (d) restricting the use of the monument or land;
    (e) prohibiting in relation to the monument or land the doing of any such thing as may be specified in the agreement; and
    (f) the making by the Secretary of State or [F177the Commission or the local authority [F178or Historic Environment Scotland] (as the case may be)] of payments in such manner, of such amounts and on such terms as may be so specified (and whether for or towards the cost of any work provided for under the agreement or in consideration of any restriction, prohibition or obligation accepted by any other party thereto);
and may contain such incidental and consequential provisions as appear to the Secretary of State or [F177the Commission or the local authority [F179or Historic Environment Scotland] (as the case may be)] to be necessary or expedient.
(5) Where an agreement under this section expressly provides that the agreement as a whole or any restriction, prohibition or obligation arising thereunder is to be binding on the successors of any party to the agreement (but not otherwise), then, as respects any monument or land in England and Wales, every person deriving title to the monument or land in question from, through or under that party shall be bound by the agreement, or (as the case may be) by that restriction, prohibition or obligation, unless he derives title by virtue of any disposition made by that party before the date of the agreement.
(6) An agreement under this section relating to any monument or land in Scotland and containing any such provision as is mentioned in subsection (5) above may be recorded in the Register of Sasines, and that subsection shall apply to any such agreement which is so recorded or (as the case may be) to any restriction, prohibition or obligation to which that provision relates.
(7) [F180. Neither—
    (a) section 84 of the M18 Law of Property Act 1925 (power of Lands Tribunal to discharge or

modify restrictive covenants); nor

(b) sections 1 and 2 of the M19 Conveyancing and Feudal Reform (Scotland) Act 1970 (power of Lands Tribunal for Scotland to vary or discharge land obligations);

shall apply to an agreement under this section.]

[F180. Section 84 of the Law of Property Act 1925 (c. 20) (power F181... to discharge or modify restrictive covenant) shall not apply to an agreement under this section.]

(8) Nothing in any agreement under this section to which the Secretary of State is a party shall be construed as operating as a scheduled monument consent.

[F182. (9) References to an ancient monument in subsection (1. A) above, and in subsection (3) above so far as it applies for the purposes of subsection (1. A), shall be construed as if the reference in section 61. (12)(b) of this Act to the Secretary of State were to the Commission.]

[F183. (9. A)References to an ancient monument in subsection (2. A), and in subsection (3) so far as it applies for the purposes of subsection (2. A), are to be construed as if the reference in section 61. (12)(b) of this Act to the Secretary of State were to Historic Environment Scotland.]

[F184. (10)References in this section to an ancient monument situated in England include any such monument situated in, on or under the seabed within the seaward limits of the United Kingdom territorial waters adjacent to England; and an order under section 33. (10) of the National Heritage Act 1983 (orders determining limits of waters adjacent to England) applies for the purposes of this subsection as it applies for the purposes of section 33. (9) of that Act.]

Amendments (Textual)

F175. S. 17. (1. A) inserted by National Heritage Act 1983 (c. 47, SIF 78), s. 41, Sch. 4 para. 43. (2)

F176. S. 17. (2. A) inserted (S.) (27.2.2015 for specified purposes, 1.10.2015 in so far as not already in force) by Historic Environment Scotland Act 2014 (asp 19), s. 31. (2), sch. 2 para. 41. (a) (with ss. 29, 30); S.S.I. 2015/31, art. 2, sch.; S.S.I. 2015/196, art. 2, sch.

F177. Words substituted by National Heritage Act 1983 (c. 47, SIF 78), s. 41, Sch. 4 para. 43. (3)

F178. Words in s. 17. (4)(f) inserted (S.) (27.2.2015 for specified purposes, 1.10.2015 in so far as not already in force) by Historic Environment Scotland Act 2014 (asp 19), s. 31. (2), sch. 2 para. 41. (b)(i) (with ss. 29, 30); S.S.I. 2015/31, art. 2, sch.; S.S.I. 2015/196, art. 2, sch.

F179. Words in s. 17. (4) inserted (S.) (27.2.2015 for specified purposes, 1.10.2015 in so far as not already in force) by Historic Environment Scotland Act 2014 (asp 19), s. 31. (2), sch. 2 para. 41. (b)(ii) (with ss. 29, 30); S.S.I. 2015/31, art. 2, sch.; S.S.I. 2015/196, art. 2, sch.

F180. S. 17. (7) substituted (S.) (28.11.2004) by Title Conditions (Scotland) Act 2003 (asp 9), ss. 122. (1), 129. (2), Sch. 14 para. 8 (with ss. 119, 121) (see S.S.I. 2003/456, art. 2)

F181. Words in s. 17. (7) omitted (1.6.2009) by virtue of The Transfer of Tribunal Functions (Lands Tribunal and Miscellaneous Amendments) Order 2009 (S.I. 2009/1307), art. 1, Sch. 1 para. 128 (with Sch. 5)

F182. S. 17. (9) inserted by National Heritage Act 1983 (c. 47, SIF 78), s. 41, Sch. 4 para. 43. (4)

F183. S. 17. (9. A) inserted (S.) (27.2.2015 for specified purposes, 1.10.2015 in so far as not already in force) by Historic Environment Scotland Act 2014 (asp 19), s. 31. (2), sch. 2 para. 41. (c) (with ss. 29, 30); S.S.I. 2015/31, art. 2, sch.; S.S.I. 2015/196, art. 2, sch.

F184. S. 17. (10) inserted (1.7.2002) by National Heritage Act 2002 (c. 14), ss. {2. (2)}, 8. (2)

Modifications etc. (not altering text)

C27. Ss. 12-17 functions made exercisable concurrently (E.W.) (with effect in accordance with art. 25. (1) of the amending S.I.) by The Cotswolds Area of Outstanding Natural Beauty (Establishment of Conservation Board) Order 2004 (S.I. 2004/1777), arts. 1, 25. (2)(xxvi) (with art. 35)

C28. Ss. 12-17 functions made exercisable concurrently (E.W.) (with effect in accordance with art. 25. (1) of the amending S.I.) by The Chilterns Area of Outstanding Natural Beauty (Establishment of Conservation Board) Order 2004 (S.I. 2004/1778), arts. 2, 25. (1), 25. (1), 25. (2)(xxvi) (with art. 35)

Marginal Citations

M181925 c. 20.

M191970 c. 35.

Powers of limited owners

18 Powers of limited owners for purposes of sections 12, 16 and 17.

(1) Subject to section 12 of this Act, a person may establish guardianship of any land under subsection (1) [F185or (1. A)] or (2) of that section or join in executing a guardianship deed for the purposes of that section notwithstanding that he is a limited owner of the land.
(2) A person may—
   (a) grant any easement, servitude or other right over land which the Secretary of State [F186or the Commission] or any local authority are authorised to acquire under section 16 of this Act; or
   (b) enter into an agreement under section 17 of this Act with respect to any land;
notwithstanding that he is a limited owner of the land.
(3) For the purposes of this section—
   (a) a body corporate or corporation sole is a limited owner of any land in which it has an interest; and
   (b) any other persons are limited owners of land in which they have an interest only if they hold that interest in one or other of the capacities mentioned in subsection (4) below.
(4) The capacities referred to in subsection (3)(b) above are the following—
   (a) as tenant for life or statutory owner within the meaning of the M20. Settled Land Act 1925;
   F187 [(b)as trustees of land;]
   (c) as liferenter or heir of entail in possession (in Scotland); and
   (d) as trustees for charities or as commissioners or trustees for ecclesiastical, collegiate or other public purposes.
(5) The M21. Trusts (Scotland) Act 1921 shall have effect as if among the powers conferred on trustees by section 4 of that Act (general powers of trustees) there were included a power to do any of the following acts in relation to the trust estate or any part of it, that is to say—
   (a) to execute a guardianship deed;
   (b) to grant any servitude or other right which the Secretary of State or any local authority are authorised to acquire under section 16 of this Act; and
   (c) to enter into an agreement under section 17 of this Act.
(6) Subject to subsection (7) below, where a person who is a limited owner of any land by virtue of holding an interest in the land in any of the capacities mentioned in subsection (4) above executes a guardianship deed in relation to the land the guardianship deed shall bind every successive owner of any estate or interest in the land.
(7) Where the land to which a guardianship deed relates is at the date of the deed subject to any incumbrance not capable of being overreached by the limited owner in exercise of any powers of sale or management conferred on him by law or under any settlement or other instrument, the deed shall not bind the incumbrancer.
(8) Subject to subsection (9) below, where an agreement under section 17 of this Act to which a limited owner is a party expressly provides that the agreement as a whole or any restriction, prohibition or obligation arising thereunder is to be binding on his successors (but not otherwise), subsections (6) and (7) above shall apply to the agreement or (as the case may be) to the restriction, prohibition or obligation in question as they apply to a guardianship deed.
(9) Subsection (8) above does not apply to an agreement relating to any land in Scotland unless it is recorded in the Register of Sasines.
Extent Information
E2. This version of this provision extends to England and Wales only; a separate version has been

created for Scotland only
Amendments (Textual)
F185. Words inserted by National Heritage Act 1983 (c. 47, SIF 78), s. 41, Sch. 4 para. 44. (2)
F186. Words inserted by National Heritage Act 1983 (c. 47, SIF 78), s. 41, Sch. 4 para. 44. (3)
F187. S. 18. (4)(b) substituted (E.W.) (1.1.1997) by 1996 c. 47, s. 25. (1), Sch. 3 para. 17. (b) (with s. 24. (2), 25. (4)); S.I. 1996/2974, art.2
Marginal Citations
M201925 c. 18.
M211921 c. 58.

18 Powers of limited owners for purposes of sections 12, 16 and 17.S

(1) Subject to section 12 of this Act, a person may establish guardianship of any land under subsection (1) [F260or (1. A)] or (2) of that section or join in executing a guardianship deed for the purposes of that section notwithstanding that he is a limited owner of the land.
(2) A person may—
    (a) grant any easement, servitude or other right over land which the Secretary of State [F261or the Commission] or any local authority are authorised to acquire under section 16 of this Act; or
    (b) enter into an agreement under section 17 of this Act with respect to any land;
notwithstanding that he is a limited owner of the land.
(3) For the purposes of this section—
    (a) a body corporate or corporation sole is a limited owner of any land in which it has an interest; and
    (b) any other persons are limited owners of land in which they have an interest only if they hold that interest in one or other of the capacities mentioned in subsection (4) below.
(4) The capacities referred to in subsection (3)(b) above are the following—
    (a) as tenant for life or statutory owner within the meaning of the M24. Settled Land Act 1925;
    (b) as trustees for sale within the meaning of the M25. Law of Property Act 1925;
    (c) as liferenter F262... in possession (in Scotland); and
    (d) as trustees for charities or as commissioners or trustees for ecclesiastical, collegiate or other public purposes.
(5) The M26. Trusts (Scotland) Act 1921 shall have effect as if among the powers conferred on trustees by section 4 of that Act (general powers of trustees) there were included a power to do any of the following acts in relation to the trust estate or any part of it, that is to say—
    (a) to execute a guardianship deed;
    (b) to grant any servitude or other right which the Secretary of State or any local authority are authorised to acquire under section 16 of this Act; and
    (c) to enter into an agreement under section 17 of this Act.
(6) Subject to subsection (7) below, where a person who is a limited owner of any land by virtue of holding an interest in the land in any of the capacities mentioned in subsection (4) above executes a guardianship deed in relation to the land the guardianship deed shall bind every successive owner of any estate or interest in the land.
(7) Where the land to which a guardianship deed relates is at the date of the deed subject to any incumbrance not capable of being overreached by the limited owner in exercise of any powers of sale or management conferred on him by law or under any settlement or other instrument, the deed shall not bind the incumbrancer.
(8) Subject to subsection (9) below, where an agreement under section 17 of this Act to which a limited owner is a party expressly provides that the agreement as a whole or any restriction, prohibition or obligation arising thereunder is to be binding on his successors (but not otherwise), subsections (6) and (7) above shall apply to the agreement or (as the case may be) to the restriction, prohibition or obligation in question as they apply to a guardianship deed.

(9) Subsection (8) above does not apply to an agreement relating to any land in Scotland unless it is recorded in the Register of Sasines.
Extent Information
E4. This version of this provision extends to Scotland only; a separate version has been created for England and Wales only
Amendments (Textual)
F260. Words inserted by National Heritage Act 1983 (c. 47, SIF 78), s. 41, Sch. 4 para. 44. (2)
F261. Words inserted by National Heritage Act 1983 (c. 47, SIF 78), s. 41, Sch. 4 para. 44. (3)
F262. Words in s. 18. (4)(c) repealed (28.11.2004) by Abolition of Feudal Tenure etc. (Scotland) Act 2000 (asp 5), ss. 71, 77. (2), Sch. 12 para. 40. (3), 13 Pt. 1 (with ss. 58, 62, 75); S.S.I. 2003/456, art. 2
Marginal Citations
M241925 c. 18.
M251925 c. 20.
M261921 c. 58.

Public access to monuments under public control

19 Public access to monuments under public control.

(1) Subject to[F188sections 13. (2. A) and 15. (3. A) of this Act and to] the following provisions of this section, the public shall have access to any monument under the ownership or guardianship of the Secretary of State [F189or the Commission] or any local authority by virtue of this Act.
(2) The Secretary of State [F190and the Commission] and any local authority may nevertheless control the times of normal public access to any monument under their ownership or guardianship by virtue of this Act and may also, if they consider it necessary or expedient to do so in the interests of safety or for the maintenance or preservation of the monument, entirely exclude the public from access to any such monument or to any part of it, for such period as they think fit: Provided that—
    (a) the power of a local authority under this subsection to control the times of normal public access to any monument shall only be exercisable by regulations under this section; and
    (b) the power of a local authority under this subsection entirely to exclude the public from access to any monument with a view to its preservation shall only be exercisable with the consent of the Secretary of State.
(3) The Secretary of State and any local authority may by regulations under [F191this subsection] regulate public access to any monument, or to all or any of the monuments, under their ownership or guardianship by virtue of this Act and any such regulations made by the Secretary of State may also apply to any monument, or to all or any of the monuments, under his control or management for any other reason.
[F192. The Secretary of State shall consult with the Commission before he makes any regulations under this subsection in relation only to monuments situated in England.]
(4) Without prejudice to the generality of subsection (3) above, regulations made by the Secretary of State or a local authority under [F193that subsection] may prescribe the times when the public are to have access to monuments to which the regulations apply and may make such provision as appears to the Secretary of State or to the local authority in question to be necessary for—
    (a) the preservation of any such monument and its amenities or of any property of the Secretary of State or local authority; and
    (b) prohibiting or regulating any act or thing which would tend to injure or disfigure any such monument or its amenities or to disturb the public in their enjoyment of it;
and may prescribe charges for the admission of the public to any such monument or to any class or description of monuments to which the regulations apply.

[F194. (4. A) The Secretary of State may by regulations under this section make such provision as appears to him necessary for prohibiting or regulating any act or thing which would tend to injure or disfigure any monument under the ownership or guardianship of the Commission by virtue of this Act or the monument's amenities or to disturb the public in their enjoyment of it.
(4. B) The Secretary of State shall consult with the Commission before he makes any regulations under subsection (4. A) above.]
(5) Without prejudice to subsections (3) and (4) above, the Secretary of State [F195and the Commission] and any local authority shall have power to make such charges as they may from time to time determine for the admission of the public to any monument under their ownership or guardianship by virtue of this Act or (in the case of the Secretary of State) to any monument otherwise under his control or management.
(6) Notwithstanding subsection (1) above, any person authorised in that behalf by the Secretary of State [F196or by the Commission] or by a local authority may refuse admission—

(a) to any monument under the ownership or guardianship of the Secretary of State or [F197the Commission or that local authority (as the case may be)] by virtue of this Act; or

(b) (in the case of the Secretary of State) to any monument otherwise under his control or management;

to any person he has reasonable cause to believe is likely to do anything which would tend to injure or disfigure the monument or its amenities or to disturb the public in their enjoyment of it.
(7) If any person contravenes or fails to comply with any provision of any regulations under this section, he shall be liable on summary conviction or, in Scotland, on conviction before a court of summary jurisdiction, to a fine not exceeding [F198level 2 on the standard scale].
(8) Regulations made by a local authority under this section shall not take effect unless they are submitted to and confirmed by the Secretary of State, and the Secretary of State may confirm any such regulations either with or without modifications.
(9) In relation to any monument under guardianship, subsection (1) above is subject to any provision to the contrary in the guardianship deed.

Amendments (Textual)
F188. Words in s. 19. (1) inserted (S.) (30.6.2011) by Historic Environment (Amendment) (Scotland) Act 2011 (asp 3), ss. 7. (4), 33. (2); S.S.I. 2011/174, art. 2, Sch.
F189. Words inserted by National Heritage Act 1983 (c. 47, SIF 78), s. 41, Sch. 4 para. 45. (2)
F190. Words inserted by National Heritage Act 1983 (c. 47, SIF 78), s. 41, Sch. 4 para. 45. (3)
F191. Words substituted by National Heritage Act 1983 (c. 47, SIF 78), s. 41, Sch. 4 para. 45. (4)
F192. Words inserted by National Heritage Act 1983 (c. 47, SIF 78), s. 41, Sch. 4 para. 45. (4)
F193. Words substituted by National Heritage Act 1983 (c. 47, SIF 78), s. 41, Sch. 4 para. 45. (5)
F194. S. 19. (4. A)(4. B) inserted by National Heritage Act 1983 (c. 47, SIF 78), s. 41, Sch. 4 para. 45. (6)
F195. Words inserted by National Heritage Act 1983 (c. 47, SIF 78), s. 41, Sch. 4 para. 45. (7)
F196. Words inserted by National Heritage Act 1983 (c. 47, SIF 78), s. 41, Sch. 4 para. 45. (8)
F197. Words substituted by National Heritage Act 1983 (c. 47, SIF 78), s. 41, Sch. 4 para. 45. (8)
F198. Words substituted by virtue of Criminal Justice Act 1982 (c. 48), s. 46 and Criminal Procedure (Scotland) Act 1975 (c. 21), s. 289. G (as inserted by Criminal Justice Act 1982 (c. 48), s. 54)

Modifications etc. (not altering text)
C29. S. 19 excluded (18.12.1996) by 1996 c. 61, s. 12, Sch. 7 para. 4. (5)
C30. S. 19 functions made exercisable concurrently (E.W.) (with effect in accordance with art. 25. (1) of the amending S.I.) by The Cotswolds Area of Outstanding Natural Beauty (Establishment of Conservation Board) Order 2004 (S.I. 2004/1777), arts. 1, 25. (2)(xxvii) (with art. 35)
C31. S. 19 functions made exercisable concurrently (with effect in accordance with art. 25. (1) of the amending S.I.) by The Chilterns Area of Outstanding Natural Beauty (Establishment of Conservation Board) Order 2004 (S.I. 2004/1778), arts. 2, 25. (1), 25. (1), 25. (2)(xxvii) (with art. 35)
C32. S. 19 excluded (22.7.2008) by Crossrail Act 2008 (c. 18), Sch. 9 para. 4. (5)

C33. S. 19. (3)(4. A) excluded (18.12.1996) by 1996 c. 61, s. 12, Sch. 7 para. 4. (6)
C34. S. 19. (6) restricted (18.12.1996) by 1996 c. 61, s. 12, Sch. 7 para. 4. (7)
C35. S. 19. (6) restricted (22.7.2008) by Crossrail Act 2008 (c. 18), Sch. 9 para. 4. (7)

20 Provision of facilities for the public in connection with ancient monuments.

(1) The Secretary of State [F199and the Commission] and any local authority may provide such facilities and information or other services for the public [F200for or in connection with affording public access]—
 (a) [F201to] [F201in or on] any monument under their ownership or guardianship by virtue of this Act; or
 (b) (in the case of the Secretary of State) [F202to] [F202in or on] any monument otherwise under his control or management;
as appear to them to be necessary or desirable.
(2) [F203. Facilities and information or other services for the public may be provided under this section in or on the monument itself or on any land associated with the monument.]
[F203. In subsection (1), references to a monument include references to any land associated with the monument.
(2. A)The facilities and services which may be provided for the public under this section include—
 (a) facilities and information or other services for or in connection with affording public access to the monument, and
 (b) facilities for the sale of goods and the provision of other services.]
(3) The Secretary of State [F204and the Commission] and any local authority shall have power to make such charges as they may from time to time determine for the use of any facility or service provided by them for the public under this section.
Amendments (Textual)
F199. Words inserted by National Heritage Act 1983 (c. 47, SIF 78), s. 41, Sch. 4 para. 46. (2)
F200. Words in s. 20. (1) repealed (S.) (30.6.2011) by Historic Environment (Amendment) (Scotland) Act 2011 (asp 3), ss. 8. (a)(i), 33. (2); S.S.I. 2011/174, art. 2, Sch.
F201. Words in s. 20. (1)(a) substituted (S.) (30.6.2011) by Historic Environment (Amendment) (Scotland) Act 2011 (asp 3), ss. 8. (a)(ii), 33. (2); S.S.I. 2011/174, art. 2, Sch.
F202. Words in s. 20. (1)(b) substituted (S.) (30.6.2011) by Historic Environment (Amendment) (Scotland) Act 2011 (asp 3), ss. 8. (a)(iii), 33. (2); S.S.I. 2011/174, art. 2, Sch.
F203. S. 20. (2)(2. A) substituted for s. 20. (2) (S.) (30.6.2011) by Historic Environment (Amendment) (Scotland) Act 2011 (asp 3), ss. 8. (b), 33. (2); S.S.I. 2011/174, art. 2, Sch.
F204. Words inserted by National Heritage Act 1983 (c. 47, SIF 78), s. 41, Sch. 4 para. 46. (3)
Modifications etc. (not altering text)
C36. S. 20 functions made exercisable concurrently (E.W.) (with effect in accordance with art. 25. (1) of the amending S.I.) by The Cotswolds Area of Outstanding Natural Beauty (Establishment of Conservation Board) Order 2004 (S.I. 2004/1777), arts. 1, 25. (2)(xxvii) (with art. 35)
C37. S. 20 functions made exercisable concurrently (with effect in accordance with art. 25. (1) of the amending S.I.) by The Chilterns Area of Outstanding Natural Beauty (Establishment of Conservation Board) Order 2004 (S.I. 2004/1778), arts. 2, 25. (1), 25. (1), 25. (2)(xxvii) (with art. 35)

Transfer of ownership and guardianship of ancient monuments

21 Transfer of ancient monuments between local authorities and Secretary of State.

(1) Subject to subsection (2) below, the Secretary of State [F205and the Commission] and any local authority may, in respect of any monument of which they are the owners or guardians by virtue of this Act or any land associated with any such monument, enter into and carry into effect any agreements for the transfer—
  (a) from the Secretary of State to the local authority;
  (b) from the local authority to the Secretary of State; or
  (c) from the local authority to another local authority; [F206or
  (d) from the Secretary of State to the Commission; or
  (e) from the Commission to the Secretary of State; or
  (f) from the Commission to the local authority; or
  (g) from the local authority to the Commission;]
of that monument or land or (as the case may be) of the guardianship of that monument or land.
(2) Where the Secretary of State [F207or the Commission] or the local authority in question are guardians of a monument or associated land, they may not enter into an agreement under this section with respect to that monument or land without the consent of the persons who are for the time being immediately affected by the operation of the guardianship deed.
[F208. (3)The Commission may not enter into an agreement under subsection (1) above in respect of a monument or land not situated in England.
(4) The Secretary of State may not enter into an agreement mentioned in subsection (1)(a) or (b) above in respect of a monument or land situated in England without consulting the Commission.
(5) The Commission may not enter into an agreement mentioned in subsection (1)(f) above without consulting the Secretary of State.
(6) The Commission may not enter into an agreement mentioned in subsection (1)(g) above without the consent of the Secretary of State.]

Amendments (Textual)
F205. Words inserted by National Heritage Act 1983 (c. 47, SIF 78), s. 41, Sch. 4 para. 47. (2)
F206. S. 21. (1)(d)–(g) inserted by National Heritage Act 1983 (c. 47, SIF 78), s. 41, Sch. 4 para. 47. (2)
F207. Words inserted by National Heritage Act 1983 (c. 47, SIF 78), s. 41, Sch. 4 para. 47. (3)
F208. S. 21. (3)–(6) inserted by National Heritage Act 1983 (c. 47, SIF 78), s. 41, Sch. 4 para. 47. (4)

Modifications etc. (not altering text)
C38. S. 21 functions made exercisable concurrently (E.W.) (with effect in accordance with art. 25. (1) of the amending S.I.) by The Cotswolds Area of Outstanding Natural Beauty (Establishment of Conservation Board) Order 2004 (S.I. 2004/1777), arts. 1, 25. (2)(xxviii) (with art. 35)
C39. S. 21 functions made exercisable concurrently (E.W.) (with effect in accordance with art. 25. (1) of the amending S.I.) by The Chilterns Area of Outstanding Natural Beauty (Establishment of Conservation Board) Order 2004 (S.I. 2004/1778), arts. 2, 25. (1), 25. (1), 25. (2)(xxviii) (with art. 35)

Ancient Monuments Boards

F20922 Ancient Monuments Boards.

. . . .
Amendments (Textual)
F209. S. 22 repealed (1.4.2006) by Ancient Monuments Board for Wales (Abolition) Order 2006 (S.I. 2006/64), arts. 1. (2), 3. (1)(a)

F210. F21123 Annual reports of Ancient Monuments Boards.

. . . .
Amendments (Textual)
F210. S. 23 repealed (1.4.2006) by Ancient Monuments Board for Wales (Abolition) Order 2006 (S.I. 2006/64), arts. 1. (2), 3. (1)(a)
F211. Words in s. 23 repealed (S.) (31.5.2003) by Public Appointments and Public Bodies etc. (Scotland) Act 2003 (asp 4), s. 21. (2), Sch. 4 para. 6. (b)(i); S.S.I. 2003/219, art. 2. (1)(c)

[F212. Local inquiriesS

Amendments (Textual)
F212. Ss. 23. A, 23. B and cross-heading inserted (27.2.2015 for specified purposes, 1.10.2015 in so far as not already in force) by Historic Environment Scotland Act 2014 (asp 19), ss. 21. (2), 31. (2) (with ss. 29, 30); S.S.I. 2015/31, art. 2, sch.; S.S.I. 2015/196, art. 2, sch.

23. ALocal inquiriesS

(1) The Scottish Ministers may hold a local inquiry for the purposes of the exercise of any of their functions under this Part of this Act.
(2) The Scottish Ministers must appoint a person to hold the inquiry and to report on it to them.
(3) Subsections (4) to (13) of section 265 of the Town and Country Planning (Scotland) Act 1997 (c.8) apply to an inquiry held by virtue of subsection (1) as they apply to an inquiry held by virtue of subsection (1) of that section.

23. BLocal inquiries: further provisionS

(1) The Scottish Ministers may by regulations make provision as to the procedure to be followed in connection with inquiries or hearings conducted under or by virtue of this Act.
(2) Regulations under subsection (1) may in particular make provision—
   (a) about the notification of an inquiry or hearing,
   (b) about the manner in which an inquiry or hearing is to be conducted,
   (c) as to procedure in connection with matters preparatory to such inquiries or hearings and in connection with matters subsequent to them.]

Miscellaneous and supplemental

24 Expenditure by Secretary of State or local authority on acquisition and preservation of ancient monuments, etc.

(1) [F213. Subject to subsection (3. A) below] The Secretary of State may defray or contribute towards the cost of the acquisition by any person of any ancient monument.
(2) [F213. Subject to subsection (3. A) below] The Secretary of State may undertake, or assist in, or defray or contribute towards the cost of the removal of any ancient monument or of any part of any such monument to another place for the purpose of preserving it, and may [F214at the request of the owner undertake, or assist in, or defray or contribute towards the cost of the preservation, maintenance and management of any ancient monument.
   [F214. (a)at the request of the owner undertake, or assist in, or
   (b) defray or contribute towards the cost of,

the preservation, maintenance and management of any ancient monument.]]
(3) [F213. Subject to subsection (3. A) below] The Secretary of State may contribute towards the cost of the provision of facilities or services for the public by a local authority under section 20 of this Act.
[F215. (3. A)As respects a monument situated in England, subsections (1) to (3) above shall apply as if "Commission" were substituted for "Secretary of State".
[F216. (3. AA)The reference in subsection (3. A) above to a monument situated in England includes any monument situated in, on or under the seabed within the seaward limits of the United Kingdom territorial waters adjacent to England; and an order under section 33. (10) of the National Heritage Act 1983 (orders determining limits of waters adjacent to England) applies for the purposes of this subsection as it applies for the purposes of section 33. (9) of that Act.]
(3. B) References to an ancient monument in subsections (1) and (2) above, as amended by subsection (3. A) above, shall be construed as if the reference in section 61. (12)(b) of this Act to the Secretary of State were to the Commission.]
(4) Any local authority may [F217at the request of the owner undertake, or assist in, or defray or contribute towards the cost of the preservation, maintenance and management of any ancient monument situated in or in the vicinity of their area.
[F217. (a)at the request of the owner undertake, or assist in, or
(b) defray or contribute towards the cost of,
the preservation, maintenance and management of any ancient monument situated in or in the vicinity of their area.]]
(5) No expenses shall be incurred by the Secretary of State [F218or the Commission] or any local authority under this section in connection with any monument which is occupied as a dwelling house by any person other than a person employed as the caretaker thereof or his family.
Amendments (Textual)
F213. Words inserted by National Heritage Act 1983 (c. 47, SIF 78), s. 41, Sch. 4 para. 48. (2)
F214. Words in s. 24. (2) substituted (S.) (30.6.2011) by Historic Environment (Amendment) (Scotland) Act 2011 (asp 3), ss. 9. (a), 33. (2); S.S.I. 2011/174, art. 2, Sch.
F215. S. 24. (3. A)(3. B) inserted by National Heritage Act 1983 (c. 47, SIF 78), s. 41, Sch. 4 para. 48. (3)
F216. S. 24. (3. AA) inserted (1.7.2002) by National Heritage Act 2002 (c. 14), ss. {2. (3)}, 8. (2)
F217. Words in s. 24. (4) substituted (S.) (30.6.2011) by Historic Environment (Amendment) (Scotland) Act 2011 (asp 3), ss. 9. (b), 33. (2); S.S.I. 2011/174, art. 2, Sch.
F218. Words inserted by National Heritage Act 1983 (c. 47, SIF 78), s. 41, Sch. 4 para. 48. (4)

25 Advice and superintendence by Secretary of State.

(1) [F219. Subject to subsection (3. A) below] [F220. The Secretary of State] [F220. Historic Environment Scotland] may give advice with reference to the treatment of any ancient monument.
(2) [F219. Subject to subsection (3. A) below] [F221. The Secretary of State] [F221. Historic Environment Scotland]may also, if in [F222his] [F222its] opinion it is advisable, superintend any work in connection with any ancient monument if invited to do so by the owner, and shall superintend any such work, whether required to do so by the owner or not, in connection with any scheduled monument, if in [F222his] [F222its] opinion it is advisable.
(3) [F219. Subject to subsection (3. A) below] [F223. The Secretary of State] [F223. Historic Environment Scotland] may make a charge for giving advice and superintendence under this section or may give it free of charge, as [F224he] [F224it] thinks fit.
[F225. (3. A)As respects a monument situated in England, subsections (1) to (3) above shall apply as if "Commission" were substituted for "Secretary of State", "their" for "his" (in each place) and "they think" for "he thinks".
(3. B) References to an ancient monument in subsections (1) and (2) above, as amended by subsection (3. A) above, shall be construed as if the reference in section 61. (12)(b) of this Act to

the Secretary of State were to the Commission.]
Amendments (Textual)
F219. Words inserted by National Heritage Act 1983 (c. 47, SIF 78), s. 41, Sch. 4 para. 49. (2)(4)(5)
F220. Words in s. 25. (1) substituted (S.) (27.2.2015 for specified purposes, 1.10.2015 in so far as not already in force) by Historic Environment Scotland Act 2014 (asp 19), s. 31. (2), sch. 2 para. 42. (a) (with ss. 29, 30); S.S.I. 2015/31, art. 2, sch.; S.S.I. 2015/196, art. 2, sch.
F221. Words in s. 25. (2) substituted (S.) (27.2.2015 for specified purposes, 1.10.2015 in so far as not already in force) by Historic Environment Scotland Act 2014 (asp 19), s. 31. (2), sch. 2 para. 42. (b)(i) (with ss. 29, 30); S.S.I. 2015/31, art. 2, sch.; S.S.I. 2015/196, art. 2, sch.
F222. Word in s. 25. (2) substituted (S.) (27.2.2015 for specified purposes, 1.10.2015 in so far as not already in force) by Historic Environment Scotland Act 2014 (asp 19), s. 31. (2), sch. 2 para. 42. (b)(ii) (with ss. 29, 30); S.S.I. 2015/31, art. 2, sch.; S.S.I. 2015/196, art. 2, sch.
F223. Words in s. 25. (3) substituted (S.) (27.2.2015 for specified purposes, 1.10.2015 in so far as not already in force) by Historic Environment Scotland Act 2014 (asp 19), s. 31. (2), sch. 2 para. 42. (c)(i) (with ss. 29, 30); S.S.I. 2015/31, art. 2, sch.; S.S.I. 2015/196, art. 2, sch.
F224. Word in s. 25. (3) substituted (S.) (27.2.2015 for specified purposes, 1.10.2015 in so far as not already in force) by Historic Environment Scotland Act 2014 (asp 19), s. 31. (2), sch. 2 para. 42. (c)(ii) (with ss. 29, 30); S.S.I. 2015/31, art. 2, sch.; S.S.I. 2015/196, art. 2, sch.
F225. S. 25. (3. A)(3. B) inserted by National Heritage Act 1983 (c. 47, SIF 78), s. 41, Sch. 4 para. 49. (3)–(5)
Modifications etc. (not altering text)
C40. S. 25. (2) restricted (18.12.1996) by 1996 c. 61, s. 12, Sch. 7 para. 4. (8)(a)
C41. S. 25. (2) restricted (22.7.2008) by Crossrail Act 2008 (c. 18), Sch. 9 para. 4. (8)(a)
C42. S. 25. (3) excluded (18.12.1996) by 1996 c. 61, s. 12, Sch. 7 para. 4. (8)(b)
C43. S. 25. (3) excluded (22.7.2008) by Crossrail Act 2008 (c. 18), Sch. 9 para. 4. (8)(b)

26 Power of entry on land believed to contain an ancient monument.

(1) A person duly authorised in writing by [F226the Secretary of State] [F226. Historic Environment Scotland] may at any reasonable time enter any land in, on or under which [F226the Secretary of State] [F226. Historic Environment Scotland] knows or has reason to believe there is an ancient monument for the purpose of inspecting the land (including any building or other structure on the land) with a view to recording any matters of archaeological or historical interest.
(2) Subject to subsection (3) below, a person entering any land in exercise of the power conferred by subsection (1) above may carry out excavations in the land for the purpose of archaeological investigation.
(3) [F227. Subject to subsection (4) below,] no excavation shall be made in exercise of the power conferred by subsection (2) above except with the consent of every person whose consent to the making of the excavation would be required apart from this section.
[F228. (4)Subsection (3) does not apply where—
(a) land is, or is to be, excavated in exercise of the power conferred by subsection (2); and
(b) [F229the Scottish Ministers know or have] [F229. Historic Environment Scotland knows or has] reason to believe that any ancient monument [F230they know or believe] [F230it knows or believes] to be in, on or under that land is or may be at risk of imminent damage or destruction.]
Amendments (Textual)
F226. Words in s. 26. (1) substituted (S.) (27.2.2015 for specified purposes, 1.10.2015 in so far as not already in force) by Historic Environment Scotland Act 2014 (asp 19), s. 31. (2), sch. 2 para. 43. (a) (with ss. 29, 30); S.S.I. 2015/31, art. 2, sch.; S.S.I. 2015/196, art. 2, sch.
F227. Words in s. 26. (3) inserted (S.) (1.12.2011) by Historic Environment (Amendment) (Scotland) Act 2011 (asp 3), ss. 10. (a), 33. (2); S.S.I. 2011/372, art. 2, Sch.

F228. S. 26. (4) added (S.) (1.12.2011) by Historic Environment (Amendment) (Scotland) Act 2011 (asp 3), ss. 10. (b), 33. (2); S.S.I. 2011/372, art. 2, Sch.
F229. Words in s. 26. (4)(b) substituted (S.) (27.2.2015 for specified purposes, 1.10.2015 in so far as not already in force) by Historic Environment Scotland Act 2014 (asp 19), s. 31. (2), sch. 2 para. 43. (b)(i) (with ss. 29, 30); S.S.I. 2015/31, art. 2, sch.; S.S.I. 2015/196, art. 2, sch.
F230. Words in s. 26. (4)(b) substituted (S.) (27.2.2015 for specified purposes, 1.10.2015 in so far as not already in force) by Historic Environment Scotland Act 2014 (asp 19), s. 31. (2), sch. 2 para. 43. (b)(ii) (with ss. 29, 30); S.S.I. 2015/31, art. 2, sch.; S.S.I. 2015/196, art. 2, sch.
Modifications etc. (not altering text)
C44. S. 26 restricted (18.12.1996) by 1996 c. 61, s. 12, Sch. 7 para. 4. (3)
C45. S. 26 restricted (22.7.2008) by Crossrail Act 2008 (c. 18), Sch. 9 para. 4. (3)

27 General provisions as to compensation for depreciation under Part I.

(1) For the purpose of assessing any compensation to which this section applies, the rules set out in section 5 of the M22. Land Compensation Act 1961 or, in relation to land in Scotland, the rules set out in section 12 of the M23. Land Compensation (Scotland) Act 1963 shall, so far as applicable and subject to any necessary modifications, have effect as they have effect for the purpose of assessing compensation for the compulsory acquisition of an interest in land.
(2) This section applies to any compensation payable under section 7 or 9 of this Act in respect of any loss or damage consisting of depreciation of the value of an interest in land.
(3) Where an interest in land is subject to a mortgage—
　(a) any compensation to which this section applies, which is payable in respect of depreciation of the value of that interest, shall be assessed as if the interest were not subject to the mortgage;
　(b) a claim for any such compensation may be made by any mortgagee of the interest, but without prejudice to the making of a claim by the person entitled to the interest;
　(c) no compensation to which this section applies shall be payable in respect of the interest of the mortgagee (as distinct from the interest which is subject to the mortgage); and
　(d) any compensation to which this section applies which is payable in respect of the interest which is subject to the mortgage shall be paid to the mortgagee, or, if there is more than one mortgagee, to the first mortgagee, and shall in either case be applied by him as if it were proceeds of sale.
Marginal Citations
M221961 c. 33.
M231963 c. 51.

28 Offence of damaging certain ancient monuments.

(1) A person who without [F231lawful] [F231reasonable] excuse destroys or damages any protected monument [F232shall be guilty of an offence if the person]—
　(a) [F233knowing that it is] [F233knew or ought to have known that it was] a protected monument; and
　(b) [F234intending] [F234intended] to destroy or damage the monument or [F235being] [F235was] reckless as to whether the monument would be destroyed or damaged;
[F236shall be guilty of an offence.]
(2) This section applies to anything done by or under the authority of the owner of the monument, other than an act for the execution of excepted works, as it applies to anything done by any other person.
In this subsection "excepted works" means works for which scheduled monument consent has been given under this Act (including any consent granted by order under section 3) [F237or for

which development consent has been granted].

(3) In this section "protected monument" means any scheduled monument and any monument under the ownership or guardianship of the Secretary of State [F238or the Commission] or a local authority by virtue of this Act.

(4) A person guilty of an offence under this section shall be liable—

(a) on summary conviction, to a fine not exceeding [F239the statutory maximum] [F239£50,000] or to imprisonment for a term not exceeding six months or both; or

(b) on conviction on indictment, to a fine or to imprisonment for a term not exceeding two years or both.

[F240. (5)In determining the amount of any fine to be imposed on a person under this section, the court shall in particular have regard to any financial benefit which has accrued or appears likely to accrue to the person in consequence of the offence.]

Amendments (Textual)

F231. Word in s. 28. (1) substituted (S.) (1.12.2011) by Historic Environment (Amendment) (Scotland) Act 2011 (asp 3), ss. 3. (3)(a), 33. (2); S.S.I. 2011/372, art. 2, Sch.

F232. Words in s. 28. (1) inserted (S.) (1.12.2011) by Historic Environment (Amendment) (Scotland) Act 2011 (asp 3), ss. 3. (3)(b), 33. (2); S.S.I. 2011/372, art. 2, Sch.

F233. Words in s. 28. (1)(a) substituted (S.) (1.12.2011) by Historic Environment (Amendment) (Scotland) Act 2011 (asp 3), ss. 3. (3)(c), 33. (2); S.S.I. 2011/372, art. 2, Sch.

F234. Word in s. 28. (1)(b) substituted (S.) (1.12.2011) by Historic Environment (Amendment) (Scotland) Act 2011 (asp 3), ss. 3. (3)(d)(i), 33. (2); S.S.I. 2011/372, art. 2, Sch.

F235. Word in s. 28. (1)(b) substituted (S.) (1.12.2011) by Historic Environment (Amendment) (Scotland) Act 2011 (asp 3), ss. 3. (3)(d)(ii), 33. (2); S.S.I. 2011/372, art. 2, Sch.

F236. Words in s. 28. (1) repealed (S.) (1.12.2011) by Historic Environment (Amendment) (Scotland) Act 2011 (asp 3), ss. 3. (3)(e), 33. (2); S.S.I. 2011/372, art. 2, Sch.

F237. Words in s. 28. (2) inserted (1.3.2010) by Planning Act 2008 (c. 29), s. 241. (8), Sch. 2 para. 18 (with s. 226); S.I. 2010/101, art. 2 (with art. 6)

F238. Words inserted by National Heritage Act 1983 (c. 47, SIF 78), s. 41, Sch. 4 para. 50

F239. Words in s. 28. (4) substituted (S.) (1.12.2011) by Historic Environment (Amendment) (Scotland) Act 2011 (asp 3), ss. 4. (3)(a), 33. (2); S.S.I. 2011/372, art. 2, Sch.

F240. S. 28. (5) added (S.) (1.12.2011) by Historic Environment (Amendment) (Scotland) Act 2011 (asp 3), ss. 4. (3)(b), 33. (2); S.S.I. 2011/372, art. 2, Sch.

Modifications etc. (not altering text)

C46. S. 28 excluded (18.12.1996) by 1996 c. 61, s. 12, Sch. 7 para. 4. (9)

C47. S. 28 excluded (22.7.2008) by Crossrail Act 2008 (c. 18), Sch. 9 para. 4. (9)

C48. S. 28. (1) savings for effects of 2011 asp 3 s. 3. (3) (S.) (1.12.2011) by The Historic Environment (Amendment) (Scotland) Act 2011 (Saving, Transitional and Consequential Provisions) Order 2011 (S.S.I. 2011/377), arts. 1. (1), 2. (b)

29 Compensation orders for damage to monuments under guardianship in England and Wales.

Where the owner or any other person is convicted of an offence involving damage to a monument situated in England and Wales which was at the time of the offence under the guardianship of the Secretary of State [F241or the Commission] or any local authority by virtue of this Act, any compensation order made under [F242section 130 of the Powers of Criminal Courts (Sentencing) Act 2000] (compensation orders against convicted persons) in respect of that damage shall be made in favour of the Secretary of State or [F243the Commission or the local authority in question (as the case may require)].

Amendments (Textual)

F241. Words inserted by National Heritage Act 1983 (c. 47, SIF 78), s. 41, Sch. 4 para. 51

F242. Words in s. 29 substituted (25.8.2000) by 2000 c. 6, ss. 165, 168. (1), Sch. 9 para. 59 (with

ss. 58, 62, 75)
F243. Words substituted by National Heritage Act 1983 (c. 47, SIF 78), s. 41, Sch. 4 para. 51

30 Disposal of land acquired under Part I.

(1) Subject to the following provisions of this section, the Secretary of State [F244or the Commission] or any local authority may dispose of any land acquired by them under section 10, 11 or 21 of this Act.
[F245. (1. A)The Secretary of State shall consult with the Commission before disposing of any land situated in England under this section.
(1. B)The Commission shall consult with the Secretary of State before disposing of any land under this section.]
(2) A local authority shall consult with the Secretary of State before disposing of any land under this section.
(3) Subject to subsection (4) below, where the land in question is or includes a monument, the Secretary of State or [F246the Commission or the local authority (as the case may be)] may only dispose of it on such terms as will in their opinion ensure the preservation of the monument.
(4) Subsection (3) above does not apply in any case where the Secretary of State or [F246the Commission or the local authority (as the case may be)] are satisfied that it is no longer practicable to preserve the monument (whether because of the cost of preserving it or otherwise).
Amendments (Textual)
F244. Words inserted by National Heritage Act 1983 (c. 47, SIF 78), s. 41, Sch. 4 para. 52. (2)
F245. S. 30. (1. A)(1. B) inserted by National Heritage Act 1983 (c. 47, SIF 78), s. 41, Sch. 4 para. 52. (3)
F246. Words substituted by National Heritage Act 1983 (c. 47, SIF 78), s. 41, Sch. 4 para. 52. (4)

31 Voluntary contributions towards expenditure under Part I.

The Secretary of State [F247, Historic Environment Scotland] or any local authority may receive voluntary contributions for or towards the cost of any expenditure incurred by them under this Part of this Act (whether in relation to any particular monument or land or otherwise).
Amendments (Textual)
F247. Words in s. 31 inserted (S.) (27.2.2015 for specified purposes, 1.10.2015 in so far as not already in force) by Historic Environment Scotland Act 2014 (asp 19), s. 31. (2), sch. 2 para. 44 (with ss. 29, 30); S.S.I. 2015/31, art. 2, sch.; S.S.I. 2015/196, art. 2, sch.

32 Interpretation of Part I.

(1) In this Part of this Act "maintenance" and "maintain" have the meanings given by section 13. (7) of this Act, and expressions to which a meaning is given for the purposes of [F248the Town and Country Planning Act 1990 or the Planning (Listed Buildings and Conservation Areas) Act 1990] or (as regards Scotland) for the purposes of [F249the Town and Country Planning (Scotland) Act 1997 or the Planning (Listed Buildings and Conservation Areas) (Scotland) Act 1997] have the same meaning as in [F248the said Acts of 1990] or (as the case may require) as in [F249the said Acts of 1997].
(2) References in this Part of this Act to a monument, in relation to the acquisition or transfer of any monument (whether under a power conferred by this Part of this Act or otherwise), include references to any interest in or right over the monument.
(3) For the purposes of this Part of this Act the Secretary of State [F250or the Commission] or a local authority are the owners of a monument by virtue of this Act if the Secretary of State or [F251the Commission or the local authority (as the case be)] have acquired it under section 10, 11

or 21 of this Act.
Amendments (Textual)
F248. Words substituted by Planning (Consequential Provisions) Act 1990 (c. 11, SIF 123:1, 2), s. 4, Sch. 2 para. 43. (1)
F249. Words in s. 32. (1) substituted (27.5.1997) by 1997 c. 11, ss. 4, 6, Sch. 2 para. 29. (1)(a).
F250. Words inserted by National Heritage Act 1983 (c. 47, SIF 78), s. 41, Sch. 4 para. 53
F251. Words substituted by National Heritage Act 1983 (c. 47, SIF 78), s. 41, Sch. 4 para. 53

General provisions as to compensation for depreciation under Part I.

27 General provisions as to compensation for depreciation under Part I.

(1) For the purpose of assessing any compensation to which this section applies, the rules set out in section 5 of the M1. Land Compensation Act 1961 or, in relation to land in Scotland, the rules set out in section 12 of the M2. Land Compensation (Scotland) Act 1963 shall, so far as applicable and subject to any necessary modifications, have effect as they have effect for the purpose of assessing compensation for the compulsory acquisition of an interest in land.
(2) This section applies to any compensation payable under section 7 or 9 of this Act in respect of any loss or damage consisting of depreciation of the value of an interest in land.
(3) Where an interest in land is subject to a mortgage—
 (a) any compensation to which this section applies, which is payable in respect of depreciation of the value of that interest, shall be assessed as if the interest were not subject to the mortgage;
 (b) a claim for any such compensation may be made by any mortgagee of the interest, but without prejudice to the making of a claim by the person entitled to the interest;
 (c) no compensation to which this section applies shall be payable in respect of the interest of the mortgagee (as distinct from the interest which is subject to the mortgage); and
 (d) any compensation to which this section applies which is payable in respect of the interest which is subject to the mortgage shall be paid to the mortgagee, or, if there is more than one mortgagee, to the first mortgagee, and shall in either case be applied by him as if it were proceeds of sale.
Marginal Citations
M11961 c. 33.
M21963 c. 51.

Disposal of land acquired under Part I.

30 Disposal of land acquired under Part I.

(1) Subject to the following provisions of this section, the Secretary of State [F1or the Commission] or any local authority may dispose of any land acquired by them under section 10, 11 or 21 of this Act.
[F2. (1. A)The Secretary of State shall consult with the Commission before disposing of any land situated in England under this section.
(1. B)The Commission shall consult with the Secretary of State before disposing of any land under this section.]

(2) A local authority shall consult with the Secretary of State before disposing of any land under this section.
(3) Subject to subsection (4) below, where the land in question is or includes a monument, the Secretary of State or [F3the Commission or the local authority (as the case may be)] may only dispose of it on such terms as will in their opinion ensure the preservation of the monument.
(4) Subsection (3) above does not apply in any case where the Secretary of State or [F3the Commission or the local authority (as the case may be)] are satisfied that it is no longer practicable to preserve the monument (whether because of the cost of preserving it or otherwise).
Amendments (Textual)
F1. Words inserted by National Heritage Act 1983 (c. 47, SIF 78), s. 41, Sch. 4 para. 52. (2)
F2. S. 30. (1. A)(1. B) inserted by National Heritage Act 1983 (c. 47, SIF 78), s. 41, Sch. 4 para. 52. (3)
F3. Words substituted by National Heritage Act 1983 (c. 47, SIF 78), s. 41, Sch. 4 para. 52. (4)

Voluntary contributions towards expenditure under Part I.

31 Voluntary contributions towards expenditure under Part I.

The Secretary of State [F1, Historic Environment Scotland] or any local authority may receive voluntary contributions for or towards the cost of any expenditure incurred by them under this Part of this Act (whether in relation to any particular monument or land or otherwise).
Amendments (Textual)
F1. Words in s. 31 inserted (S.) (27.2.2015 for specified purposes, 1.10.2015 in so far as not already in force) by Historic Environment Scotland Act 2014 (asp 19), s. 31. (2), sch. 2 para. 44 (with ss. 29, 30); S.S.I. 2015/31, art. 2, sch.; S.S.I. 2015/196, art. 2, sch.

Interpretation of Part I.

32 Interpretation of Part I.

(1) In this Part of this Act "maintenance" and "maintain" have the meanings given by section 13. (7) of this Act, and expressions to which a meaning is given for the purposes of [F1the Town and Country Planning Act 1990 or the Planning (Listed Buildings and Conservation Areas) Act 1990] or (as regards Scotland) for the purposes of [F2the Town and Country Planning (Scotland) Act 1997 or the Planning (Listed Buildings and Conservation Areas) (Scotland) Act 1997] have the same meaning as in [F1the said Acts of 1990] or (as the case may require) as in [F2the said Acts of 1997].
(2) References in this Part of this Act to a monument, in relation to the acquisition or transfer of any monument (whether under a power conferred by this Part of this Act or otherwise), include references to any interest in or right over the monument.
(3) For the purposes of this Part of this Act the Secretary of State [F3or the Commission] or a local authority are the owners of a monument by virtue of this Act if the Secretary of State or [F4the Commission or the local authority (as the case be)] have acquired it under section 10, 11 or 21 of this Act.
Amendments (Textual)
F1. Words substituted by Planning (Consequential Provisions) Act 1990 (c. 11, SIF 123:1, 2), s. 4,

Sch. 2 para. 43. (1)
F2. Words in s. 32. (1) substituted (27.5.1997) by 1997 c. 11, ss. 4, 6, Sch. 2 para. 29. (1)(a).
F3. Words inserted by National Heritage Act 1983 (c. 47, SIF 78), s. 41, Sch. 4 para. 53
F4. Words substituted by National Heritage Act 1983 (c. 47, SIF 78), s. 41, Sch. 4 para. 53

Part 1A Inventories of gardens and designed landscapes and of battlefields

[F1. Part 1. ASInventories of gardens and designed landscapes and of battlefields

Amendments (Textual)
F1. Pt. 1. A inserted (S.) (30.6.2011) by Historic Environment (Amendment) (Scotland) Act 2011 (asp 3), ss. 11, 33. (2); S.S.I. 2011/174, art. 2, Sch.

32. AInventory of gardens and designed landscapesS

(1) [F2. The Scottish Ministers] [F2. Historic Environment Scotland] must compile and maintain (in such form as [F3they think] [F3it thinks] fit) an inventory of such gardens and designed landscapes as appear to [F4them] [F4it] to be of national importance.
(2) In subsection (1), references to gardens and designed landscapes are to grounds which have been laid out for artistic effect and, in appropriate cases, include references to any buildings, land, or water on, adjacent, or contiguous to such grounds.
(3) [F5. The Scottish Ministers] [F5. Historic Environment Scotland] may, from time to time, modify the inventory so as to—
    (a) add an entry relating to grounds mentioned in subsection (2);
    (b) remove an entry relating to such grounds;
    (c) amend an entry relating to such grounds (whether by excluding anything previously included as part of the grounds or adding anything not previously so included, or otherwise).
(4) As soon as reasonably practicable after including any grounds in the inventory in exercise of [F6their] [F6its] duty under subsection (1), or modifying the inventory under subsection (3), [F7the Scottish Ministers] [F7. Historic Environment Scotland] must—
    (a) inform—
(i) the owner of the grounds;
(ii) (if the owner is not the occupier) the occupier of the grounds; and
(iii) any local authority in whose area the grounds are situated,
of the inclusion or modification; and
    (b) where the grounds are so included, or the inventory is modified as mentioned in paragraph (a) or (c) of subsection (3), send to any person or any local authority informed under paragraph (a) of this subsection a copy of the entry or, as the case may be, of the amended entry in the inventory relating to the grounds.
(5) [F8. The Scottish Ministers] [F8. Historic Environment Scotland] must from time to time publish, in such manner as [F9they think] [F9it thinks] fit, a list of all the gardens and designed landscapes which are for the time being included in the inventory.
Amendments (Textual)
F2. Words in s. 32. A(1) substituted (S.) (27.2.2015 for specified purposes, 1.10.2015 in so far as not already in force) by Historic Environment Scotland Act 2014 (asp 19), s. 31. (2), sch. 2 para. 37. (a)(i) (with ss. 29, 30); S.S.I. 2015/31, art. 2, sch.; S.S.I. 2015/196, art. 2, sch.
F3. Words in s. 32. A(1) substituted (S.) (27.2.2015 for specified purposes, 1.10.2015 in so far as

not already in force) by Historic Environment Scotland Act 2014 (asp 19), s. 31. (2), sch. 2 para. 37. (a)(ii) (with ss. 29, 30); S.S.I. 2015/31, art. 2, sch.; S.S.I. 2015/196, art. 2, sch.
F4. Word in s. 32. A(1) substituted (S.) (27.2.2015 for specified purposes, 1.10.2015 in so far as not already in force) by Historic Environment Scotland Act 2014 (asp 19), s. 31. (2), sch. 2 para. 37. (a)(iii) (with ss. 29, 30); S.S.I. 2015/31, art. 2, sch.; S.S.I. 2015/196, art. 2, sch.
F5. Words in s. 32. A(3) substituted (S.) (27.2.2015 for specified purposes, 1.10.2015 in so far as not already in force) by Historic Environment Scotland Act 2014 (asp 19), s. 31. (2), sch. 2 para. 37. (b) (with ss. 29, 30); S.S.I. 2015/31, art. 2, sch.; S.S.I. 2015/196, art. 2, sch.
F6. Word in s. 32. A(4) substituted (S.) (27.2.2015 for specified purposes, 1.10.2015 in so far as not already in force) by Historic Environment Scotland Act 2014 (asp 19), s. 31. (2), sch. 2 para. 37. (c)(i) (with ss. 29, 30); S.S.I. 2015/31, art. 2, sch.; S.S.I. 2015/196, art. 2, sch.
F7. Words in s. 32. A(4) substituted (S.) (27.2.2015 for specified purposes, 1.10.2015 in so far as not already in force) by Historic Environment Scotland Act 2014 (asp 19), s. 31. (2), sch. 2 para. 37. (c)(ii) (with ss. 29, 30); S.S.I. 2015/31, art. 2, sch.; S.S.I. 2015/196, art. 2, sch.
F8. Words in s. 32. A(5) substituted (S.) (27.2.2015 for specified purposes, 1.10.2015 in so far as not already in force) by Historic Environment Scotland Act 2014 (asp 19), s. 31. (2), sch. 2 para. 37. (d)(i) (with ss. 29, 30); S.S.I. 2015/31, art. 2, sch.; S.S.I. 2015/196, art. 2, sch.
F9. Words in s. 32. A(5) substituted (S.) (27.2.2015 for specified purposes, 1.10.2015 in so far as not already in force) by Historic Environment Scotland Act 2014 (asp 19), s. 31. (2), sch. 2 para. 37. (d)(ii) (with ss. 29, 30); S.S.I. 2015/31, art. 2, sch.; S.S.I. 2015/196, art. 2, sch.
Modifications etc. (not altering text)
C1. S. 32. A savings for effects of 2014 asp 19, Sch. 2 para. 37 (S.) (1.10.2015) by The Historic Environment Scotland Act 2014 (Saving, Transitional and Consequential Provisions) Order 2015 (S.S.I. 2015/239), arts. 1. (1), 10

32. BInventory of battlefieldsS

(1) [F10. The Scottish Ministers] [F10. Historic Environment Scotland] must compile and maintain (in such form as [F11they think] [F11it thinks] fit) an inventory of such battlefields as appear to [F12them] [F12it] to be of national importance.
(2) In this section, "battlefield" means—
   (a) an area of land over which a battle was fought; or
   (b) an area of land on which any significant activities relating to a battle occurred (whether or not the battle was fought over that area).
(3) Subsections (3) to (5) of section 32. A apply to an inventory compiled and maintained under subsection (1) of this section as they apply to an inventory compiled and maintained under subsection (1) of that section; and, for the purposes of that application, references to gardens and designed landscapes, and to grounds referred to by those expressions, are to be construed as references to a battlefield.]
Amendments (Textual)
F10. Words in s. 32. B(1) substituted (S.) (27.2.2015 for specified purposes, 1.10.2015 in so far as not already in force) by Historic Environment Scotland Act 2014 (asp 19), s. 31. (2), sch. 2 para. 38. (a) (with ss. 29, 30); S.S.I. 2015/31, art. 2, sch.; S.S.I. 2015/196, art. 2, sch.
F11. Words in s. 32. B(1) substituted (S.) (27.2.2015 for specified purposes, 1.10.2015 in so far as not already in force) by Historic Environment Scotland Act 2014 (asp 19), s. 31. (2), sch. 2 para. 38. (b) (with ss. 29, 30); S.S.I. 2015/31, art. 2, sch.; S.S.I. 2015/196, art. 2, sch.
F12. Word in s. 32. B(1) substituted (S.) (27.2.2015 for specified purposes, 1.10.2015 in so far as not already in force) by Historic Environment Scotland Act 2014 (asp 19), s. 31. (2), sch. 2 para. 38. (c) (with ss. 29, 30); S.S.I. 2015/31, art. 2, sch.; S.S.I. 2015/196, art. 2, sch.
Modifications etc. (not altering text)
C2. S. 32. B savings for effects of 2014 asp 19, Sch. 2 para. 38 (S.) (1.10.2015) by The Historic Environment Scotland Act 2014 (Saving, Transitional and Consequential Provisions) Order 2015

(S.S.I. 2015/239), arts. 1. (1), 10

Part II Archaeological Areas

Part II Archaeological Areas

Modifications etc. (not altering text)
C1. Pt. II (ss. 33-41) extended (E.W.) (19.9.1995) by 1995 c. 25, ss. 70, 125. (2), Sch. 9 para.10. (1) (with ss. 7. (6), 115, 117, Sch. 8 para. 7)

33 Designation of areas of archaeological importance.

(1) The Secretary of State may from time to time by order designate as an area of archaeological importance any area which appears to him to merit treatment as such for the purposes of this Act [F1; but, where the area in question is situated in England, he shall consult with the Commission before doing so.]
(2) A local authority may from time to time by order designate as an area of archaeological importance any area within the area of that local authority which appears to them to merit treatment as such for the purposes of this Act [F2; but, where the area in question is situated in England, the authority shall first notify the Commission of their intention to do so.]
[F3. (2. A)The Commission may from time to time by order designate as an area of archaeological importance any area in Greater London which appears to them to merit treatment as such for the purposes of this Act.]
(3) An order under this section designating an area as an area of archaeological importance (whether made by the Secretary of State or by a local authority [F4or by the Commission]) is referred to below in this Act as a designation order.
(4) The Secretary of State may at any time by order vary or revoke a designation order, but his power to vary such an order is confined to reducing the area designated by the order.
[F5. The Secretary of State shall consult with the Commission before varying or revoking an order relating to an area situated in England.]
(5) A designation order relating to an area in England and Wales shall be a local land charge.
(6) Schedule 2 to this Act shall have effect with respect to the making, and with respect to the variation and revocation, of designation orders.
Amendments (Textual)
F1. Words inserted by National Heritage Act 1983 (c. 47, SIF 78), s. 41, Sch. 4 para. 54. (2)
F2. Words inserted by National Heritage Act 1983 (c. 47, SIF 78), s. 41, Sch. 4 para. 54. (3)
F3. S. 33. (2. A) inserted by Local Government Act 1985 (c. 51, SIF 81:1), s. 6, Sch. 2 para. 2. (2)(a)
F4. Words inserted by Local Government Act 1985 (c. 51, SIF 81:1), s. 6, Sch. 2 para. 2. (2)(b)
F5. Words inserted by National Heritage Act 1983 (c. 47, SIF 78), s. 41, Sch. 4 para. 54. (4)

34 Investigating authorities for areas of archaeological importance.

(1) The Secretary of State may at any time appoint any person whom he considers to be competent to undertake archaeological investigations to exercise in relation to any area of archaeological importance the functions conferred by the following provisions of this Part of this Act on the investigating authority for an area of archaeological importance, and any such appointment shall be on such terms and for such period as the Secretary of State thinks fit.

[F6. The Secretary of State shall consult with the Commission before making an appointment under this subsection in relation to an area situated in England.]

(2) A person's appointment as investigating authority may be cancelled at any time by the Secretary of State [F7; but, where the appointment was made in relation to an area situated in England, he shall consult with the Commission before cancelling the appointment.]

(3) On appointing or cancelling the appointment of any person as investigating authority for an area of archaeological importance, the Secretary of Sate shall notify each local authority in whose area the area of archaeological importance in question is wholly or partly situated [F8; and, if the area is wholly or partly situated in Greater London, he shall also notify the Commission.]

(4) Where there is for the time being no person holding appointment under this section as the investigating authority for an area of archaeological importance, the functions of the investigating authority for that area under this Part of this Act shall be exercisable by the [F9. Commission (in the case of an area situated in England) or the Secretary of State (in any other case)].

(5) A person duly authorised in writing by any person by whom the functions of an investigating authority under this Part of this Act are for the time being exercisable may act on his behalf in the exercise of those functions.

Amendments (Textual)

F6. Words inserted by National Heritage Act 1983 (c. 47, SIF 78), s. 41, Sch. 4 para. 55. (2)
F7. Words inserted by National Heritage Act 1983 (c. 47, SIF 78), s. 41, Sch. 4 para. 55. (3)
F8. Words inserted by Local Government Act 1985 (c. 51, SIF 81:1), s. 6, Sch. 2 para. 2. (3)
F9. Words substituted by National Heritage Act 1983 (c. 47, SIF 78), s. 41, Sch. 4 para. 55. (4)

35 Notice required of operations in areas of archaeological importance.

(1) Subject to section 37 of this Act, if any person carries out, or causes or permits to be carried out, on land in an area of archaeological importance any operations to which this section applies—

   (a) without having first served a notice relating to those operations which complies with subsections (4) and (5) below; or

   (b) within six weeks of serving such a notice;

he shall be guilty of an offence.

(2) Subject to section 37 of this Act, this section applies to any of the following operations, that is to say—

   (a) operations which disturb the ground;

   (b) flooding operations; and

   (c) tipping operations.

(3) In this Part of this Act the person carrying out or proposing to carry out any operations is referred to, in relation to those operations, as "the developer", and a notice complying with subsections (4) and (5) below is referred to as an "operations notice".

(4) A notice required for the purposes of this section—

   (a) shall specify the operations to which it relates, the site on which they are to be carried out, the date on which it is proposed to begin them and, where the operations are to be carried out after clearance of the site, the developer's estimated date for completion of the clearance operations;

   (b) shall be accompanied by a certificate in the prescribed form which satisfies the requirements of section 36 of this Act; and

   (c) shall be in the prescribed form.

(5) A notice required for the purposes of this section shall be served by the developer—

   (a) in the case of land in England F10. . ., on the district council or London borough council or (as the case may be) on each district council or London borough council in whose area the site of the operations is wholly or partly situated;

   F11[(aa)in the case of land in Wales, on the council of each county or county borough in which the site of the operations is wholly or partly situated;]

(b) in the case of land in Scotland, on the local authority or (as the case may be) on each local authority in whose area the site of the operations is wholly or partly situated; or

(c) in a case where the developer is any such council or local authority, on the Secretary of State.

(6) Regulations made by the Secretary of State may prescribe the steps to be taken by any council or local authority on whom an operations notice is served in accordance with subsection (5) above.

(7) Where an operations notice is served with respect to operations which are to be carried out after clearance of any site, the developer shall notify the investigating authority for the area of archaeological importance in question of the clearance of the site immediately on completion of the clearance operations.

(8) If in a case falling within subsection (7) above the developer carries out, or causes or permits to be carried out, any of the operations to which the operations notice relates without having first notified the investigating authority of the clearance of the site in accordance with that subsection, this section shall have effect in relation to those operations as if the operations notice had not been served.

(9) A person guilty of an offence under this section shall be liable—

(a) on summary conviction or, in Scotland, on conviction before a court of summary jurisdiction, to a fine not exceeding the statutory maximum; or

(b) on conviction on indictment to a fine.

(10) Without prejudice to section 222 of the M1. Local Government Act 1972, any such council as is mentioned in subsection (5)(a) above may institute proceedings for an offence under this section in respect of operations on any site situated partly in their area notwithstanding that the operations are confined to a part of the site outside their area; and if it appears to any such council or, in Scotland, to any local authority—

(a) that any operations are being, or are about to be, carried out in contravention of this section on any site situated wholly or partly in their area; and

(b) that the site contains or is likely to contain anything of archaeological or historical interest which will be disturbed, damaged, destroyed or removed without proper archaeological investigation if operations are carried out on the site without regard for the provisions of this Part of this Act;

that council or local authority may take proceedings in the High Court or, in Scotland, in any court of competent jurisdiction for the purpose of securing an injunction or interdict prohibiting those operations from being carried out in contravention of this section.

[F12. (11)This section shall have effect, in relation to any land within the Broads (as defined by the Norfolk and Suffolk Broads Act 1988), as if the Broads Authority were the district council (to the exclusion of the authority which is otherwise the district council for the area in question) and the Broads were its local authority area.]

Amendments (Textual)

F10. Words in s. 35. (5)(a) repealed (1.4.1996) by 1994 c. 19, s. 66. (6)(8), Sch. 16 para. 56. (2), Sch.18 (with ss. 54. (5)(7), 55. (5), Sch. 17 paras. 22. (1), 23. (2)); S.I. 1996/396, art. 4, Sch.2

F11. S. 35. (5)(aa) inserted (1.4.1996) by 1994 c. 19, s. 66. (6), Sch. 16 para. 56. (2) (with ss. 54. (5)(7), 55. (5), Sch. 17 paras. 22. (1), 23. (2)); S.I. 1996/396, art. 4, Sch.2

F12. S. 35. (11) added (E.W.) by Norfolk and Suffolk Broads Act 1988 (c. 4, SIF 81:1), ss. 2. (5)(6), 23. (2), 27. (2), Sch. 3 para. 30. (2), Sch. 7

Modifications etc. (not altering text)

C2. S. 35 excluded by S.I. 1984/1286, art. 2. (1)

C3. S. 35 extended (E.W.)(19.9.1995) by 1995 c. 25, ss. 70, 125, Sch. 9 para. 10. (2)(with ss. 7. (6), 115, 117, Sch. 8 para. 7).

C4. S. 35 excluded (18.12.1996) by 1996 c. 61, s. 12, Sch. 7 para. 4. (10)

C5. S. 35 excluded (22.7.2008) by Crossrail Act 2008 (c. 18), Sch. 9 para. 4. (10)

Marginal Citations

M11972 c. 70.

36 Certificate to accompany operations notice under section 35.

(1) A person is qualified to issue a certificate for the purposes of section 35. (4)(b) of this Act if he either—

(a) has an interest in the site of the operations which (apart from any restrictions imposed by law) entitles him to carry out the operations in question; or

(b) has a right to enter on and take possession of that site under section 11. (1) or (2) of the M2. Compulsory Purchase Act 1965 (powers of entry on land subject to compulsory purchase) or, in the case of a site in Scotland, under paragraph 3. (1) of Schedule 2 to the M3. Acquisition of Land (Authorisation Procedure) (Scotland) Act 1947.

(2) Statutory undertakers are qualified to issue a certificate for the purposes of section 35. (4)(b) of this Act if they are entitled by or under any enactment to carry out the operations in question.

(3) Any such certificate—

(a) shall be signed by or on behalf of a person or persons qualified in accordance with subsection (1) or (2) above to issue it;

(b) shall state that the person issuing the certificate has an interest within paragraph (a) or (as the case may be) a right within paragraph (b) of subsection (1) above or, in the case of a certificate issued by statutory undertakers, shall state that it is so issued and specify the enactment by or under which they are entitled to carry out the operations in question; and

(c) if the person issuing the certificate is not the developer, shall state that he has authorised the developer to carry out the operations.

(4) If any person issues a certificate which purports to comply with the requirements of this section and which contains a statement which he knows to be false or misleading in a material particular, or recklessly issues a certificate which purports to comply with those requirements and which contains a statement which is false or misleading in a material particular, he shall be guilty of an offence and liable on summary conviction or, in Scotland, on conviction before a court of summary jurisdiction, to a fine not exceeding [F13level 3 on the standard scale].

Amendments (Textual)

F13. Words substituted by virtue of Criminal Justice Act 1982 (c. 48), s. 46 and Criminal Procedure (Scotland) Act 1975 (c. 21), s. 289. G (as inserted by Criminal Justice Act 1982 (c. 48), s. 54)

Marginal Citations

M21965 c. 56.

M31947 c. 42.

37 Exemptions from offence under section 35.

(1) Section 35 of this Act does not apply to any operations carried out with the consent of the investigating authority for the area of archaeological importance in question.

[F14. (1. A)Section 35 does not apply to the carrying out of any operations for which development consent has been granted.]

(2) The Secretary of State may by order direct that section 35 shall not apply to the carrying out, or to the carrying out by any class or description of persons specified in the order, of operations of any class or description so specified; and an exemption conferred by an order under this subsection may be either unconditional or subject to any conditions specified in the order.

(3) The Secretary of State may direct that any exemption conferred by an order under subsection (2) above shall not apply to the carrying out on any land specified in the direction, or to the carrying out on any land so specified by any class or description of persons so specified, of operations of any class or description so specified, and may withdraw any direction given under this subsection.

[F15. The Secretary of State shall consult with the Commission before giving or withdrawing a direction under this subsection in relation to land situated in England.]

(4) A direction under subsection (3) above shall not take effect until notice of it has been served on the occupier or (if there is no occupier) on the owner of the land in question.
(5) In any proceedings for an offence under section 35 consisting in carrying out, or causing or permitting to be carried out, any operations which disturb the ground, it shall be a defence for the accused to prove that he took all reasonable precautions and exercised all due diligence to avoid or prevent disturbance of the ground.
(6) In any proceedings for an offence under section 35 it shall be a defence for the accused to prove either—
    (a) that he did not know and had no reason to believe that the site of the operations was within an area of archaeological importance;
    (b) that the operations were urgently necessary in the interests of safety or health and that notice in writing of the need for the operations was given to the Secretary of State as soon as reasonably practicable.
Amendments (Textual)
F14. S. 37. (1. A) inserted (1.3.2010) by Planning Act 2008 (c. 29), s. 241. (8), Sch. 2 para. 19 (with s. 226); S.I. 2010/101, art. 2 (with art. 6)
F15. Words inserted by National Heritage Act 1983 (c. 47, SIF 78), s. 41, Sch. 4 para. 56

38 Powers of investigating authority to enter and excavate site of operations covered by an operations notice.

(1) Where an operations notice is served with respect to any operations, the investigating authority for the area of archaeological importance in which the site of the operations is situated shall thereupon have a right to enter, at any reasonable time, the site and any land giving access to the site, for either or both of the following purposes, that is to say—
    (a) for the purpose of inspecting the site (including any buildings or other structures on the site) with a view to recording any matters of archaeological or historical interest and determining whether it would be desirable to carry out any excavations in the site; and
    (b) for the purpose of observing any operations carried out on the site with a view to examining and recording any objects or other material of archaeological or historical interest, and recording any matters of archaeological or historical interest, discovered during the course of those operations.
(2) Where—
    (a) an operations notice is served with respect to any operations; and
    (b) the investigating authority for the area of archaeological importance in which the site of the operations is situated serves notice in accordance with subsection (3) below of its intention to excavate the site;
the investigating authority shall have a right to carry out excavations in the site for the purpose of archaeological investigation at any time during the period allowed for excavation in accordance with subsection (4) below.
(3) The investigating authority shall only have a right to excavate the site of any operations in accordance with subsection (2) above if before the end of the period of four weeks beginning with the date of service of the operations notice the authority—
    (a) serves notice in the prescribed form of its intention to excavate on the developer; and
    (b) serves a copy of that notice on any council (in England and Wales) or local authority (in Scotland) served with the operations notice and also (unless the functions of the investigating authority are for the time being exercisable by the Secretary of State) on the Secretary of State.
[F16and
    (c) where the site in question is situated in England, serves a copy of that notice on the Commission (unless the investigating authority is for the time being the Commission).]
(4) The period allowed for excavation under subsection (2) above is the period of four months and two weeks beginning—

(a) with the date immediately following the end of the period of six weeks beginning with the date of service of the operations notice; or

(b) where the operations specified in the operations notice are to be carried out after clearance of the site, with the date of receipt of the notification of clearance of the site required under section 35. (7) of this Act or with the date first mentioned in paragraph (a) above (whichever last occurs); or

(c) with any earlier date agreed between the investigating authority and the developer.

(5) Where—

(a) the investigating authority has served notice of its intention to excavate the site in accordance with subsection (3) above; and

(b) the period of six weeks beginning with the date of service of the operations notice has expired;

the investigating authority shall have a right to carry out excavations in the site for the purpose of archaeological investigation notwithstanding that the period allowed for excavation in accordance with subsection (4) above has not yet begun, but only if the authority does not thereby obstruct the execution on the site by the developer of clearance operations or any other operations to which section 35 of this Act does not apply.

(6) The investigating authority may at any reasonable time enter the site and any land giving access to the site for the purpose of exercising a right to excavate the site in accordance with subsection (2) or (5) above.

(7) If operations to which the operations notice relates are carried out on the site at a time when the investigating authority has a right to excavate the site in accordance with subsection (2) or (5) above section 35 of this Act shall have effect in relation to those operations as if the operations notice had not been served (subject, however, to any exemption or defence conferred by or under section 37 of this Act).

(8) The Secretary of State may at any time direct—

(a) that an investigating authority shall comply with any conditions specified in the direction in exercising any of its powers under the preceding provisions of this section in relation to any site; or

(b) that any such power shall cease to be exercisable by an investigating authority in relation to the whole or any part of any site;

and may vary or revoke any direction given under paragraph (a) above.

[F17. The Secretary of State shall consult with the Commission before giving, varying or revoking a direction under this subsection in relation to a site situated in England.]

(9) On giving a direction under subsection (8) above the Secretary of State shall serve a copy of the direction on each of the following persons, that is to say—

(a) the investigating authority;

(b) any council (in England and Wales) or local authority (in Scotland) served with the operations notice in question;

(c) the developer; and

(d) any person other than the developer by whom the certificate accompanying the operations notice in accordance with section 35. (4)(b) of this Act was issued;

and on varying or revoking any such direction the Secretary of State shall notify the same persons (giving particulars of the effect of any variation).

[F18. (10) On giving a direction under subsection (8) above in relation to a site situated in England the Secretary of State shall send a copy of the direction to the Commission (if the investigating authority is not the Commission).

(11) On varying or revoking a direction given under subsection (8) above in relation to a site situated in England the Secretary of State shall notify the Commission (giving particulars of the effect of any variation) if the investigating authority is not the Commission.]

Amendments (Textual)

F16. S. 38. (3)(c) inserted by National Heritage Act 1983 (c. 47, SIF 78), s. 41, Sch. 4 para. 57. (2)(5)

F17. Words inserted by National Heritage Act 1983 (c. 47, SIF 78), s. 41, Sch. 4 para. 57. (3)
F18. S. 38. (10)(11) inserted by National Heritage Act 1983 (c. 47, SIF 78), s. 41, Sch. 4 para. 57. (4)

39 Power of investigating authority to investigate in advance of operations notice any site which may be acquired compulsorily.

(1) If an authority possessing compulsory purchase powers notifies the investigating authority for any area of archaeological importance that it proposes to carry out, or to authorise someone else to carry out, on any site in the area, any operations of a description mentioned in section 35. (2) of this Act (other than exempt operations), the investigating authority shall thereupon have a right to enter, at any reasonable time, the site and any land giving access to the site, for the purpose mentioned in section 38. (1)(a) of this Act.
In this subsection "exempt operations" means operations excluded from the application of section 35 by an order under section 37 of this Act.
(2) The right of an investigating authority to enter any site by virtue of subsection (1) above shall cease at the end of the period of one month beginning with the day on which it is first exercised.
(3) Section 38. (8) of this Act shall apply in relation to the power of entry under this section as it applies in relation to the powers of an investigating authority under that section.
(4) Section 38. (9) of this Act shall not apply in relation to a direction under section 38. (8) with respect to the exercise of the power of entry under this section, but on giving any such direction the Secretary of State shall serve a copy of the direction on each of the following persons, that is to say—
  (a) the investigating authority;
  (b) the authority possessing compulsory purchase powers; and
  (c) the owner and (if the owner is not the occupier) the occupier of the site in question; [F19and
  (d) where the site in question is situated in England, the Commission (if the investigating authority is not the Commission);]
and on varying or revoking any such direction the Secretary of State shall notify the same persons (giving particulars of the effect of any variation).
(5) In this section "authority possessing compulsory purchase powers" means any person or body of persons who could be or have been authorised to acquire an interest in land compulsorily.
Amendments (Textual)
F19. S. 39. (4)(d) inserted by National Heritage Act 1983 (c. 47, SIF 78), s. 41, Sch. 4 para. 58
Modifications etc. (not altering text)
C6. S. 39. (1) amended (18.12.1996) by 1996 c. 61, s. 12, Sch. 7 para. 4. (11)
C7. S. 39. (1) modified (22.7.2008) by Crossrail Act 2008 (c. 18), Sch. 9 para. 4. (11)

40 Other powers of entry on site of operations covered by an operations notice.

Where an operations notice is served with respect to any operations—
  (a) any person duly authorised in writing by the Secretary of State may at any reasonable time enter the site of the operations for the purpose of inspecting the site (including any building or other structure on the site) and recording any matters of archaeological or historical interest observed in the course of that inspection; and
  (b) any person duly authorised in writing by the Royal Commission on Historical Monuments may at any reasonable time enter the site for the purpose of inspecting any building or other structure on the site and recording any matters of archaeological or historical interest observed in the course of that inspection.

41 Interpretation of Part II.

(1) In this Part of this Act—
(a) "the developer" and "operations notice" have the meanings respectively given by section 35.(3) of this Act;
(b) references to a London borough council include references to the Common Council of the City of London;
(c) references to operations on any land include references to operations in, under or over the land in question;
(d) references to the clearance of any site are references to the demolition and removal of any existing building or other structure on the site and the removal of any other materials thereon so as to clear the surface of the land (but do not include the levelling of the surface or the removal of materials from below the surface); and
(e) references to clearance operations are references to operations undertaken for the purpose of or in connection with the clearance of any site.
(2) For the purposes of this Part of this Act, the investigating authority for an area of archaeological importance is the person for the time being holding appointment as such under section 34 of this Act or (if there is no such person) the [F20. Commission (in a case where the area is situated in England) or the Secretary of State (in any other case)].
Amendments (Textual)
F20. Words substituted by National Heritage Act 1983 (c. 47, SIF 78), s. 41, Sch. 4 para. 59

Interpretation of Part II.

41 Interpretation of Part II.

(1) In this Part of this Act—
(a) "the developer" and "operations notice" have the meanings respectively given by section 35.(3) of this Act;
(b) references to a London borough council include references to the Common Council of the City of London;
(c) references to operations on any land include references to operations in, under or over the land in question;
(d) references to the clearance of any site are references to the demolition and removal of any existing building or other structure on the site and the removal of any other materials thereon so as to clear the surface of the land (but do not include the levelling of the surface or the removal of materials from below the surface); and
(e) references to clearance operations are references to operations undertaken for the purpose of or in connection with the clearance of any site.
(2) For the purposes of this Part of this Act, the investigating authority for an area of archaeological importance is the person for the time being holding appointment as such under section 34 of this Act or (if there is no such person) the [F1. Commission (in a case where the area is situated in England) or the Secretary of State (in any other case)].
Amendments (Textual)
F1. Words substituted by National Heritage Act 1983 (c. 47, SIF 78), s. 41, Sch. 4 para. 59

Part III Miscellaneous and Supplemental

Part III Miscellaneous and Supplemental

42 Restrictions on use of metal detectors.

(1) If a person uses a metal detector in a protected place without the written consent [F1of Historic Environment Scotland (in the case of a place situated in Scotland),] of the [F2. Commission (in a case of a place situated in England) or of the Secretary of State (in any other case)] he shall be guilty of an offence and liable on summary conviction or, in Scotland, on conviction before a court of summary jurisdiction, to a fine not exceeding [F3level 3 on the standard scale].

(2) In this section—
"metal detector" means any device designed or adapted for detecting or locating any metal or mineral in the ground; and
"protected place" means any place which is either—
   (a) the site of a scheduled monument or of any monument under the ownership or guardianship of the Secretary of State [F4, Historic Environment Scotland] [F5or the Commission] or a local authority by virtue of this Act; or
   (b) situated in an area of archaeological importance.

F6. (3)If a person without [F7written consent] removes any object of archaeological or historical interest which he has discovered by the use of a metal detector in a protected place he shall be guilty of an offence and liable on summary conviction to a fine not exceeding the statutory maximum or on conviction on indictment to a fine.
[F8. The reference in this subsection to written consent is to that [F6of Historic Environment Scotland (where the place in question is situated in Scotland),] of the Commission (where the place in question is situated in England) or of the Secretary of State (in any other case)]

(4) A consent granted by [F9. Historic Environment Scotland,] the Secretary of State [F10or the Commission] for the purposes of this section may be granted either unconditionally or subject to conditions.

(5) If any person—
   (a) in using a metal detector in a protected place in accordance with any consent granted by [F11. Historic Environment Scotland,] the Secretary of State [F10or the Commission] for the purposes of this section; or
   (b) in removing or otherwise dealing with any object which he has discovered by the use of a metal detector in a protected place in accordance with any such consent;
fails to comply with any condition attached to the consent, he shall be guilty of an offence and liable, in a case falling within paragraph (a) above, to the penalty provided by subsection (1) above, and in a case falling within paragraph (b) above, to the penalty provided by subsection (3) above.

(6) In any proceedings for an offence under subsection (1) above, it shall be a defence for the accused to [F12prove] [F12show] that he used the metal detector for a purpose other than detecting or locating objects of archaeological or historical interest.

(7) In any proceedings for an offence under subsection (1) or (3) above, it shall be a defence for the accused to [F13prove that he had taken all reasonable precautions] [F13show that—
   (a) he had taken all reasonable steps]
to find out whether the place where he used the metal detector was a protected place [F14and did not believe that it was.] [F14; and
   (b) he did not know and had no reason to believe that that place was a protected place]

Amendments (Textual)

F1. Words in s. 42. (1) inserted (S.) (27.2.2015 for specified purposes, 1.10.2015 in so far as not already in force) by Historic Environment Scotland Act 2014 (asp 19), s. 31. (2), sch. 2 para. 45. (a) (with ss. 29, 30); S.S.I. 2015/31, art. 2, sch.; S.S.I. 2015/196, art. 2, sch.

F2. Words substituted by National Heritage Act 1983 (c. 47, SIF 78), s. 41, Sch. 4 para. 60. (2)(6)

F3. Words substituted by virtue of Criminal Justice Act 1982 (c. 48), s. 46 and Criminal Procedure (Scotland) Act 1975 (c. 21), s. 289. G (as inserted by Criminal Justice Act 1982 (c. 48), s. 54)
F4. Words in s. 42. (2) inserted (S.) (27.2.2015 for specified purposes, 1.10.2015 in so far as not already in force) by Historic Environment Scotland Act 2014 (asp 19), s. 31. (2), sch. 2 para. 45. (b) (with ss. 29, 30); S.S.I. 2015/31, art. 2, sch.; S.S.I. 2015/196, art. 2, sch.
F5. Words inserted by National Heritage Act 1983 (c. 47, SIF 78), s. 41, Sch. 4 para. 60. (3)(6)
F6. Words in s. 42. (3) inserted (S.) (27.2.2015 for specified purposes, 1.10.2015 in so far as not already in force) by Historic Environment Scotland Act 2014 (asp 19), s. 31. (2), sch. 2 para. 45. (c) (with ss. 29, 30); S.S.I. 2015/31, art. 2, sch.; S.S.I. 2015/196, art. 2, sch.
F7. Words substituted by National Heritage Act 1983 (c. 47, SIF 78), s. 41, Sch. 4 para. 60. (4)(6)
F8. Words inserted by National Heritage Act 1983 (c. 47, SIF 78), s. 41, Sch. 4 para. 60. (4)(6)
F9. Words in s. 42. (4) inserted (S.) (27.2.2015 for specified purposes, 1.10.2015 in so far as not already in force) by Historic Environment Scotland Act 2014 (asp 19), s. 31. (2), sch. 2 para. 45. (d) (with ss. 29, 30); S.S.I. 2015/31, art. 2, sch.; S.S.I. 2015/196, art. 2, sch.
F10. Words inserted by National Heritage Act 1983 (c. 47, SIF 78), s. 41, Sch. 4 para. 60. (5)(6)
F11. Words in s. 42. (5)(a) inserted (S.) (27.2.2015 for specified purposes, 1.10.2015 in so far as not already in force) by Historic Environment Scotland Act 2014 (asp 19), s. 31. (2), sch. 2 para. 45. (e) (with ss. 29, 30); S.S.I. 2015/31, art. 2, sch.; S.S.I. 2015/196, art. 2, sch.
F12. Word in s. 42. (6) substituted (S.) (1.12.2011) by Historic Environment (Amendment) (Scotland) Act 2011 (asp 3), ss. 3. (4)(a), 33. (2); S.S.I. 2011/372, art. 2, Sch.
F13. Words in s. 42. (7) substituted (S.) (1.12.2011) by Historic Environment (Amendment) (Scotland) Act 2011 (asp 3), ss. 3. (4)(b)(i), 33. (2); S.S.I. 2011/372, art. 2, Sch.
F14. Words in s. 42. (7) substituted (S.) (1.12.2011) by Historic Environment (Amendment) (Scotland) Act 2011 (asp 3), ss. 3. (4)(b)(ii), 33. (2); S.S.I. 2011/372, art. 2, Sch.
Modifications etc. (not altering text)
C1. S. 42 savings for effects of 2011 asp 3 s. 3. (4) (S.) (1.12.2011) by The Historic Environment (Amendment) (Scotland) Act 2011 (Saving, Transitional and Consequential Provisions) Order 2011 (S.S.I. 2011/377), arts. 1. (1), 2. (c)
C2. S. 42. (1) excluded (18.12.1996) by 1996 c. 61, s. 12, Sch. 7 para. 4. (12)
C3. S. 42. (1) excluded (22.7.2008) by Crossrail Act 2008 (c. 18), Sch. 9 para. 4. (12)
C4. S. 42. (1) savings for effects of 2014 asp 19, Sch. 2 para. 45. (a) (1.10.2015) by The Historic Environment Scotland Act 2014 (Saving, Transitional and Consequential Provisions) Order 2015 (S.S.I. 2015/239), arts. 1. (1), 11
C5. S. 42. (3) excluded (18.12.1996) by 1996 c. 61, s. 12, Sch. 7 para. 4. (13)
C6. S. 42. (3) excluded (22.7.2008) by Crossrail Act 2008 (c. 18), Sch. 9 para. 4. (13)

Powers of entry

43 Power of entry for survey and valuation.

(1) Any person authorised under this section may at any reasonable time enter any land for the purpose of surveying it, or estimating its value, in connection with any proposal to acquire that or any other land under this Act or in connection with any claim for compensation under this Act in respect of any such acquisition or for any damage to that or any other land.
(2) A person is authorised under this section if he is an officer of the Valuation Office of the Inland Revenue Department or a person duly authorised in writing by the Secretary of State [F15, Historic Environment Scotland] or other authority proposing to make the acquisition which is the occasion of the survey or valuation or (as the case may be) from whom in accordance with this Act compensation in respect of the damage is recoverable.
(3) Subject to section 44. (9) of this Act, the power to survey land conferred by this section shall be construed as including power to search and bore for the purposes of ascertaining the nature of

the subsoil or the presence of minerals therein.
Amendments (Textual)
F15. Words in s. 43. (2) inserted (S.) (27.2.2015 for specified purposes, 1.10.2015 in so far as not already in force) by Historic Environment Scotland Act 2014 (asp 19), s. 31. (2), sch. 2 para. 46 (with ss. 29, 30); S.S.I. 2015/31, art. 2, sch.; S.S.I. 2015/196, art. 2, sch.

44 Supplementary provisions with respect to powers of entry.

(1) A person may not in the exercise of any power of entry under this Act, other than that conferred by section 43, enter any building or part of a building occupied as a dwelling house without the consent of the occupier.

(2) Subject to the following provisions of this subsection, a person may not in the exercise of any power of entry under this Act demand admission as of right to any land which is occupied unless prior notice of the intended entry has been given to the occupier—

(a) where the purpose of the entry is to carry out any works on the land (other than excavations in exercise of the power under section 26 or 38 of this Act), not less than fourteen days before the day on which admission is demanded; or

(b) in any other case, not less than twenty-four hours before admission is demanded.

This subsection does not apply in relation to the power of entry under section 5 of this Act.

(3) A person seeking to enter any land in exercise of any power of entry under this Act shall, if so required by or on behalf of the owner or occupier thereof, produce evidence of his authority before entering.

(4) Any power of entry under this Act shall be construed as including power for any person entering any land in exercise of the power of entry to take with him any assistance or equipment reasonably required for the purpose to which his entry relates and to do there anything reasonably necessary for carrying out that purpose.

(5) Without prejudice to subsection (4) above, where a person enters any land in exercise of any power of entry under this Act for the purpose of carrying out any archaeological investigation or examination of the land, he may take and remove such samples of any description as appear to him to be reasonably required for the purpose of archaelolgical analysis.

(6) Subject to subsection (7) below, where any works are being carried out on any land in relation to which any power of entry under this Act is exercisable, a person acting in the exercise of that power shall comply with any reasonable requirements or conditions imposed by the person by whom the works are being carried out for the purpose of preventing interference with or delay to the works.

(7) Any requirements or conditions imposed by a person by whom any works are being carried out shall not be regarded as reasonable for the purposes of subsection (6) above if compliance therewith would in effect frustrate the exercise of the power of entry or the purpose of the entry; and that subsection does not apply where the works in question are being carried out in contravention of section 2. (1) or (6) or 35 of this Act.

(8) Any person who intentionally obstructs a person acting in the exercise of any power of entry under this Act shall be guilty of an offence and liable on summary conviction or, in Scotland, on conviction before a court of summary jurisdiction, to a fine not exceeding [F16level 3 on the standard scale]

(9) Where under section 43 of this Act a person proposes to carry out any works authorised by virtue of subsection (3) of that section—

(a) he shall not carry out those works unless notice of his intention to do so was included in the notice required by subsection (2)(a) above; and

(b) if the land in question is held by statutory undertakers, and those undertakers object to the proposed works on the grounds that the carrying out thereof would be seriously detrimental to the carrying on of their undertaking, the works shall not be carried out except with the authority of the Secretary of State.

Amendments (Textual)
F16. Words substituted by virtue of Criminal Justice Act 1982 (c. 48), s. 46 and Criminal Procedure (Scotland) Act 1975 (c. 21), s. 289. G (as inserted by Criminal Justice Act 1982 (c. 48), s. 54)

Financial provisions

45 Expenditure on archaeological investigation.

(1) The Secretary of State may undertake, or assist in, or defray or contribute towards the cost of, an archaeological investigation of any land [F17)(other than land in England)] which he considers may contain an ancient monument or anything else of archaeological or historical interest.
[F18. (1. A) The Commission may undertake, or assist in, or defray or contribute towards the cost of, an archaeological investigation of any land in England which they consider may contain an ancient monument or anything else of archaeological or historical interest; and the reference to an ancient monument in this subsection shall be construed as if the reference in section 61. (12)(b) of this Act to the Secretary of State were to the Commission.]
(2) Any local authority may undertake, or assist in, or defray or contribute towards the cost of, an archaeological investigation of any land in or in the vicinity of their area, being land which they consider may contain an ancient monument or anything else of archaeological or historical interest.
(3) The Secretary of State [F19or the Commission] or any local authority may publish the results of any archaeological investigation undertaken, assisted, or wholly or partly financed by them under this section in such manner and form as they think fit.
(4) Without prejudice to the application, by virtue of section 53 of this Act, of any other provision of this Act to land which is not within Great Britain, the powers conferred by this section shall be exercisable in relation to any such land which forms part of the sea bed within the seaward limits of United Kingdom territorial waters adjacent to the coast of Great Britain [F20. (or, as regards the powers mentioned in subsection (1. A) above, England)].
Amendments (Textual)
F17. Words inserted by National Heritage Act 1983 (c. 47, SIF 78), s. 41, Sch. 4 para. 61. (2)
F18. S. 45. (1. A) inserted by National Heritage Act 1983 (c. 47, SIF 78), s. 41, Sch. 4 para. 61. (3)
F19. Words inserted by National Heritage Act 1983 (c. 47, SIF 78), s. 41, Sch. 4 para. 61. (4)
F20. Words inserted by National Heritage Act 1983 (c. 47, SIF 78), s. 41, Sch. 4 para. 61. (5)
Modifications etc. (not altering text)
C7. S. 45. (2)(3) extended (E.W.) (19.9.1995) by 1995 c. 25, ss. 70, 125. (2), Sch. 9 para.10. (3) (with ss. 7. (6), 115, 117, Sch. 8 para. 7)

[F2145. ADevelopment and understanding of matters of historic, etc. interest: grants and loansS

(1) The Scottish Ministers may make grants or loans for the purpose of defraying in whole or in part any expenditure incurred, or to be incurred—
    (a) in or in connection with;
    (b) with a view to the promotion of,
the development or understanding of matters of historic, architectural, traditional, artistic or archaeological interest.
(2) A grant or loan under this section may be made subject to such conditions (including conditions as to repayment) as the Scottish Ministers consider appropriate.
F22. (3). . . . .]

Amendments (Textual)
F21. S. 45. A inserted (S.) (30.6.2011) by Historic Environment (Amendment) (Scotland) Act 2011 (asp 3), ss. 12, 33. (2); S.S.I. 2011/174, art. 2, Sch.
F22. S. 45. A(3) repealed (1.10.2015) by Historic Environment Scotland Act 2014 (asp 19), ss. 20. (3), 31. (2) (with ss. 29, 30); S.S.I. 2015/196, art. 2, sch.

46 Compensation for damage caused by exercise of certain powers under this Act.

(1) Subject to subsection (2) below, where, in the exercise in relation to any land of any power to which this section applies, any damage has been caused to that land or to any chattels on that land, any person interested in that land or those chattels may recover compensation in respect of that damage from [F23. Historic Environment Scotland,] the Secretary of State [F24or the Commission] or other authority by or on whose behalf the power was exercised.
(2) Where any such damage is caused in the exercise of any such power by or on behalf of any person for the time being holding appointment as the investigating authority for an area of archaeological importance under section 34 of this Act, compensation shall be recoverable in accordance with this section from the [F25. Commission (if the area in question is situated in England) or from the Secretary of State (in any other case).]
(3) This section applies to any power to enter, or to do anything, on any land under any of the following sections of this Act, that is to say, sections 6, [F266. A] 26, 38, 39, 40 and 43.
(4) References in subsection (1) above to chattels shall be construed in relation to Scotland as references to moveables.
Amendments (Textual)
F23. Words in s. 46. (1) inserted (S.) (27.2.2015 for specified purposes, 1.10.2015 in so far as not already in force) by Historic Environment Scotland Act 2014 (asp 19), s. 31. (2), sch. 2 para. 47 (with ss. 29, 30); S.S.I. 2015/31, art. 2, sch.; S.S.I. 2015/196, art. 2, sch.
F24. Words inserted by National Heritage Act 1983 (c. 47, SIF 78), s. 41, Sch. 4 para. 62. (2)
F25. Words substituted by National Heritage Act 1983 (c. 47, SIF 78), s. 41, Sch. 4 para. 62. (3)(5)
F26. Word inserted by National Heritage Act 1983 (c. 47, SIF 78), s. 41, Sch. 4 para. 62. (4)

47 General provisions with respect to claims for compensation under this Act.

(1) Any claim for compensation under this Act shall be made within the time and in the manner prescribed.
(2) Any question of disputed compensation under this Act shall be referred to and determined by the [F27. Upper Tribunal or] (in the case of any land situated in Scotland) by the Lands Tribunal for Scotland.
(3) In relation to the determination of any such question, the provisions of [F28section] 4 of the M1. Land Compensation Act 1961 or (as the case may be) of Sections 9 and 11 of the M2. Land Compensation (Scotland) Act 1963 shall apply, but the references in section 4 of the Act of 1961 and section 11 of the Act of 1963 to the acquiring authority shall be construed as references to the authority by whom the compensation claimed is payable under this Act.
Amendments (Textual)
F27. Words in s. 47. (2) substituted (1.6.2009) by The Transfer of Tribunal Functions (Lands Tribunal and Miscellaneous Amendments) Order 2009 (S.I. 2009/1307), art. 1, Sch. 1 para. 129. (a) (with Sch. 5)
F28. Word in s. 47. (3) substituted (1.6.2009) by The Transfer of Tribunal Functions (Lands Tribunal and Miscellaneous Amendments) Order 2009 (S.I. 2009/1307), art. 1, Sch. 1 para. 129.

(b) (with Sch. 5)
Marginal Citations
M1 1961 c 33.
M2 1963 c 51.

48 Recovery of grants for expenditure in conservation areas and on historic buildings.

F29. (1). . . . .

X1. (2)After section 4 of the M3. Historic Buildings and Ancient Monuments Act 1953 (grants for preservation of historic buildings, their contents and adjoining land) there shall be inserted the following section —

"4. A Recovery of grants under section 4.

(1) This section applies to any grant under section 4 of this Act made on terms that it shall be recoverable under this section ; but any such grant shall only be regarded for the purposes of this section as so made if before or on making the grant the Secretary of State gives to the grantee notice in writing —
   (a) summarising the effect of this section ; and
   (b) specifying the period during which the grant is to be recoverable in accordance with subsection (4) below in the case of a grant made for the purpose there mentioned.

(2) The period specified under subsection (1)(b) above in the case of any grant shall be a period beginning with the day on which the grant is made and ending not more than ten years after that day.

(3) If any condition subject to which a grant to which this section applies was made is contravened or not complied with, the Secretary of State may recover the amount of the grant or such part of it as he thinks fit from the grantee.

(4) If, during the period specified under subsection (1)(b) above in the case of a grant to which this section applies made to any person for the purpose of defraying in whole or in part any expenditure on the repair, maintenance or upkeep of any property, the grantee disposes in any manner mentioned in subsection (5) below of the interest, or any part thereof, held by him in the property on the day on which the grant is made (referred to below in this section as "the relevant interest"), the Secretary of State may recover the amount of the grant or such part of it as he thinks fit from the grantee.

(5) Subsection (4) above only applies where the grantee disposes of the relevant interest or any part of it by way of sale or exchange or lease for a term of not less than twenty-one years.

(6) If a person becomes entitled by way of gift from the grantee, whether directly or indirectly (but otherwise than by will) to a part of the relevant interest, a disposal by the donee in any manner mentioned in subsection (5) above of the interest so acquired by him in the property, or any part of that interest, shall be treated for the purposes of subsection (4) above as a disposal by the grantee of a part of the relevant interest.

(7) If a person becomes entitled by way of any such gift to the whole of the relevant interest subsection (4) above shall have effect (except for the purpose of determining the relevant interest) as if the donee were the grantee.

(8) Nothing in subsection (3) or (4) above shall be taken as conferring on the Secretary of State a right to recover (by virtue of a breach of more than one condition or disposals of several parts of an interest in property) amounts in the aggregate exceeding the amount of the grant."

Editorial Information

X1. The text of s. 48. (2) is in the form in which it was originally enacted: it was not reproduced in Statutes in Force and does not reflect any amendments or repeals which may have been made prior to 1.2.1991.

Amendments (Textual)

F29. S. 48. (1) repealed (27.5.1997) by 1997 c. 11, ss. 3, 6. (2), Sch. 1 Pt.I (with s. 5, Sch. 3)

Marginal Citations
M31953 c.49.

49 Grants to the Architectural Heritage Fund.

(1) The Secretary of State may make grants to the [F30. Architectural Heritage Fund].
[F31. (1. A)The Commission may make grants to the Architectural Heritage Fund for the purpose of enabling it to perform its functions in, or in relation to, England.]
(2) A grant under this section may be made subject to such conditions as the Secretary of State [F32or the Commission (as the case may be)] may think fit to impose.
[F33. (3)In this section "the Architectural Heritage Fund" means the institution registered under that name under [F34the Charities Act 1993] [F34the Charities Act 2011]]
Amendments (Textual)
F30. Words substituted by National Heritage Act 1983 (c. 47, SIF 78), s. 41, Sch. 4 para. 63. (2)
F31. S. 49. (1. A) inserted by National Heritage Act 1983 (c. 47, SIF 78), s. 41, Sch. 4 para. 63. (3)
F32. Words inserted by National Heritage Act 1983 (c. 47, SIF 78), s. 41, Sch. 4 para. 63. (4)
F33. S. 49. (3) inserted by National Heritage Act 1983 (c. 47, SIF 78), s. 41, Sch. 4 para. 63. (5)
F34. Words in s. 49. (3) substituted (E.W.) (14.3.2012) by Charities Act 2011 (c. 25), s. 355, Sch. 7 para. 36 (with s. 20. (2), Sch. 8)

Application to special cases

50 Application to Crown land.

(1) Notwithstanding any interest of the Crown in Crown land, but subject to the following provisions of this section—
   (a) a monument which for the time being is Crown land may be included in the Schedule; and
   (b) any restrictions or powers imposed or conferred by any of the provisions of this Act shall apply and be exercisable in relation to Crown land and in relation to anything done on Crown land otherwise than by or on behalf of the Crown, but not so as to affect any interest of the Crown therein.
[F35. (1. A)For the purposes of subsection (1)(b), anything done by Historic Environment Scotland on Crown land, in relation to which it has functions by virtue of a delegation by the Scottish Ministers under section 3 of the Historic Environment Scotland Act 2014 (asp 19), is not to be treated as done by or on behalf of the Crown.]
(2) Except with the consent of the appropriate authority—
   (a) no power under this Act to enter, or to do anything, on any land shall be exercisable in relation to land which for the time being is Crown land; and
   (b) no interest in land which for the time being is Crown land shall be acquired compulsorily under Part I of this Act.
(3) In relation to any operations proposed to be carried out on Crown land otherwise than by or on behalf of the Crown, an operations notice served under section 35 of this Act shall not be effective for the purposes of that section unless it is accompanied by a certificate from the appropriate authority in the prescribed form consenting to the exercise in relation to that land in connection with those operations of the powers conferred by sections 38 and 40 of this Act.
(4) In this section "Crown land" means land in which there is a Crown interest or a Duchy interest; "Crown interest" means an interest belonging to Her Majesty in right of the Crown, or belonging to a Government department, or held in trust for Her Majesty for the purposes of a Government department, and includes any estate or interest held in right of the Prince and Steward of Scotland; "Duchy interest" means an interest belonging to Her Majesty in right of the Duchy of Lancaster,

or belonging to the Duchy of Cornwall; and for the purposes of this section "the appropriate authority", in relation to any land—

(a) in the case of land belonging to Her Majesty in right of the Crown and forming part of the Crown Estate, means the Crown Estate Commissioners, and, in relation to any other land belonging to Her Majesty in right of the Crown, means the Government department having the management of that land;

(b) in relation to land belonging to Her Majesty in right of the Duchy of Lancaster, means the Chancellor of the Duchy;

(c) in relation to land belonging to the Duchy of Cornwall, means such person as the Duke of Cornwall, or the possessor for the time being of the Duchy of Cornwall, appoints;

(d) in the case of land belonging to a Government department or held in trust for Her Majesty for the purposes of a Government department, means that department;

and, if any question arises as to what authority is the appropriate authority in relation to any land, that question shall be referred to the Treasury, whose decision shall be final.

In this subsection "Government department" includes any Minister of the Crown.

Amendments (Textual)

F35. S. 50. (1. A) inserted (S.) (27.2.2015 for specified purposes, 1.10.2015 in so far as not already in force) by Historic Environment Scotland Act 2014 (asp 19), s. 31. (2), sch. 2 para. 48 (with ss. 29, 30); S.S.I. 2015/31, art. 2, sch.; S.S.I. 2015/196, art. 2, sch.

Modifications etc. (not altering text)

C8. S. 50 modified (17.7.1992) by S.I. 1992/1732, arts. 1, 3. (1).

S. 50 extended (17.7.1992) by S.I. 1992/1732, arts. 1, 3. (1)(a).

C9. S. 50. (4)(a) modified (17.7.1992) by S.I. 1992/1732, arts. 1, 3. (2).

51 Ecclesiastical Property.

(1) Without prejudice to the provisions of the M4. Acquisition of Land (Authorisation Procedure) Act 1946 with respect to notices served under that Act, where under any of the provisions of this Act a notice is required to be served on an owner of land, and the land is ecclesiastical property, a like notice shall be served on the [F36. Church Commissioners] [F36. Diocesan Board of Finance for the diocese in which the land is situated].

(2) [F37. Where the fee simple of any ecclesiastical property is in abeyance, the fee simple] [F37. Where any ecclesiastical property is vested in the incumbent of a benefice which is vacant it] shall for the purposes of this Act be treated as being vested in the [F36. Church Commissioners] [F36. Diocesan Board of Finance for the diocese in which the land is situated].

(3) Any sum which under section 7, 9 or 46 of this Act is payable in relation to land which is ecclesiastical property and apart from this subsection would be payable to an incumbent, shall be paid to the [F36. Church Commissioners] [F36. Diocesan Board of Finance for the diocese in which the land is situated], to be applied for the purposes for which the proceeds of a sale by agreement of the land would be applicable under any enactment or Measure authorising, or disposing of the proceeds of, such a sale.

(4) Where any sum is recoverable under section 8 of this Act in respect of land which is ecclesiastical property the [F36. Church Commissioners] [F36. Diocesan Board of Finance for the diocese in which the land is situated] may apply any money or securities held by [F38them] [F38it] in the payment of that sum.

(5) In this section "ecclesiastical property" means land belonging to an ecclesiastical benefice of the Church of England, or being or forming part of a church subject to the jurisdiction of a bishop of any diocese of the Church of England or the site of such a church, or being or forming part of a burial ground subject to such jurisdiction.

Amendments (Textual)

F36. Words in s. 51 substituted (E.) (1.10.2006) by Church of England (Miscellaneous Provisions) Measure 2006 (No. 1), s. 16. (2), Sch. 5 para. 20. (a); 2006 No. 2, Instrument made by

Archbishops
F37. Words in s. 51. (2) substituted (E.) (1.10.2006) by Church of England (Miscellaneous Provisions) Measure 2006 (No. 1), s. 16. (2), Sch. 5 para. 20. (b); 2006 No. 2, Instrument made by Archbishops
F38. Word in s. 51. (4) substituted (E.) (1.10.2006) by Church of England (Miscellaneous Provisions) Measure 2006 (No. 1), s. 16. (2), Sch. 5 para. 20. (a); 2006 No. 2, Instrument made by Archbishops
Marginal Citations
M41946 c. 49.

52 Application to the Isles of Scilly.

The Secretary of State may, after consultation with the Council of the Isles of Scilly, by order provide for the application to those Isles of the provisions of this Act—
    (a) as if those Isles were a district and the Council of the Isles were the council of that district; and
    (b) in other respects subject to such modifications as may be specified in the order.

[F3952. A The Broads.

Parts I and II and section 45. (2) and (3) of this Act shall apply, in relation to the Broads (as defined by the Norfolk and Suffolk Broads Act 1988), as if the Broads Authority were a local authority.]
Amendments (Textual)
F39. S. 52. A inserted (E.W.) by Norfolk and Suffolk Broads Act 1988 (c. 4, SIF 81:1), ss. 2. (5)(6), 23. (2), 27. (2), Sch. 3 para. 30. (1), Sch. 7

53 Monuments in territorial waters.

(1) A monument situated in, on or under the sea bed within the seaward limits of United Kingdom territorial waters adjacent to the coast of Great Britain (referred to below in this section as a monument in territorial waters) may be included in the Schedule under section 1. (3) of this Act, and the remaining provisions of this Act shall extend accordingly to any such monument which is a scheduled monument (but not otherwise).
(2) The entry in the Schedule relating to any monument in territorial waters shall describe the monument as lying off the coast of England, or of Scotland, or of Wales; and any such monument shall be treated for the purposes of this Act as situated in the country specified for the purposes of this subsection in the entry relating to the monument in the Schedule.
(3) In relation to any monument in territorial waters which is under the ownership or guardianship of the Secretary of State [F40or the Commission] or any local authority by virtue of this Act, references in this Act to land associated with the monument (or to associated land) include references to any part of the sea bed occupied by the Secretary of State [F40or by the Commission] or by a local authority for any such purpose relating to the monument as is mentioned in section 15. (1) of this Act.
(4) Without prejudice to any jurisdiction exercisable apart from this subsection, proceedings for any offence under this Act committed in United Kingdom territorial waters adjacent to the coast of Great Britain may be taken, and the offence may for all incidental purposes be treated as having been committed, in any place in Great Britain.
(5) It is hereby declared that, notwithstanding that by virtue of this section this Act may affect individuals or bodies corporate outside the United Kingdom, it applies to any individual whether or not he is a British subject, and to any body corporate whether or not incorporated under the law

of any part of the United Kingdom.

(6) A constable shall on any monument in territorial waters have all the powers, protection and privileges which he has in the area for which he acts as constable.

(7) References in this section to the sea bed do not include the seashore or any other land which, though covered (intermittently or permanently) by the sea, is within Great Britain.

Amendments (Textual)

F40. Words inserted by National Heritage Act 1983 (c. 47, SIF 78), s. 41, Sch. 4 para. 64

Supplemental

54 Treatment and preservation of finds.

(1) Where a person enters any land in exercise of any power of entry under this Act for any of the following purposes, that is to say—

(a) to carry out any excavations in the land or any operations affecting any ancient monument situated in, on or under the land;

(b) to observe any operations on the land in exercise of the power under section 6. (3)(a) or (4)(b) [F41or 6. A(2)(a)] or 38. (1)(b) of this Act; or

(c) to carry out any archaeological examination of the land;

he may take temporary custody of any object of archaeological or historical interest discovered during the course of those excavations or operations or (as the case may be) during the course of that examination, and remove it from its site for the purpose of examining, testing, treating, recording or preserving it.

F42. (2)The Secretary of State or other authority by or on whose behalf the power of entry was exercised may not retain the object without the consent of the owner beyond such period as may be reasonably required for the purpose of examining and recording it and carrying out any test or treatment which appears to the Secretary of State or to that other authority to be desirable for the purpose of archaeological investigation or analysis or with a view to restoring or preserving the object.

(3) Nothing in this section shall affect any right of the Crown [F43under the Treasure Act 1996].

Extent Information

E1. This version of this provision extends to England and Wales only; a separate version has been created for Scotland only

Amendments (Textual)

F41. Words inserted by National Heritage Act 1983 (c. 47, SIF 78), s. 41, Sch. 4 para. 65

F42. Words in s. 54. (2) inserted (S.) (27.2.2015 for specified purposes, 1.10.2015 in so far as not already in force) by Historic Environment Scotland Act 2014 (asp 19), s. 31. (2), sch. 2 para. 49 (with ss. 29, 30); S.S.I. 2015/31, art. 2, sch.; S.S.I. 2015/196, art. 2, sch.

F43. Words in s. 54. (3) substituted (E.W.) (24.9.1997 with effect in relation to any treasure found after the commencement of 1996 c. 24, s. 4) by 1996 c. 24, s. 14. (2)(4); S.I. 1997/1977, art.2

54 Treatment and preservation of finds.S

(1) Where a person enters any land in exercise of any power of entry under this Act for any of the following purposes, that is to say—

(a) to carry out any excavations in the land or any operations affecting any ancient monument situated in, on or under the land;

(b) to observe any operations on the land in exercise of the power under section 6. (3)(a) or (4)(b) [F82or 6. A(2)(a)] or 38. (1)(b) of this Act; or

(c) to carry out any archaeological examination of the land;

he may take temporary custody of any object of archaeological or historical interest discovered during the course of those excavations or operations or (as the case may be) during the course of that examination, and remove it from its site for the purpose of examining, testing, treating, recording or preserving it.

(2) The Secretary of State [F42, Historic Environment Scotland] or other authority by or on whose behalf the power of entry was exercised may not retain the object without the consent of the owner beyond such period as may be reasonably required for the purpose of examining and recording it and carrying out any test or treatment which appears to the Secretary of State [F42, Historic Environment Scotland] or to that other authority to be desirable for the purpose of archaeological investigation or analysis or with a view to restoring or preserving the object.

(3) Nothing in this section shall affect any right of the Crown in relation to treasure trove.

Extent Information

E3. This version of this provision extends to Scotland only; a separate version has been created for England and Wales only

Amendments (Textual)

F42. Words in s. 54. (2) inserted (S.) (27.2.2015 for specified purposes, 1.10.2015 in so far as not already in force) by Historic Environment Scotland Act 2014 (asp 19), s. 31. (2), sch. 2 para. 49 (with ss. 29, 30); S.S.I. 2015/31, art. 2, sch.; S.S.I. 2015/196, art. 2, sch.

F82. Words inserted by National Heritage Act 1983 (c. 47, SIF 78), s. 41, Sch. 4 para. 65

55 Proceedings for questioning validity of certain orders, etc.

(1) If any person—

(a) is aggrieved by any order to which this section applies and desires to question the validity of that order, on the grounds that it is not within the powers of this Act, or that any of the relevant requirements have not been complied with in relation to it; or

(b) is aggrieved by any action on the part of the Secretary of State [F44or Historic Environment Scotland] to which this section applies and desires to question the validity of that action, on the grounds that is is not within the powers of this Act, or that any of the relevant requirements have not been complied with in relation to it;

he may, within six weeks from the relevant date, make an application under this section to the High Court or (in Scotland) to the Court of Session.

(2) This section applies to any designation order and to any order under section 33 (4) of this Act varying or revoking a designation order.

(3) This section applies to action on the part of the Secretary of State [F45or Historic Environment Scotland] of [F46either] [F46any] of the following descriptions, that is to say—

(a) [F47any decision of the Secretary of State on an application for scheduled monument consent; and]

[F47any decision of the Scottish Ministers on an application for scheduled monument consent referred to them under section 3. B,

(aa) any decision of the Scottish Ministers on an appeal under this Act,]

(b) [F48the giving by the Secretary of State of any direction under section 4] [F48the making by Historic Environment Scotland of any order under section 4 or by the Scottish Ministers of any order under section 4. A] of this Act modifying or revoking a scheduled monument consent.

(4) In subsection (1) above "the relevant date" means—

(a) in relation to an order, the date on which notice of the making of the order is published (or, as the case may be, first published) in accordance with Schedule 2 to this Act; and

(b) in relation to any action on the part of the Secretary of State [F49or Historic Environment Scotland] , the date on which that action is taken.

(5) On any application under this section the High Court or (in Scotland) the Court of Session—

(a) may by interim order suspend the operation of the order or action, the validity whereof is questioned by the application, until the final determination of the proceedings;

(b) if satisfied that the order or action in question is not within the powers of this Act, or that the interests of the applicant have been substantially prejudiced by a failure to comply with any of the relevant requirements in relation thereto, may quash that order or action in whole or in part.

(6) In this section "the relevant requirements" means—

(a) in relation to any order to which this section applies, any requirements of this Act or of any regulations made under this Act which are applicable to that order; and

(b) in relation to any action to which this section applies, any requirements of this Act or of the M5. Tribunals and Inquiries Act [F501992] or of any regulations or rules made under this Act or under that Act which are applicable to that action.

(7) Except as provided by this section, the validity of any order or action to which this section applies shall not be questioned in any legal proceedings whatsoever; but nothing in this section shall affect the exercise of any jurisdiction of any court in respect of any refusal or failure on the part of the Secretary of State [F51or Historic Environment Scotland] to take a decision on an application for scheduled monument consent.

Amendments (Textual)

F44. Words in s. 55. (1)(b) inserted (S.) (27.2.2015 for specified purposes, 1.10.2015 in so far as not already in force) by Historic Environment Scotland Act 2014 (asp 19), s. 31. (2), sch. 2 para. 50. (a) (with ss. 29, 30); S.S.I. 2015/31, art. 2, sch.; S.S.I. 2015/196, art. 2, sch.

F45. Words in s. 55. (3) inserted (S.) (27.2.2015 for specified purposes, 1.10.2015 in so far as not already in force) by Historic Environment Scotland Act 2014 (asp 19), s. 31. (2), sch. 2 para. 50. (b)(i) (with ss. 29, 30); S.S.I. 2015/31, art. 2, sch.; S.S.I. 2015/196, art. 2, sch.

F46. Word in s. 55. (3) substituted (S.) (27.2.2015 for specified purposes, 1.10.2015 in so far as not already in force) by Historic Environment Scotland Act 2014 (asp 19), s. 31. (2), sch. 2 para. 50. (b)(ii) (with ss. 29, 30); S.S.I. 2015/31, art. 2, sch.; S.S.I. 2015/196, art. 2, sch.

F47. S. 55. (3)(a)(aa) substituted for s. 55. (3)(a) (S.) (27.2.2015 for specified purposes, 1.10.2015 in so far as not already in force) by Historic Environment Scotland Act 2014 (asp 19), s. 31. (2), sch. 2 para. 50. (b)(iii) (with ss. 29, 30); S.S.I. 2015/31, art. 2, sch.; S.S.I. 2015/196, art. 2, sch.

F48. Words in s. 55. (3)(b) substituted (S.) (27.2.2015 for specified purposes, 1.10.2015 in so far as not already in force) by Historic Environment Scotland Act 2014 (asp 19), s. 31. (2), sch. 2 para. 50. (b)(iv) (with ss. 29, 30); S.S.I. 2015/31, art. 2, sch.; S.S.I. 2015/196, art. 2, sch.

F49. Words in s. 55. (4)(b) inserted (S.) (27.2.2015 for specified purposes, 1.10.2015 in so far as not already in force) by Historic Environment Scotland Act 2014 (asp 19), s. 31. (2), sch. 2 para. 50. (c) (with ss. 29, 30); S.S.I. 2015/31, art. 2, sch.; S.S.I. 2015/196, art. 2, sch.

F50. Words in s. 55. (6)(b) substituted (1.10.1992) by Tribunals and Inquiries Act 1992 (c. 53), ss. 18. (1), 19. (2), Sch. 3 para.12.

F51. Words in s. 55. (7) inserted (S.) (27.2.2015 for specified purposes, 1.10.2015 in so far as not already in force) by Historic Environment Scotland Act 2014 (asp 19), s. 31. (2), sch. 2 para. 50. (d) (with ss. 29, 30); S.S.I. 2015/31, art. 2, sch.; S.S.I. 2015/196, art. 2, sch.

Modifications etc. (not altering text)

C10. S. 55 savings for effects of 2014 asp 19, Sch. 2 para. 50 (S.) (1.10.2015) by The Historic Environment Scotland Act 2014 (Saving, Transitional and Consequential Provisions) Order 2015 (S.S.I. 2015/239), arts. 1. (1), 12

Marginal Citations

M51971 c. 62.

56 Service of documents.

(1) Any notice or other document required or authorised to be served under this Act may be served either—

(a) by delivering it to the person on whom it is to be served; or

(b) by leaving it at the usual or last known place of abode of that person or, in a case where an address for service has been given by that person, at that address; or

(c) by sending it in a pre-paid registered letter, or by the recorded delivery service, addressed to that person at his usual or last known place of abode or, in a case where an address for service has been given by that person, at that address; or

(d) in the case of an incorporated company or body, by delivering it to the secretary or clerk of the company or body at their registered or principal office, or sending it in a pre-paid registered letter, or by the recorded delivery service, addressed to the secretary or clerk of the company or body at that office.

(2) Where any such notice or document is required or authorised to be served on any person as being the owner or occupier of any monument or other land—

(a) it may be addressed to the "owner" or (as the case may require) to the "occupier" of that monument or land (describing it) without further name or description; and

(b) if the usual or last known place of abode of the person in question cannot be found, it may be served by being affixed conspicuously to the monument or to some object on the site of the monument or (as the case may be) on the land.

57 Power to require information as to interests in land.

(1) For the purpose of enabling the Secretary of State [F52or Historic Environment Scotland] [F53or the Commission] or a local authority to exercise any function under this Act, the Secretary of State [F52or Historic Environment Scotland] [F53or the Commission] or the local authority may require the occupier of any land and any person who, either directly or indirectly, receives rent in respect of any land to state in writing the nature of his interest therein, and the name and address of any other person known to him as having an interest therein, whether as a freeholder, owner [F54of the dominium utile,] mortgagee, lessee, or otherwise.

(2) Any person who, having been required under this section to give any information, fails without reasonable excuse to give that information, shall be guilty of an offence and liable on summary conviction or, in Scotland, on conviction before a court of summary jurisdiction, to a fine not exceeding [F55level 3 on the standard scale].

(3) Any person who, having been so required to give any information, knowingly makes any mis-statement in respect of it, shall be guilty of an offence and liable—

(a) on summary conviction or, in Scotland, on conviction before a court of summary jurisdiction, to a fine not exceeding the statutory maximum; or

(b) on conviction on indictment to a fine.

Amendments (Textual)

F52. Words in s. 57. (1) inserted (S.) (27.2.2015 for specified purposes, 1.10.2015 in so far as not already in force) by Historic Environment Scotland Act 2014 (asp 19), s. 31. (2), sch. 2 para. 51 (with ss. 29, 30); S.S.I. 2015/31, art. 2, sch.; S.S.I. 2015/196, art. 2, sch.

F53. Words inserted by National Heritage Act 1983 (c. 47, SIF 78), s. 41, Sch. 4 para. 66

F54. Words in s. 57. (1) repealed (S.) (28.11.2004) by Abolition of Feudal Tenure etc. (Scotland) Act 2000 (asp 5), ss. 71, 77. (2), Sch. 12 para. 40. (4), 13 Pt. 1 (with ss. 58, 62, 75); S.S.I. 2003/456, art. 2

F55. Words substituted by virtue of Criminal Justice Act 1982 (c. 48), s. 46 and Criminal Procedure (Scotland) Act 1975 (c. 21), s. 289. G (as inserted by Criminal Justice Act 1982 (c. 48), s. 54)

58 Offences by corporations.

(1) Where an offence under this Act which has been committed by a body corporate is proved to have been committed with the consent or connivance of, or to be attributable to any neglect on the part of, a director, manager, secretary or other similar officer of the body corporate, or any person who was purporting to act in any such capacity, he, as well as the body corporate, shall be guilty of that offence and be liable to be proceeded against accordingly.

(2) In subsection (1) above the expression "director", in relation to any body corporate established by or under an enactment for the purpose of carrying on under national ownership an industry or part of an industry or undertaking, being a body corporate whose affairs are managed by the members thereof, means a member of that body corporate.

59 Prosecution of offences: Scotland.

Notwithstanding anything in [F56section 136 of the Criminal Procedure (Scotland) Act 1995], summary proceedings in Scotland for an offence under this Act may be commenced at any time within one year from the date on which evidence sufficient in the opinion of the prosecutor to warrant proceedings came to his knowledge; and a certificate purporting to be signed by the prosecutor stating that date shall be conclusive.
Amendments (Textual)
F56. Words in s. 59 substituted (1.4.1996) by 1995 c. 40, ss. 5, 7. (2), Sch. 4 para. 24. (2)

60 Regulations and orders.

[F57. (A1)Any power conferred by this Act to make regulations or orders includes power to make such incidental, supplemental, consequential, transitory, transitional or saving provision as the Scottish Ministers consider necessary or expedient.]
(1) Any order or regulations made under this Act may make different provision for different cases to which the order or (as the case may be) the regulations apply.
(2) Any power of the Secretary of State to make regulations under this Act, and the power to make orders under sections 3, 37, 52, 61 and 65 of this Act shall be exercisable by statutory instrument; and any statutory instrument containing any such regulations or order, other than one containing regulations under section 19 of this Act, shall be subject to annulment in pursuance of a resolution of either House of Parliament.
Amendments (Textual)
F57. S. 60. (A1) inserted (S.) (30.6.2011) by Historic Environment (Amendment) (Scotland) Act 2011 (asp 3), ss. 13, 33. (2); S.S.I. 2011/174, art. 2, Sch.

61 Interpretation.

F58. (1)In this Act—
"ancient monument" has the meaning given by subsection (12) below;
"area of archaeological importance" means an area designated as such under section 33 of this Act;
F59["the Commission" means the Historic Buildings and Monuments Commission for England;]
"designation order" means an order under that section;
[F60 " development consent " means development consent under the Planning Act 2008;]
"enactment" includes an enactment in any local or private Act of Parliament, and an order, rule, regulation, byelaw or scheme made under an Act of Parliament;
"flooding operations" means covering land with water or any other liquid or partially liquid substance;
"functions" includes powers and duties;
"guardianship deed" has the meaning given by section 12. (6) of this Act;
"land" means—
    (a) in England and Wales, any corporeal hereditament;
    (b) in Scotland, any heritable property;
including a building or a monument and, in relation to any acquisition of land, includes any interest in or right over land;

"local authority" means—
   (a) in England F61. . ., the council of a county or district,. . . F62 the council of a London borough, and the Common Council of the City of London;
   F63 [(aa)in Wales, the council of a county or county borough;]
   (b) in Scotland, the planning authority within the meaning of Part IX of the M6. Local Government (Scotland) Act 1973;
"monument" has the meaning given by subsection (7) below;
"owner", in relation to any land in England and Wales means (except for the purposes of paragraph 2. (1) of Schedule 1 to this Act and any regulations made for the purposes of that paragraph) a person, other than a mortgagee not in possession, who, whether in his own right or as trustee for any other person, is entitled to receive the rack rent of the land, or where the land is not let at a rack rent, would be so entitled if it were so let;
"possession" includes receipt of rents and profits or the right to receive rents and profits (if any);
"prescribed" means prescribed by regulations made by the Secretary of State;
"the Schedule" has the meaning given by section 1. (1) of this Act;
"scheduled monument" has the meaning given by section 1. (11) of this Act and references to "scheduled monument consent" shall be construed in accordance with section 2. (3) and 3. (5) of this Act;
F64. . .
"tipping operations" means tipping soil or spoil or depositing building or other materials or matter (including waste materials or refuse) on any land; and
[F65"universal postal service provider" means a universal service provider within the meaning of [F66. Part 3 of the Postal Services Act 2011]; and references to the provision of a universal postal service shall be construed in accordance with [F67that Part].]
- "works" includes operations of any description and, in particular (but without prejudice to the generality of the preceding provision) flooding or tipping operations and any operations undertaken for purposes of agriculture (within the meaning of [F68the Town and Country Planning Act 1990] or, as regards Scotland, [F69the Town and Country Planning (Scotland) Act 1997] or forestry (including afforestation).
(2) In this Act "statutory undertakers" means—
   (a) persons authorised by any enactment to carry on any railway, light railway, tramway, road transport, water transport, canal, inland navigation, dock, harbour, pier or lighthouse undertaking, or any undertaking for the supply of . . . F70, . . . F71[F72or hydraulic power];
   (b) . . . F73the Civil Aviation Authority, the F74. . ., [F75a universal postal service provider in connection with the provision of a universal postal service] and any other authority, body or undertakers which by virtue of any enactment are to be treated as statutory undertakers for any of the purposes of [F76the Town and Country Planning Act 1990] or of [F69the Town and Country Planning (Scotland) Act 1997]; and
   (c) any other authority, body or undertakers specified in an order made by the Secretary of State under this paragraph.
[F77. (2. A)The undertaking of a universal postal service provider so far as relating to the provision of a universal postal service shall be taken to be his statutory undertaking for the purposes of this Act; and references in this Act to his undertaking shall be construed accordingly.]
(3) For the purposes of sections 14. (1) and 21. (2) of this Act and paragraph 6. (1)(b) and (2)(b) of Schedule 3 to this Act a person shall be taken to be immediately affected by the operation of a guardianship deed relating to any land if he is bound by that deed and is in possession or occupation of the land.
(4) For the purposes of this Act "archaeological investigation" means any investigation of any land, objects or other material for the purpose of obtaining and recording any information of archaeological or historical interest and (without prejudice to the generality of the preceding provision) includes in the case of an archaeological investigation of any land—
   (a) any investigation for the purpose of discovering and revealing and (where appropriate) recovering and removing any objects or other material of archaeological or historical interest

situated in, on or under the land; and

(b) examining, testing, treating, recording and preserving any such objects or material discovered during the course of any excavations or inspections carried out for the purposes of any such investigation.

(5) For the purposes of this Act, an archaeological examination of any land means any examination or inspection of the land (including any buildings or other structures thereon) for the purpose of obtaining and recording any information of archaeological or historical interest.

(6) In this Act references to land associated with any monument (or to associated land) shall be construed in accordance with section 15. (6) of this Act.

(7) "Monument" means (subject to subsection (8) below)—

(a) any building, structure or work, whether above or below the surface of the land, and any cave or excavation;

(b) any site comprising the remains of any such building, structure or work or of any cave or excavation; and

(c) any site comprising, or comprising the remains of, any vehicle, vessel, aircraft or other movable structure or part thereof which neither constitutes nor forms part of any work which is a monument within paragraph (a) above;

and any machinery attached to a monument shall be regarded as part of the monument if it could not be detached without being dismantled.

(8) Subsection (7)(a) above does not apply to any ecclesiastical building for the time being used for ecclesiastical purposes, and subsection (7)(c) above does not apply—

(a) to a site comprising any object or its remains unless the situation of that object or its remains in that particular site is a matter of public interest;

(b) to a site comprising, or comprising the remains of, any vessel which is protected by an order under section 1 of the M7. Protection of Wrecks Act 1973 designating an area round the site as a restricted area.

F78. (9)For the purposes of this Act, the site of a monument includes not only the land in or on which it is situated but also any land comprising or adjoining it which appears to the Secretary of State [F79or the Commission] or a local authority, in the exercise in relation to that monument of any of their functions under this Act, to be essential for the monument's support and preservation.

(10) References in this Act to a monument include references—

(a) to the site of the monument in question; and

(b) to a group of monuments or any part of a monument or group of monuments.

(11) References in this Act to the site of a monument—

(a) are references to the monument itself where it consists of a site; and

(b) in any other case include references to the monument itself.

(12) "Ancient monument" means—

(a) any scheduled monument; and

(b) any other monument which in the opinion of the Secretary of State is of public interest by reason of the historic, architectural, traditional, artistic or archaeological interest attaching to it.

(13) In this section "remains" includes any trace or sign of the previous existence of the thing in question.

Extent Information

E2. This version of this provision extends to England and Wales only; a separate version has been created for Scotland only.

Amendments (Textual)

F58. Words in s. 61. (1) inserted (30.6.2011 for specified purposes, 1.12.2011 in so far as not already in force) by Historic Environment (Amendment) (Scotland) Act 2011 (asp 3), ss. 6. (3), 33. (2); S.S.I. 2011/174, art. 2, Sch.; S.S.I. 2011/372, art. 2, Sch.

F59. Definition inserted by National Heritage Act 1983 (c. 47, SIF 78), s. 41, Sch. 4 para. 67. (2)

F60. Words in s. 61. (1) inserted (1.3.2010) by Planning Act 2008 (c. 29), s. 241. (8), Sch. 2 para. 20 (with s. 226); S.I. 2010/101, art. 2 (with art. 6)

F61. Words in s. 61. (1)(a) repealed (1.4.1996) by 1994 c. 19, s. 66. (6)(8), Sch. 16 para. 56. (3),

Sch. 18 (with ss. 54. (5)(7), 55. (5), Sch. 17 paras. 22. (1), 23. (2)); S.I. 1996/396, art. 4, Sch. 2
F62. Words repealed by Local Government Act 1985 (c. 51, SIF 81:1), s. 102, Sch. 17
F63. S. 61. (1)(aa) inserted (1.4.1996) by 1994 c. 19, s. 66. (6), Sch. 16 para. 56. (3) (with ss. 54. (5)(7), 55. (5), Sch. 17 paras. 22. (1), 23. (2)); S.I. 1996/396, art. 4, Sch. 2
F64. The definition of "statutory maximum" in s. 61. (1) repealed (5.11.1993) by 1993 c. 50, s. 1. (1), Sch. 1 Pt. XIV Group 2
F65. S. 61. (1): definition of "universal postal provider" inserted (26.3.01) by S.I. 2001/1149, art. 3. (1), Sch. 1 para. 45. (2)
F66. Words in s. 61. (1) substituted (1.10.2011) by Postal Services Act 2011 (c. 5), s. 93. (2)(3), Sch. 12 para. 103. (a); S.I. 2011/2329, art. 3
F67. Words in s. 61. (1) substituted (1.10.2011) by Postal Services Act 2011 (c. 5), s. 93. (2)(3), Sch. 12 para. 103. (b); S.I. 2011/2329, art. 3
F68. Words substituted by Planning (Consequential Provisions) Act 1990 (c. 11, SIF 123:1, 2), s. 4, Sch. 2 para. 43. (2)
F69. Words in s. 61. (1)(2)(b) substituted (27.5.1997) by 1997 c. 11, ss. 4, 6. (2), Sch. 2 para. 29. (2)
F70. Word repealed by Electricity Act 1989 (c.29, SIF 44:1), s. 112. (3)(4), Sch. 17 para. 35, Sch. 18
F71. Word repealed by Gas Act 1986 (c.44, SIF 44:2), s. 67. (3)(4), Sch. 8 para. 17, Sch. 9 Pt. I
F72. Words in s. 61. (2)(a) substituted (E.W.) by Water Act 1989 (c. 15, SIF 130), ss. 58. (7), 101. (1), 146. (6), 160. (1)(2)(4), 189. (4)-(10), 190, 193. (1), Sch. 25 para. 58, Sch. 26 paras. 3. (1)(2), 17, 40. (4), 57. (6), 58
F73. Words repealed by Airports Act 1986 (c. 31, SIF 9), s. 83. (5), Sch. 6 Pt. I
F74. Words in s. 61. (2)(b) repealed (31.10.1994) by virtue of 1994 c. 21, s. 67, Sch. 9 para. 22, Sch. 11 Pt. II; S.I. 1994/2553, art. 2
F75. Words in s. 61. (2)(b) substituted (26.3.01) by S.I. 2001/1149, art. 3. (1), Sch. 1 para. 45. (3)
F76. Words substituted by Planning (Consequential Provisions) Act 1990 (c. 11, SIF 123:1, 2), s. 4, Sch. 2 para. 43. (2)
F77. S. 61. (2. A) inserted (26.3.01) by S.I. 2001/1149, art. 3. (1), Sch. 1 para. 45. (4)
F78. Words in s. 61. (9) inserted (27.2.2015 for specified purposes, 1.10.2015 in so far as not already in force) by Historic Environment Scotland Act 2014 (asp 19), s. 31. (2), sch. 2 para. 52 (with ss. 29, 30); S.S.I. 2015/31, art. 2, sch.; S.S.I. 2015/196, art. 2, sch.
F79. Words inserted by National Heritage Act 1983 (c. 47, SIF 78), s. 41, Sch. 4 para. 67. (3)
Marginal Citations
M61973 c. 65.
M71973 c. 33.

61 Interpretation.S

(1) In this Act—
"ancient monument" has the meaning given by subsection (12) below;
"area of archaeological importance" means an area designated as such under section 33 of this Act;
F83["the Commission" means the Historic Buildings and Monuments Commission for England;]
"designation order" means an order under that section;
[F60 " development consent " means development consent under the Planning Act 2008;]
"enactment" includes an enactment in any local or private Act of Parliament, and an order, rule, regulation, byelaw or scheme made under an Act of Parliament;
"flooding operations" means covering land with water or any other liquid or partially liquid substance;
"functions" includes powers and duties;
"guardianship deed" has the meaning given by section 12. (6) of this Act;

"land" means—
   (a) in England and Wales, any corporeal hereditament;
   (b) in Scotland, any heritable property;
including a building or a monument and, in relation to any acquisition of land, includes any interest in or right over land;
"local authority" means—
   (a) in England F84. . ., the council of a county or district, . . . F85 the council of a London borough, and the Common Council of the City of London;
   F86 [(aa)in Wales, the council of a county or county borough;]
   (b) in Scotland, the planning authority within the meaning of Part IX of the M8. Local Government (Scotland) Act 1973;
"monument" has the meaning given by subsection (7) below;
"owner", in relation to any land in England and Wales means (except for the purposes of paragraph 2. (1) of Schedule 1 to this Act and any regulations made for the purposes of that paragraph) a person, other than a mortgagee not in possession, who, whether in his own right or as trustee for any other person, is entitled to receive the rack rent of the land, or where the land is not let at a rack rent, would be so entitled if it were so let;
[F58 " period for compliance " is to be construed in accordance with section 9. B(1) and (2);]
"possession" includes receipt of rents and profits or the right to receive rents and profits (if any);
"prescribed" means prescribed by regulations made by the Secretary of State;
"the Schedule" has the meaning given by section 1. (1) of this Act;
"scheduled monument" has the meaning given by section 1. (11) of this Act and references to "scheduled monument consent" shall be construed in accordance with section 2. (3) and 3. (5) of this Act;
F87. . .
"tipping operations" means tipping soil or spoil or depositing building or other materials or matter (including waste materials or refuse) on any land; and
[F88"universal postal service provider" means a universal service provider within the meaning of [F66. Part 3 of the Postal Services Act 2011]; and references to the provision of a universal postal service shall be construed in accordance with [F67that Part].]
   - "works" includes operations of any description and, in particular (but without prejudice to the generality of the preceding provision) flooding or tipping operations and any operations undertaken for purposes of agriculture (within the meaning of [F89the Town and Country Planning Act 1990] or, as regards Scotland, [F90the Town and Country Planning (Scotland) Act 1997] or forestry (including afforestation).
(2) In this Act "statutory undertakers" means—
   (a) persons authorised by any enactment to carry on any railway, light railway, tramway, road transport, water transport, canal, inland navigation, dock, harbour, pier or lighthouse undertaking, or any undertaking for the supply of . . . F91, . . . F92 hydraulic power or water ;
   (b) . . . F93the Civil Aviation Authority, the F94. . ., [F95a universal postal service provider in connection with the provision of a universal postal service]and any other authority, body or undertakers which by virtue of any enactment are to be treated as statutory undertakers for any of the purposes of [F96the Town and Country Planning Act 1990] or of [F90the Town and Country Planning (Scotland) Act 1997]; and
   (c) any other authority, body or undertakers specified in an order made by the Secretary of State under this paragraph.
[F97. (2. A)The undertaking of a universal postal service provider so far as relating to the provision of a universal postal service shall be taken to be his statutory undertaking for the purposes of this Act; and references in this Act to his undertaking shall be construed accordingly.]
(3) For the purposes of sections 14. (1) and 21. (2) of this Act and paragraph 6. (1)(b) and (2)(b) of Schedule 3 to this Act a person shall be taken to be immediately affected by the operation of a guardianship deed relating to any land if he is bound by that deed and is in possession or occupation of the land.

(4) For the purposes of this Act "archaeological investigation" means any investigation of any land, objects or other material for the purpose of obtaining and recording any information of archaeological or historical interest and (without prejudice to the generality of the preceding provision) includes in the case of an archaeological investigation of any land—

(a) any investigation for the purpose of discovering and revealing and (where appropriate) recovering and removing any objects or other material of archaeological or historical interest situated in, on or under the land; and

(b) examining, testing, treating, recording and preserving any such objects or material discovered during the course of any excavations or inspections carried out for the purposes of any such investigation.

(5) For the purposes of this Act, an archaeological examination of any land means any examination or inspection of the land (including any buildings or other structures thereon) for the purpose of obtaining and recording any information of archaeological or historical interest.

(6) In this Act references to land associated with any monument (or to associated land) shall be construed in accordance with section 15. (6) of this Act.

(7) "Monument" means (subject to subsection (8) below)—

(a) any building, structure or work, whether above or below the surface of the land, and any cave or excavation;

(b) any site comprising the remains of any such building, structure or work or of any cave or excavation; F98...

(c) any site comprising, or comprising the remains of, any vehicle, vessel, aircraft or other movable structure or part thereof which neither constitutes nor forms part of any work which is a monument within paragraph (a) above;[F99 and

(d) any site (other than one falling within paragraph (b) or (c) above) comprising any thing, or group of things, that evidences previous human activity;]

and any machinery attached to a monument shall be regarded as part of the monument if it could not be detached without being dismantled.

(8) Subsection (7)(a) above does not apply to any ecclesiastical building for the time being used for ecclesiastical purposes, and subsection (7)(c) above does not apply—

(a) to a site comprising any object or its remains unless the situation of that object or its remains in that particular site is a matter of public interest;

F100. (b). . . . .

(9) For the purposes of this Act, the site of a monument includes not only the land in or on which it is situated but also any land comprising or adjoining it which appears to the Secretary of State [F78or Historic Environment Scotland] [F101or the Commission] or a local authority, in the exercise in relation to that monument of any of their functions under this Act, to be essential for the monument's support and preservation.

(10) References in this Act to a monument include references—

(a) to the site of the monument in question; and

(b) to a group of monuments or any part of a monument or group of monuments.

(11) References in this Act to the site of a monument—

(a) are references to the monument itself where it consists of a site; and

(b) in any other case include references to the monument itself.

(12) "Ancient monument" means—

(a) any scheduled monument; and

(b) any other monument which in the opinion of the Secretary of State is of public interest by reason of the historic, architectural, traditional, artistic or archaeological interest attaching to it.

(13) In this section "remains" includes any trace or sign of the previous existence of the thing in question.

Extent Information

E4. This version of this provision extends to Scotland only; a separate version has been created for England and Wales only.

Amendments (Textual)

F58. Words in s. 61. (1) inserted (30.6.2011 for specified purposes, 1.12.2011 in so far as not already in force) by Historic Environment (Amendment) (Scotland) Act 2011 (asp 3), ss. 6. (3), 33. (2); S.S.I. 2011/174, art. 2, Sch.; S.S.I. 2011/372, art. 2, Sch.
F60. Words in s. 61. (1) inserted (1.3.2010) by Planning Act 2008 (c. 29), s. 241. (8), Sch. 2 para. 20 (with s. 226); S.I. 2010/101, art. 2 (with art. 6)
F66. Words in s. 61. (1) substituted (1.10.2011) by Postal Services Act 2011 (c. 5), s. 93. (2)(3), Sch. 12 para. 103. (a); S.I. 2011/2329, art. 3
F67. Words in s. 61. (1) substituted (1.10.2011) by Postal Services Act 2011 (c. 5), s. 93. (2)(3), Sch. 12 para. 103. (b); S.I. 2011/2329, art. 3
F78. Words in s. 61. (9) inserted (27.2.2015 for specified purposes, 1.10.2015 in so far as not already in force) by Historic Environment Scotland Act 2014 (asp 19), s. 31. (2), sch. 2 para. 52 (with ss. 29, 30); S.S.I. 2015/31, art. 2, sch.; S.S.I. 2015/196, art. 2, sch.
F83. Definition inserted by National Heritage Act 1983 (c. 47, SIF 78), s. 41, Sch. 4 para. 67. (2)
F84. Words in s. 61. (1)(a) repealed (1.4.1996) by 1994 c. 19, s. 66. (6)(8), Sch. 16 para. 56. (3), Sch. 18 (with ss. 54. (5)(7), 55. (5), Sch. 17 paras. 22. (1), 23. (2)); S.I. 1996/396, art. 4, Sch. 2
F85. Words repealed by Local Government Act 1985 (c. 51, SIF 81:1), s. 102, Sch. 17
F86. S. 61. (1)(aa) inserted (1.4.1996) by 1994 c. 19, s. 66. (6), Sch. 16 para. 56. (3) (with ss. 54. (5)(7), 55. (5), Sch. 17 paras. 22. (1), 23. (2)); S.I. 1996/396, art. 4, Sch. 2
F87. The definition of "statutory maximum" in s. 61. (1) repealed (5.11.1993) by 1993 c. 50, s. 1. (1), Sch. 1 Pt. XIV Group 2
F88s. 61. (1): definition of "universal postal service" inserted (26.3.01) by S.I. 2001/1149, art. 3. (1), Sch. 1 para. 45. (2)
F89. Words substituted by Planning (Consequential Provisions) Act 1990 (c. 11, SIF 123:1, 2), s. 4, Sch. 2 para. 43. (2)
F90. Words in s. 61. (1)(2)(b) substituted (27.5.1997) by 1997 c. 11, ss. 4, 6. (2), Sch. 2 para. 29. (2)
F91. Word repealed by Electricity Act 1989 (c.29, SIF 44:1), s. 112. (3)(4), Sch. 17 para. 35, Sch. 18
F92. Word repealed by Gas Act 1986 (c.44, SIF 44:2), s. 67. (3)(4), Sch. 8 para. 17, Sch. 9 Pt. I
F93. Words repealed by Airports Act 1986 (c. 31, SIF 9), s. 83. (5), Sch. 6 Pt. I
F94. Words in s. 61. (2)(b) repealed (31.10.1994) by virtue of 1994 c. 21, s. 67, Sch. 9 para. 22, Sch. 11 Pt. II; S.I. 1994/2553, art. 2
F95. Words in s. 61. (2)(b) substituted (26.3.01) by S.I. 2001/1149, art. 3. (1), Sch. 1 para. 45. (3)
F96. Words substituted by Planning (Consequential Provisions) Act 1990 (c. 11, SIF 123:1, 2), s. 4, Sch. 2 para. 43. (2)
F97. S. 61. (2. A) inserted (26.3.01) by S.I. 2001/1149, art. 3. (1), Sch. 1 para. 45. (4)
F98. Word in s. 61. (7) repealed (1.12.2011) by Historic Environment (Amendment) (Scotland) Act 2011 (asp 3), ss. 14. (a)(i), 33. (2); S.S.I. 2011/372, art. 2, Sch.
F99. S. 61. (7)(d) and word inserted (1.12.2011) by Historic Environment (Amendment) (Scotland) Act 2011 (asp 3), ss. 14. (a)(ii), 33. (2); S.S.I. 2011/372, art. 2, Sch.
F100. S. 61. (8)(b) repealed (1.12.2011) by Historic Environment (Amendment) (Scotland) Act 2011 (asp 3), ss. 14. (b), 33. (2); S.S.I. 2011/372, art. 2, Sch.
F101. Words inserted by National Heritage Act 1983 (c. 47, SIF 78), s. 41, Sch. 4 para. 67. (3)
Marginal Citations
M81973 c. 65.

62 Special provision for Scotland.

(1) –(3). F80
(4) In this Act, in relation to any land in Scotland, "occupier" means an occupier with an interest in that land which is heritable and, if there is no such occupier, the owner thereof shall be deemed to be the occupier.

(5) In relation to land in Scotland, any reference in this Act—
   (a) to a mortgage shall be construed as a reference to a heritable security;
   (b) to a mortgagee shall be construed as a reference to a creditor in a heritable security; and
   (c) to a first mortgagee shall be construed as a reference to a creditor in a heritable security which ranks prior to any other heritable security over the same land.
Amendments (Textual)
F80. Ss. 62. (1)–(3), 63 repealed by Statute Law (Repeals) Act 1981 (c. 19), Sch. 1 Pt. IV

63. . . . . F81.

Amendments (Textual)
F81. Ss. 62. (1)–(3), 63 repealed by Statute Law (Repeals) Act 1981 (c. 19), Sch. 1 Pt. IV

64 Transitional provisions, consequential amendments and repeals.

(1) Schedule 3 to this Act shall have effect for the purposes of the transition to the provisions of this Act from the law previously in force.
X2. (2)The enactments specified in Schedule 4 to this Act shall have effect subject to the amendments specified in that Schedule, being amendments consequential on the provisions of this Act.
X2. (3)The enactments specified in Schedule 5 to this Act are hereby repealed to the extent specified in the third column of that Schedule.
Editorial Information
X2. The text of s. 64. (2)(3) is in the form in which it was originally enacted: it was not reproduced in Statutes in Force and does not reflect any amendments or repeals which may have been made prior to 1.2.1991.

65 Short title, commencement and extent.

(1) This Act may be cited as the Ancient Monuments and Archaeological Areas Act 1979.
(2) This Act shall come into force on such day as may be appointed by order of the Secretary of State, and different days may be appointed for different purposes; and a reference in any provision of this Act to the commencement of this Act is a reference to the day appointed for the coming into force of that provision.
(3) This Act does not extend to Northern Ireland.
Subordinate Legislation Made
P1. Power of appointment conferred by s. 65. (2) exercised: S.I. 1979/786, 1981/1300, 1981/1466 and 1982/362

Schedules

Schedule 1. Control of Works Affecting Scheduled Monuments

Sections 2 and 4.

Part I Applications for Scheduled Monument Consent

1. (1)Provision may be made by regulations under this Act with respect to the form and manner in which applications for scheduled monument consent are to be made, the particulars to be included therein and the information to be provided by applicants or (as the case may be) by [F1the Secretary of State] [F1. Historic Environment Scotland] in connection therewith.
[F2. (1. A)The Scottish Ministers may by regulations make provision as to—
(a) the manner in which scheduled monument consent is to be granted;
(b) the form and content of scheduled monument consent.]
(2) Any scheduled monument consent (including scheduled monument consent granted by order under section 3 of this Act) shall (except so far as it otherwise provides) enure for the benefit of the monument and of all persons for the time being interested therein.
Amendments (Textual)
F1. Words in Sch. 1 para. 1. (1) substituted (S.) (27.2.2015 for specified purposes, 1.10.2015 in so far as not already in force) by Historic Environment Scotland Act 2014 (asp 19), s. 31. (2), sch. 2 para. 14. (2) (with ss. 29, 30); S.S.I. 2015/31, art. 2, sch.; S.S.I. 2015/196, art. 2, sch.
F2. Sch. 1 para. 1. (1. A) inserted (S.) (30.6.2011 for specified purposes, 1.12.2011 in so far as not already in force) by Historic Environment (Amendment) (Scotland) Act 2011 (asp 3), ss. 15. (2), 33. (2); S.S.I. 2011/174, art. 2, Sch.; S.S.I. 2011/372, art. 2, Sch.
Modifications etc. (not altering text)
C1. Sch. 1 para. 1 savings for effects of 2014 asp 19, Sch. 2 para. 14 (S.) (1.10.2015) by The Historic Environment Scotland Act 2014 (Saving, Transitional and Consequential Provisions) Order 2015 (S.S.I. 2015/239), arts. 1. (1), 6
2. (1)[F3. The Secretary of State may refuse to entertain an application for scheduled monument consent unless it is accompanied by one or other of the following certificates signed by or on behalf of the applicant, that is to say—
(a) a certificate stating that, at the beginning of the period of twenty-one days ending with the application, no person other than the applicant was the owner of the monument;
(b) a certificate stating that the applicant has given the requisite notice of the application to all the persons other than the applicant who, at the beginning of that period, were owners of the monument;
(c) a certificate stating that the applicant is unable to issue a certificate in accordance with either of the preceding paragraphs, that he has given the requisite notice of the application to such one or more of the persons mentioned in paragraph (b) above as are specified in the certificate, that he has taken such steps as are reasonably open to him to ascertain the names and addresses of the remainder of those persons and that he has been unable to do so;
(d) a certificate stating that the applicant is unable to issue a certificate in accordance with paragraph (a) above, that he has taken such steps as are reasonably open to him to ascertain the names and addresses of the persons mentioned in paragraph (b) above and that he has been unable to do so.]
[F3[F4. The Scottish Ministers] [F4. Historic Environment Scotland] may refuse to entertain an application for scheduled monument consent unless it is accompanied by a certificate as to the interests in the monument to which the application relates.]
(2) [F5. Any certificate issued for the purposes of sub-paragraph (1) above—
(a) shall contain such further particulars of the matters to which the certificate relates as may be prescribed by regulations made for the purposes of this paragraph; and
(b) shall be in such form as may be so prescribed;
and any reference in that sub-paragraph to the requisite notice is a reference to a notice in the form so prescribed.]
[F5. The Scottish Ministers may by regulations—
(a) make provision as to the notice of any application for scheduled monument consent to be given to any person (other than the applicant) who, at the beginning of the period of 21 days ending with

the date of the application, was the owner of the monument;
(b) make provision for publicising applications for scheduled monument consent;
(c) make provision as to—
(i) the form and content of certificates such as are mentioned in sub-paragraph (1) and notices such as are mentioned in paragraph (a);
(ii) service of such notices;
(d) make provision as to such further particulars of the matters to which such certificates relate as may be prescribed;
(e) require an applicant for scheduled monument consent to certify, in such form as may be prescribed, or to provide evidence, that any requirements of the regulations have been satisfied.
(2. A)Regulations under sub-paragraph (2) may make different provision for different classes of case.]
(3) Regulations made for the purposes of this paragraph may make provision as to who, in the case of any monument, is to be treated as the owner for those purposes.
(4) If any person issues a certificate which purports to comply with the requirements of this paragraph[or regulations made under it] and which contains a statement which he knows to be false or misleading in a material particular, or recklessly issues a certificate which purports to comply with those requirements and which contains a statement which is false or misleading in a material particular, he shall be guilty of an offence and liable on summary conviction or, in Scotland, on conviction before a court of summary jurisdiction, to a fine not exceeding [F6level 3 on the standard scale].

Amendments (Textual)

F3. Para. 2. (2)(2. A) Sch. 1 para. 2. (1) substituted for Sch. 1 para. 2. (1)para. 2. (2) (S.) (30.6.2011 for specified purposes, 1.12.2011 in so far as not already in force) by Historic Environment (Amendment) (Scotland) Act 2011 (asp 3), ss. 15. (3)(a), 33. (2); S.S.I. 2011/174, art. 2, Sch.; S.S.I. 2011/372, art. 2, Sch.; S.S.I. 2011/174, art. 2, Sch.; S.S.I. 2011/372, art. 2, Sch.
F4. Words in Sch. 1 para. 2. (1) substituted (27.2.2015 for specified purposes, 1.10.2015 in so far as not already in force) by Historic Environment Scotland Act 2014 (asp 19), s. 31. (2), sch. 2 para. 14. (3) (with ss. 29, 30); S.S.I. 2015/31, art. 2, sch.; S.S.I. 2015/196, art. 2, sch.
F5. Sch. 1 para. 2. (2)(2. A) substituted for Sch. 1 para. 2. (2) (S.) (30.6.2011 for specified purposes) by Historic Environment (Amendment) (Scotland) Act 2011 (asp 3), ss. 15. (3)(a), 33. (2); S.S.I. 2011/174, art. 2, Sch.
F6 Words substituted by virtue of Criminal Justice Act 1982 (c. 48) , s. 46 and Criminal Procedure (Scotland) Act 1975 (c. 21) , s. 289. G (as inserted by Criminal Justice Act 1982 (c. 48) , s. 54)

Modifications etc. (not altering text)

C2 Sch. 1 para. 2 modified (1.1.1993) by S.I. 1992/3138 , reg. 4. (2) , Sch. 2 para.1 .
C3 Sch. 1 para. 2 modified (S.) (28.12.2007) by The Transport and Works (Scotland) Act 2007 (Consents under Enactments) Regulations 2007 (S.S.I. 2007/569) , regs. 1 , 6. (2)
C4. Sch. 1 para. 2 savings for effects of 2014 asp 19, Sch. 2 para. 14. (S.) (1.10.2015) by The Historic Environment Scotland Act 2014 (Saving, Transitional and Consequential Provisions) Order 2015 (S.S.I. 2015/239), arts. 1. (1), 6
C5. Sch. 1 para. 2. (1)(2) savings for effects of 2011 asp 3 s. 15. (3) (S.) (1.12.2011) by The Historic Environment (Amendment) (Scotland) Act 2011 (Saving, Transitional and Consequential Provisions) Order 2011 (S.S.I. 2011/377), arts. 1. (1), 3
C6. Words in Sch. 1 para. 1. (4) inserted (S.) (30.6.2011 for specified purposes, 1.12.2011 in so far as not already in force) by Historic Environment (Amendment) (Scotland) Act 2011 (asp 3), ss. 15. (3)(b), 33. (2); S.S.I. 2011/174, art. 2, Sch.; S.S.I. 2011/372, art. 2, Sch.

[F72. AAs soon as practicable after receiving an application for scheduled monument consent in relation to a monument situated in England, the Secretary of State shall send a copy of the application to the Commission.]

Amendments (Textual)

F7. Para. 2. A inserted by National Heritage Act 1983 (c. 47, SIF 78), s. 41, Sch. 4 para. 68. (2)
[F8 2. B (1)Where sub-paragraph (2) or (3) applies, [F9. Historic Environment Scotland] may

refuse to entertain an application for scheduled monument consent.S
(2) This sub-paragraph applies where—
(a) within the period of 2 years ending with the date the application is received, [F10. Historic Environment Scotland has or] the Scottish Ministers have refused [F11or the Scottish Ministers have dismissed an appeal against the refusal of, or an appeal under section 4. B(3) in respect of,] a similar application; and
(b) in [F12its] opinion there has been no significant change in any material considerations since the similar application was refused [F13or the appeal was dismissed] .
(3) This sub-paragraph applies where the application is made at a time when a similar application is under consideration.
(4) For the purposes of this paragraph, an application for scheduled monument consent is to be taken to be similar to another such application only if the scheduled monument and the works to which the applications relate are, in the opinion of [F14. Historic Environment Scotland] , the same or substantially the same.]
Amendments (Textual)
F8. Sch. 1 para. 2. B inserted (S.) (1.12.2011, 1.12.2011 in so far as not already in force) by Historic Environment (Amendment) (Scotland) Act 2011 (asp 3), ss. 16, 33. (2); S.S.I. 2011/372, art. 2, Sch.
F9. Words in Sch. 1 para. 2. B(1) substituted (27.2.2015 for specified purposes, 1.10.2015 in so far as not already in force) by Historic Environment Scotland Act 2014 (asp 19), s. 31. (2), sch. 2 para. 14. (4)(a) (with ss. 29, 30); S.S.I. 2015/31, art. 2, sch.; S.S.I. 2015/196, art. 2, sch.
F10. Words in Sch. 1 para. 2. B(2)(a) inserted (27.2.2015 for specified purposes, 1.10.2015 in so far as not already in force) by Historic Environment Scotland Act 2014 (asp 19), s. 31. (2), sch. 2 para. 14. (4)(b)(i) (with ss. 29, 30); S.S.I. 2015/31, art. 2, sch.; S.S.I. 2015/196, art. 2, sch.
F11. Words in Sch. 1 para. 2. B(2)(a) inserted (27.2.2015 for specified purposes, 1.10.2015 in so far as not already in force) by Historic Environment Scotland Act 2014 (asp 19), s. 31. (2), sch. 2 para. 14. (4)(b)(ii) (with ss. 29, 30); S.S.I. 2015/31, art. 2, sch.; S.S.I. 2015/196, art. 2, sch.
F12. Word in Sch. 1 para. 2. B(2)(b) substituted (27.2.2015 for specified purposes, 1.10.2015 in so far as not already in force) by Historic Environment Scotland Act 2014 (asp 19), s. 31. (2), sch. 2 para. 14. (4)(c)(i) (with ss. 29, 30); S.S.I. 2015/31, art. 2, sch.; S.S.I. 2015/196, art. 2, sch.
F13. Words in Sch. 1 para. 2. B(2)(b) inserted (27.2.2015 for specified purposes, 1.10.2015 in so far as not already in force) by Historic Environment Scotland Act 2014 (asp 19), s. 31. (2), sch. 2 para. 14. (4)(c)(ii) (with ss. 29, 30); S.S.I. 2015/31, art. 2, sch.; S.S.I. 2015/196, art. 2, sch.
F14. Words in Sch. 1 para. 2. B(4) substituted (27.2.2015 for specified purposes, 1.10.2015 in so far as not already in force) by Historic Environment Scotland Act 2014 (asp 19), s. 31. (2), sch. 2 para. 14. (4)(d) (with ss. 29, 30); S.S.I. 2015/31, art. 2, sch.; S.S.I. 2015/196, art. 2, sch.
Modifications etc. (not altering text)
C7. Sch. 1 para. 2. B(1) restricted (S.) (1.12.2011) by The Historic Environment (Amendment) (Scotland) Act 2011 (Saving, Transitional and Consequential Provisions) Order 2011 (S.S.I. 2011/377), arts. 1. (1), 4
C8. Sch. 1 para. 2. B savings for effects of 2014 asp 19, Sch. 2 para. 14 (S.) (1.10.2015) by The Historic Environment Scotland Act 2014 (Saving, Transitional and Consequential Provisions) Order 2015 (S.S.I. 2015/239), arts. 1. (1), 6
[F152. C(1)If Historic Environment Scotland, on an application to it for scheduled monument consent, intends to grant that consent, it must, where sub-paragraph (2) applies, first notify the Scottish Ministers of the application.S
(2) This sub-paragraph applies where—
(a) regulations, or
(b) directions given to Historic Environment Scotland by the Scottish Ministers,
provide that the application must be so notified.
(3) The Scottish Ministers may within the period of 28 days beginning with the date of the notification—
(a) direct the reference of the application to them under section 3. B, or

(b) give notice to Historic Environment Scotland that they require further time in which to consider whether to require such a reference.

(4) Historic Environment Scotland must not grant scheduled monument consent until—

(a) the period mentioned in sub-paragraph (3) has expired without the Scottish Ministers directing the reference of the application to them or giving notice under paragraph (b) of that sub-paragraph, or

(b) the Scottish Ministers have notified Historic Environment Scotland that they do not intend to require the reference of the application.

Amendments (Textual)

F15. Sch. 1 paras. 2. C, 2. D inserted (S.) (27.2.2015 for specified purposes, 1.10.2015 in so far as not already in force) by Historic Environment Scotland Act 2014 (asp 19), s. 31. (2), sch. 2 para. 14. (5) (with ss. 29, 30); S.S.I. 2015/31, art. 2, sch.; S.S.I. 2015/196, art. 2, sch.

2. DThe Scottish Ministers may give directions to Historic Environment Scotland requiring it, in such cases or classes of case as may be specified in the directions, to notify to Ministers and to such other persons as may be so specified—S

(a) any applications made to it for scheduled monument consent, and

(b) the decisions taken on those applications.]

Amendments (Textual)

F15. Sch. 1 paras. 2. C, 2. D inserted (S.) (27.2.2015 for specified purposes, 1.10.2015 in so far as not already in force) by Historic Environment Scotland Act 2014 (asp 19), s. 31. (2), sch. 2 para. 14. (5) (with ss. 29, 30); S.S.I. 2015/31, art. 2, sch.; S.S.I. 2015/196, art. 2, sch.

3. (1)The Secretary of State [F16or Historic Environment Scotland] may grant scheduled monument consent in respect of all or any part of the works to which an application for scheduled monument consent relates.

[F17. (2)Before determining whether or not to grant scheduled monument consent on any application therefor, the Secretary of State [F18shall] [F18may] either—

(a) cause a public local inquiry to be held; or

(b) afford to the applicant, and to any other person to whom it appears to the Secretary of State expedient to afford it, an opportunity of appearing before and being heard by a person appointed by the Secretary of State for the purpose.]

[F17. The Scottish Ministers may by regulations make provision for the procedure to be followed by Historic Environment Scotland in considering and determining applications for scheduled monument consent.]

[F17. (3)Before determining whether or not to grant scheduled monument consent on any application therefor the Secretary of State—

(a) shall in every case consider any representations made by any person with respect to that application before the time when he considers his decision thereon (whether in consequence of any notice given to that person in accordance with any requirements of regulations made by virtue of paragraph 2 above or of any publicity given to the application by the Secretary of State, or otherwise); and

(b) shall also, if any inquiry or hearing has been held in accordance with sub-paragraph (2) above, consider the report of the person who held it. [F19and

(c) shall, if the monument in question is situated in England, consult with the Commission.]

(4) The Secretary of State [F20or, as the case may be, Historic Environment Scotland] shall serve notice of [F21his] [F21the] decision with respect to the application on the applicant and on every person who has made representations [F22to him] with respect to the application.]

Amendments (Textual)

F16. Words in Sch. 1 para. 3. (1) inserted (S.) (27.2.2015 for specified purposes, 1.10.2015 in so far as not already in force) by Historic Environment Scotland Act 2014 (asp 19), s. 31. (2), sch. 2 para. 14. (6)(a) (with ss. 29, 30); S.S.I. 2015/31, art. 2, sch.; S.S.I. 2015/196, art. 2, sch.

F17. Sch. 1 para. 3. (2) substituted for Sch. 1 para. 3. (2)(3) (S.) (27.2.2015 for specified purposes, 1.10.2015 in so far as not already in force) by Historic Environment Scotland Act 2014 (asp 19), s. 31. (2), sch. 2 para. 14. (6)(b) (with ss. 29, 30); S.S.I. 2015/31, art. 2, sch.; S.S.I. 2015/196, art. 2,

sch.
F18. Word in Sch. 1 para. 3. (2) substituted (S.) (1.12.2011) by Historic Environment (Amendment) (Scotland) Act 2011 (asp 3), ss. 17, 33. (2); S.S.I. 2011/372, art. 2, Sch.
F19. Para. 3. (3)(c) inserted by National Heritage Act 1983 (c. 47, SIF 78), s. 41, Sch. 4 para. 68. (3)
F20. Words in Sch. 1 para. 3. (4) inserted (S.) (27.2.2015 for specified purposes, 1.10.2015 in so far as not already in force) by Historic Environment Scotland Act 2014 (asp 19), s. 31. (2), sch. 2 para. 14. (6)(c)(i) (with ss. 29, 30); S.S.I. 2015/31, art. 2, sch.; S.S.I. 2015/196, art. 2, sch.
F21. Word in Sch. 1 para. 3. (4) substituted (S.) (27.2.2015 for specified purposes, 1.10.2015 in so far as not already in force) by Historic Environment Scotland Act 2014 (asp 19), s. 31. (2), sch. 2 para. 14. (6)(c)(ii) (with ss. 29, 30); S.S.I. 2015/31, art. 2, sch.; S.S.I. 2015/196, art. 2, sch.
F22. Words in Sch. 1 para. 3. (4) repealed (S.) (27.2.2015 for specified purposes, 1.10.2015 in so far as not already in force) by Historic Environment Scotland Act 2014 (asp 19), s. 31. (2), sch. 2 para. 14. (6)(c)(iii) (with ss. 29, 30); S.S.I. 2015/31, art. 2, sch.; S.S.I. 2015/196, art. 2, sch.
Modifications etc. (not altering text)
C9. Sch. 1 para. 3 savings for effects of 2014 asp 19, Sch. 2 para. 14 (S.) (1.10.2015) by The Historic Environment Scotland Act 2014 (Saving, Transitional and Consequential Provisions) Order 2015 (S.S.I. 2015/239), arts. 1. (1), 6
4[F23. (1)Subsections (2) to (5) of section 250 of the M1. Local Government Act 1972 (evidence and costs at local inquiries) shall apply to a public local inquiry held in pursuance of paragraph 3. (2) above in relation to a monument situated in England and Wales as they apply where a Minister or the Secretary of State causes an inquiry to be held under subsection (1) of that section.
(2) Subsections (2) to (8) of section 210 of the M2. Local Government (Scotland) Act 1973 (evidence and expenses at local inquiries) shall apply to a public local inquiry held in pursuance of paragraph 3. (2) above in relation to a monument situated in Scotland as they apply where a Minister or the Secretary of State causes an inquiry to be held under subsection (1) of that section.]
Amendments (Textual)
F23. Sch. 1 para. 4 repealed (S.) (27.2.2015 for specified purposes, 1.10.2015 in so far as not already in force) by Historic Environment Scotland Act 2014 (asp 19), s. 31. (2), sch. 2 para. 14. (7) (with ss. 29, 30); S.S.I. 2015/31, art. 2, sch.; S.S.I. 2015/196, art. 2, sch.
Modifications etc. (not altering text)
C10. Sch. 1 para. 4 savings for effects of 2014 asp 19, Sch. 2 para. 14 (S.) (1.10.2015) by The Historic Environment Scotland Act 2014 (Saving, Transitional and Consequential Provisions) Order 2015 (S.S.I. 2015/239), arts. 1. (1), 6
Marginal Citations
M11972 c. 70.
M21973 c. 65.

Part II Modification and Revocation of Scheduled Monument Consent

5[F24. (1)Before giving a direction under section 4 of this Act modifying or revoking a scheduled monument consent the Secretary of State shall serve a notice of proposed modification or revocation on—
(a) the owner of the monument and (if the owner is not the occupier) the occupier of the monument; and
(b) any other person who in the opinion of the Secretary of State would be affected by the proposed modification or revocation.
[F25. (1. A)Where the monument in question is situated in England, the Secretary of State shall consult with the Commission before serving a notice under this paragraph, and on serving such a notice he shall send a copy of it to the Commission.]
(2) A notice under this paragraph shall—

(a) contain a draft of the proposed modification or revocation and a brief statement of the reasons therefor; and
(b) specify the time allowed by sub-paragraph (5) below for making objections to the proposed modification or revocation and the manner in which any such objections can be made.
(3) Where the effect of a proposed modification (or any part of it) would be to exclude any works from the scope of the scheduled monument consent in question or in any manner to affect the execution of any of the works to which the consent relates, the notice under this paragraph relating to that proposed modification shall indicate that the works affected must not be executed after the receipt of the notice or (as the case may require) must not be so executed in a manner specified in the notice.
(4) A notice of proposed revocation under this paragraph shall indicate that the works to which the scheduled monument consent in question relates must not be executed after receipt of the notice.
(5) A person served with a notice under this paragraph may make an objection to the proposed modification or revocation at any time before the end of the period of twenty-eight days beginning with the date on which the notice was served.]
Amendments (Textual)
F24. Sch. 1 paras. 5-9 repealed (S.) (27.2.2015 for specified purposes, 1.10.2015 in so far as not already in force) by Historic Environment Scotland Act 2014 (asp 19), s. 31. (2), sch. 2 para. 15. (a) (with ss. 29, 30); S.S.I. 2015/31, art. 2, sch.; S.S.I. 2015/196, art. 2, sch.
F25. Para. 5. (1. A) inserted by National Heritage Act 1983 (c. 47, SIF 78), s. 41, Sch. 4 para. 68. (4)
Modifications etc. (not altering text)
C11. Sch. 1 paras. 5-9 savings for effects of 2014 asp 19, Sch. 2 para. 15. (a) (S.) (1.10.2015) by The Historic Environment Scotland Act 2014 (Saving, Transitional and Consequential Provisions) Order 2015 (S.S.I. 2015/239), arts. 1. (1), 7
6[F24. (1)If no objection to a proposed modification or revocation is duly made by a person served with notice thereof in accordance with paragraph 5 above, or if all objections so made are withdrawn, the Secretary of State may give a direction under section 4 of this Act modifying or revoking the scheduled monument consent in question in accordance with the notice.
(2) If any objection duly made as mentioned in sub-paragraph (1) above is not withdrawn, then, before giving a direction under section 4 of this Act with respect to the proposed modification or revocation, the Secretary of State shall either—
(a) cause a public local inquiry to be held; or
(b) afford to any such person an opportunity of appearing before and being heard by a person appointed by the Secretary of State for the purpose.
(3) If any person by whom an objection has been made avails himself of the opportunity of being heard, the Secretary of State shall afford to each other person served with notice of the proposed modification or revocation in accordance with paragraph 5 above, and to any other person to whom it appears to the Secretary of State expedient to afford it, an opportunity of being heard on the same occasion.
(4) Before determining in a case within sub-paragraph (2) above whether to give a direction under section 4 of this Act modifying or revoking the scheduled monument consent in accordance with the notice, the Secretary of State—
(a) shall in every case consider any objections duly made as mentioned in sub-paragraph (1) above and not withdrawn; and
(b) shall also, if any inquiry or hearing has been held in accordance with sub-paragraph (2) above, consider the report of the person who held it.
(5) After considering any objections and report he is required to consider in accordance with sub-paragraph (4) above the Secretary of State may give a direction under section 4 of this Act modifying or revoking the scheduled monument consent either in accordance with the notice or with any variation appearing to him to be appropriate.]
Amendments (Textual)
F24. Sch. 1 paras. 5-9 repealed (S.) (27.2.2015 for specified purposes, 1.10.2015 in so far as not

already in force) by Historic Environment Scotland Act 2014 (asp 19), s. 31. (2), sch. 2 para. 15. (a) (with ss. 29, 30); S.S.I. 2015/31, art. 2, sch.; S.S.I. 2015/196, art. 2, sch.
Modifications etc. (not altering text)
C11. Sch. 1 paras. 5-9 savings for effects of 2014 asp 19, Sch. 2 para. 15. (a) (S.) (1.10.2015) by The Historic Environment Scotland Act 2014 (Saving, Transitional and Consequential Provisions) Order 2015 (S.S.I. 2015/239), arts. 1. (1), 7

7[F24. As soon as may be after giving a direction under section 4 of this Act the Secretary of State shall send a copy of the direction to each person served with notice of its proposed effect in accordance with paragraph 5 above and to any other person afforded an opportunity of being heard in accordance with paragraph 6. (3) above.]

Amendments (Textual)
F24. Sch. 1 paras. 5-9 repealed (S.) (27.2.2015 for specified purposes, 1.10.2015 in so far as not already in force) by Historic Environment Scotland Act 2014 (asp 19), s. 31. (2), sch. 2 para. 15. (a) (with ss. 29, 30); S.S.I. 2015/31, art. 2, sch.; S.S.I. 2015/196, art. 2, sch.
Modifications etc. (not altering text)
C11. Sch. 1 paras. 5-9 savings for effects of 2014 asp 19, Sch. 2 para. 15. (a) (S.) (1.10.2015) by The Historic Environment Scotland Act 2014 (Saving, Transitional and Consequential Provisions) Order 2015 (S.S.I. 2015/239), arts. 1. (1), 7

8[F24. (1)Where in accordance with sub-paragraph (3) of paragraph 5 above a notice under that paragraph indicates that any works specified in the notice must not be executed after receipt of the notice, the works so specified shall not be regarded as authorised under Part I of this Act at any time after the relevant service date.
(2) Where in accordance with that sub-paragraph a notice under that paragraph indicates that any works specified in the notice must not be executed after receipt of the notice in a manner so specified, the works so specified shall not be regarded as authorised under Part I of this Act if executed in that manner at any time after the relevant service date.
(3) Where in accordance with sub-paragraph (4) of paragraph 5 above a notice under that paragraph indicates that the works to which the scheduled monument consent relates must not be executed after receipt of the notice, those works shall not be regarded as authorised under Part I of this Act at any time after the relevant service date.
(4) The preceding provisions of this paragraph shall cease to apply in relation to any works affected by a notice under paragraph 5 above—
(a) if within the period of twenty-one months beginning with the relevant service date the Secretary of State gives a direction with respect to the modification or revocation proposed by that notice in accordance with paragraph 6 above, on the date when he gives that direction;
(b) if within that period the Secretary of State serves notice on the occupier or (if there is no occupier) on the owner of the monument that he has determined not to give such a direction, on the date when he serves that notice; and
(c) in any other case, at the end of that period.
(5) In this paragraph "the relevant service date" means, in relation to a notice under paragraph 5 above with respect to works affecting any monument, the date on which that notice was served on the occupier or (if there is no occupier) on the owner of the monument.]

Amendments (Textual)
F24. Sch. 1 paras. 5-9 repealed (S.) (27.2.2015 for specified purposes, 1.10.2015 in so far as not already in force) by Historic Environment Scotland Act 2014 (asp 19), s. 31. (2), sch. 2 para. 15. (a) (with ss. 29, 30); S.S.I. 2015/31, art. 2, sch.; S.S.I. 2015/196, art. 2, sch.
Modifications etc. (not altering text)
C11. Sch. 1 paras. 5-9 savings for effects of 2014 asp 19, Sch. 2 para. 15. (a) (S.) (1.10.2015) by The Historic Environment Scotland Act 2014 (Saving, Transitional and Consequential Provisions) Order 2015 (S.S.I. 2015/239), arts. 1. (1), 7

9[F24. (1)Subject to sub-paragraph (2) below, subsections (2) to (5) of section 250 of the M3. Local Government Act 1972 (evidence and costs at local inquiries) shall apply to a public local inquiry held in pursuance of paragraph 6. (2) above as they apply where a Minister or the

Secretary of State causes an inquiry to be held under subsection (1) of that section.
(2) Subsection (4) of that section (costs of the Minister causing the inquiry to be held to be defrayed by such local authority or party to the inquiry as the Minister may direct) shall not apply except in so far as the Secretary of State is of opinion, having regard to the object and result of the inquiry, that his costs should be defrayed by any party thereto.
(3) In the application of this paragraph to Scotland, in sub-paragraph (1) for the words "subsections (2) to (5) of section 250 of the M4. Local Government Act 1972 (evidence and costs at local inquiries)" there shall be substituted the words "subsections (2) to (8) of section 210 of the M5. Local Government (Scotland) Act 1973 (evidence and expenses at local inquiries)", and in sub-paragraph (2) for the words "subsection (4) of that section (costs" there shall be substituted the words "subsection (7) of that section (expenses".]
Amendments (Textual)
F24. Sch. 1 paras. 5-9 repealed (S.) (27.2.2015 for specified purposes, 1.10.2015 in so far as not already in force) by Historic Environment Scotland Act 2014 (asp 19), s. 31. (2), sch. 2 para. 15. (a) (with ss. 29, 30); S.S.I. 2015/31, art. 2, sch.; S.S.I. 2015/196, art. 2, sch.
Modifications etc. (not altering text)
C11. Sch. 1 paras. 5-9 savings for effects of 2014 asp 19, Sch. 2 para. 15. (a) (S.) (1.10.2015) by The Historic Environment Scotland Act 2014 (Saving, Transitional and Consequential Provisions) Order 2015 (S.S.I. 2015/239), arts. 1. (1), 7
Marginal Citations
M3 1972 c. 70.
M4 1972 c. 70.
M5 1973 c. 65.
[F26 10. (1) Except as provided for in paragraph 11, an order made by Historic Environment Scotland under section 4 modifying or revoking a scheduled monument consent does not take effect unless it is confirmed by the Scottish Ministers.S
(2) Where Historic Environment Scotland submits an order to the Scottish Ministers for confirmation, it must serve notice on—
(a) the owner of the scheduled monument affected,
(b) where the owner is not the occupier of the monument, the occupier, and
(c) any other person who in its opinion will be affected by the order.
(3) The notice must specify the period (which must not be less than 28 days after its service) within which any person on whom it is served may require an opportunity of appearing before and being heard by a person appointed by the Scottish Ministers for the purpose.
(4) If within that period a person on whom the notice is served so requires, the Scottish Ministers must, before they confirm the order, give such an opportunity both to that person and to Historic Environment Scotland.
(5) The Scottish Ministers may confirm any such order submitted to them either without modification or subject to such modifications as they consider expedient.
Amendments (Textual)
F26. Sch. 1 paras. 10, 11 inserted (27.2.2015 for specified purposes, 1.10.2015 in so far as not already in force) by Historic Environment Scotland Act 2014 (asp 19), s. 31. (2), sch. 2 para. 15. (b) (with ss. 29, 30); S.S.I. 2015/31, art. 2, sch.; S.S.I. 2015/196, art. 2, sch.
Modifications etc. (not altering text)
C12. Sch. 1 para. 10 savings for effects of 2014 asp 19, Sch. 2 para. 15. (b) (S.) (1.10.2015) by The Historic Environment Scotland Act 2014 (Saving, Transitional and Consequential Provisions) Order 2015 (S.S.I. 2015/239), arts. 1. (1), 7
11. (1) Where sub-paragraph (2) applies, Historic Environment Scotland—S
(a) need not submit the order under section 4 modifying or revoking the scheduled monument consent to the Scottish Ministers for approval,
(b) must instead take the steps mentioned in sub-paragraph (3).
(2) This sub-paragraph applies where—
(a) the owner of the scheduled monument affected,

(b) where the owner is not the occupier of the monument, the occupier, and
(c) all other persons who in Historic Environment Scotland's opinion will be affected by the order, have notified Historic Environment Scotland in writing that they do not object to the order.
(3) The steps referred to in sub-paragraph (1)(b) are—
(a) advertising in the prescribed manner the fact that the order has been made,
(b) serving notice to the same effect on the persons mentioned in sub-paragraph (2), and
(c) sending a copy of any such advertisement to the Scottish Ministers not more than 3 days after its publication.
(4) The advertisement under sub-paragraph (3)(a) must specify—
(a) the period within which persons affected by the order may give notice to the Scottish Ministers that they require an opportunity of appearing before and being heard by a person appointed by the Scottish Ministers for the purpose, and
(b) the period at the end of which, if no such notice is given to the Scottish Ministers, the order may take effect by virtue of this paragraph and without being confirmed by the Scottish Ministers.
(5) The period referred to in sub-paragraph (4)(a) must not be less than 28 days from the date on which the advertisement first appears.
(6) The period referred to in sub-paragraph (4)(b) must not be less than 14 days from the end of the period referred to in sub-paragraph (4)(a).
(7) The notice under sub-paragraph (3)(b) must include a statement to the effect that no compensation is payable under section 9 in respect of an order which takes effect by virtue of this paragraph.
(8) The order takes effect at the end of the period referred to in sub-paragraph (4)(b) without being confirmed by the Scottish Ministers if—
(a) no person claiming to be affected by the order has given notice to the Scottish Ministers as mentioned in sub-paragraph (4)(a) within the period referred to in that sub-paragraph, and
(b) the Scottish Ministers have not directed that the order be submitted to them for confirmation.]
Amendments (Textual)
F26. Sch. 1 paras. 10, 11 inserted (27.2.2015 for specified purposes, 1.10.2015 in so far as not already in force) by Historic Environment Scotland Act 2014 (asp 19), s. 31. (2), sch. 2 para. 15. (b) (with ss. 29, 30); S.S.I. 2015/31, art. 2, sch.; S.S.I. 2015/196, art. 2, sch.
Modifications etc. (not altering text)
C13. Sch. 1 para. 11 savings for effects of 2014 asp 19, Sch. 2 para. 15. (b) (S.) (1.10.2015) by The Historic Environment Scotland Act 2014 (Saving, Transitional and Consequential Provisions) Order 2015 (S.S.I. 2015/239), arts. 1. (1), 7

Schedule 2. DETERMINATION OF CERTAIN APPEALS BY PERSON APPOINTED BY THE SCOTTISH MINISTERS

(introduced by sections 1. E(4), 4. D(6) and 9. CB(4))
Amendments (Textual)
F1. Sch. 1. A inserted (27.2.2015 for specified purposes, 1.10.2015 in so far as not already in force) by Historic Environment Scotland Act 2014 (asp 19), s. 31. (2), sch. 2 para. 34 (with ss. 29, 30); S.S.I. 2015/31, art. 2, sch.; S.S.I. 2015/196, art. 2, sch.

Determination of appeals by appointed personS

1. (1)The Scottish Ministers may by regulations prescribe classes of appeals under sections 1. C, 4. B and 9. C which are to be determined by a person appointed by the Scottish Ministers for the

purpose.S
(2) Those classes of appeals are to be so determined except in such classes of case—
(a) as may for the time being be prescribed, or
(b) as may be specified in directions given by the Scottish Ministers.
(3) Regulations under sub-paragraph (1) may provide for the giving of publicity to any directions given by the Scottish Ministers under this paragraph.
(4) This paragraph does not affect any provision made by or under this Act that an appeal is to lie to, or a notice of an appeal is to be served on, the Scottish Ministers.
(5) A person appointed under this paragraph is referred to in this schedule as an "appointed person".

Powers and duties of appointed personS

2. (1)An appointed person is to have the same powers and duties—S
(a) in relation to an appeal under section 1. C as the Scottish Ministers have under section 1. D,
(b) in relation to an appeal under section 4. B as the Scottish Ministers have under section 4. C,
(c) in relation to an appeal under section 9. C as the Scottish Ministers have under section 9. CA.
(2) Where an appeal has been determined by an appointed person, the decision is to be treated as a decision of the Scottish Ministers.
(3) Except as provided for by section 55, the decision of an appointed person on any appeal is final.

Determination of appeals by the Scottish MinistersS

3. (1)The Scottish Ministers may, if they think fit, direct that an appeal which would otherwise fall to be determined by an appointed person is instead to be determined by them.S
(2) Such a direction must—
(a) state the reasons for which it is given, and
(b) be served on the appellant.
(3) Where an appeal under section 1. C, 4. B or 9. C falls to be determined by the Scottish Ministers by virtue of a direction under this paragraph, the provisions of this Act which are relevant to the appeal are to apply, subject to sub-paragraph (4), as if this schedule had never applied to it.
(4) In determining the appeal, the Scottish Ministers may take into account any report made to them by any person previously appointed to determine the appeal.
4. (1)The Scottish Ministers may by a further direction revoke a direction under paragraph 3 at any time before the determination of the appeal.S
(2) Such a further direction must—
(a) state the reasons for which it is given, and
(b) be served on—
(i) the person, if any, previously appointed to determine the appeal, and
(ii) the appellant.
(3) Where such a further direction has been given, the provisions of this schedule relevant to the appeal are to apply, subject to sub-paragraph (4), as if no direction under paragraph 3 had been given.
(4) Anything done by or on behalf of the Scottish Ministers in connection with the appeal which might have been done by the appointed person (including any arrangements made for the holding of a hearing or local inquiry) is, unless that person directs otherwise, to be treated as having been done by that person.

Appointment of another person to determine appealS

5. (1)At any time before the appointed person has determined the appeal the Scottish Ministers may—S
(a) revoke the appointment, and
(b) appoint another person under paragraph 1 to determine the appeal instead.
(2) Where such a new appointment is made, the consideration of the appeal or any inquiry or other hearing in connection with it is to be begun afresh.
(3) Nothing in sub-paragraph (2) requires any person to be given an opportunity of making fresh representations or modifying or withdrawing any representations already made.

Local inquiries and hearingsS

6. (1)Whether or not the parties to an appeal have asked for an opportunity to appear and be heard, an appointed person—S
(a) may hold a local inquiry in connection with the appeal, and
(b) must do so if the Scottish Ministers so direct.
(2) Where an appointed person—
(a) holds a hearing, or
(b) holds an inquiry by virtue of this paragraph,
an assessor may be appointed by the Scottish Ministers to sit with the appointed person at the hearing or inquiry to advise the appointed person on any matters arising.
(3) Subject to sub-paragraph (4), the expenses of any such hearing or inquiry are to be paid by the Scottish Ministers.
(4) Subsections (4) to (13) of section 265 of the Town and Country Planning (Scotland) Act 1997 (c.8) apply to an inquiry held under this paragraph as they apply to an inquiry held under that section.
(5) The appointed person has the same power to make orders under subsection (9) of that section in relation to proceedings under this schedule which do not give rise to an inquiry as the person has in relation to such an inquiry.
(6) For the purposes of this paragraph, references to the Minister in subsections (9) and (12) of that section are to be read as references to the appointed person.

Supplementary provisionsS

7. The functions of determining an appeal and doing anything in connection with it conferred by this schedule on an appointed person who is a member of the staff of the Scottish Administration are to be treated for the purposes of the Scottish Public Services Ombudsman Act 2002 (asp 11) as functions conferred on the Scottish Ministers.]S

Schedule 3. Designation Orders

Section 33.

Designation orders by the Secretary of State

1. (1)A designation order made by the Secretary of State shall describe by reference to a map the area affected.
(2) The map shall be to such a scale, and the order in such form, as the Secretary of State considers appropriate.
2. Before making a designation order the Secretary of State shall—

(a) consult each of the local authorities concerned; and
[F1. (aa)consult with the Commission (if the area which would be designated by the order is situated in England); and]
(b) publish notice of his proposal to make the order;
in accordance with paragraph 3 below.
Amendments (Textual)
F1. Para. 2. (aa) inserted by National Heritage Act 1983 (c. 47, SIF 78), s. 41, Sch. 4 para. 69. (2)
3. (1)The [F2consultations required by sub-paragraphs (a)(aa)] of paragraph 2 above shall precede the publication of the notice required by sub-paragraph (b) of that paragraph.
(2) The notice required by paragraph 2. (b) above—
(a) shall be published in two successive weeks in the London Gazette and in one or more local newspapers circulating in the locality in which the area affected is situated;
(b) shall state that the Secretary of State proposes to make the order, describing the area affected and the effect of the order; and
(c) shall indicate where (in accordance with paragraphs 4 and 5 below) a copy of the draft order and of the map to which it refers may be inspected.
Amendments (Textual)
F2. Words substituted by National Heritage Act 1983 (c. 47, SIF 78), s. 41, Sch. 4 para. 69. (3)
4. Copies of the draft order and of the map to which it refers—
(a) shall be deposited with each of the local authorities concerned on or before the date on which notice of the Secretary of State's proposal to make the order is first published in accordance with paragraph 3. (2)(a) above; and
[F3. (aa)shall be sent to the Commission (if the area which would be designated by the order is situated in England); and]
(b) shall be kept available for public inspection by each of those authorities, free of charge, at reasonable hours and at a convenient place, until the Secretary of State makes the order or notifies the local authority in question that he has determined not to make it.
Amendments (Textual)
F3. Para. 4. (aa) inserted by National Heritage Act 1983 (c. 47, SIF 78), s. 41, Sch. 4 para. 69. (4)
5. Copies of the draft order and of the map to which it refers shall similarly be kept available by the Secretary of State, until he makes the order or determines not to make it.
6. The Secretary of State may make the order, either without modifications or with such modification only as consists in reducing the area affected, at any time after the end of the period of six weeks beginning with the date on which notice of his proposal to make the order is first published in accordance with paragraph 3. (2)(a) above.
7. On making the order, the Secretary of State shall—
(a) publish notice in two successive weeks in the London Gazette and in one or more local newspapers circulating in the locality in which the area affected is situated, stating that the order has been made and describing the area affected and the effect of the order; and
(b) deposit a copy of the order and of the map to which it refers with each local authority concerned. [F4and
(c) send to the Commission a copy of the order and of the map to which it refers (if the area designated is situated in England).]
Amendments (Textual)
F4. Para. 7. (c) inserted by National Heritage Act 1983 (c. 47, SIF 78), s. 41, Sch. 4 para. 69. (5)

Designation orders by a local authority

8. (1)A designation order made by a local authority shall describe by reference to a map the area affected.
(2) The map shall be to such a scale, and the order in such form as may be prescribed.
9. Before making a designation order a local authority shall—

(a) consult any other local authority concerned; and
(b) publish notice of their proposal to make the order;
in accordance with paragraph 10 below.
[F59. ABefore making a designation order a local authority shall notify the Commission of their proposal to make the order, if the area which would be designated by the order is situated in England.]
Amendments (Textual)
F5. Para. 9. A inserted by National Heritage Act 1983 (c. 47, SIF 78), s. 41, Sch. 4 para. 69. (6)
10. (1)The consultation required by sub-paragraph (a) of paragraph 9 above shall precede the publication of the notice required by sub-paragraph (b) of that paragraph.
(2) The notice required by paragraph 9. (b) above shall be in the prescribed form and shall otherwise comply with paragraph 3. (2) above (with the necessary modifications).
11. Copies of the draft order and of the map to which it refers—
(a) shall be deposited with each of the local authorities concerned (other than the local authority proposing to make the order) on or before the date on which notice of the proposal to make the order is first published in accordance with paragraph 3. (2)(a) above as applied by paragraph 10 above; and
(b) shall be kept available for public inspection by each of the local authorities concerned, free of charge at reasonable hours and at a convenient place, until the local authority proposing to make the order either make it or determine not to make it and, in the case of any other local authority concerned, notify that local authority of their determination.
12. The local authority may make the order, either without modifications or with such modification only as consists in reducing the area affected, and submit it to the Secretary of State for confirmation, at any time after the end of the period of six weeks beginning with the date on which notice of their proposal to make the order is first published in accordance with paragraph 3. (2)(a) above as applied by paragraph 10 above.
13. A designation order made by a local authority shall not take effect unless it is confirmed by the Secretary of State, and the Secretary of State may confirm any such order either without modifications or with such modification only as consists in reducing the area affected.
14. If the Secretary of State confirms the order the local authority shall on being notified that the order has been confirmed—
(a) publish notice of the making of the order in the manner and form prescribed; and
(b) deposit a copy of the order and of the map to which it refers with any other local authority concerned. [F6and
(c) send to the Commission a copy of the order and of the map to which it refers, if the area designated is situated in England.]
Amendments (Textual)
F6. Para. 14. (c) inserted by National Heritage Act 1983 (c. 47, SIF 78), s. 41, Sch. 4 para. 69. (7)
15. The Secretary of State may by regulations prescribe the procedure to be followed by a local authority in submitting a designation order for confirmation by the Secretary of State.

[F7 Designation orders by the Commission]

Amendments (Textual)
F7. Para. 15. A inserted by Local Government Act 1985 (c. 51, SIF 81:1), s. 6, Sch. 2 para. 2. (4)
[F815. A Paragraphs 8, 9, 10 to 13, 14. (a) and (b) and 15 above shall have effect in relation to a designation order made by the Commission as if—
(a) in paragraphs 8. (1), 12, 13 and 15 the references to a local authority were a reference to the Commission;
(b) in paragraphs 9 and 14 the first reference to a local authority were a reference to the Commission, and the word "other" were omitted; and
(c) in paragraph 11—

(i) in sub-paragraph (a) the words in brackets were omitted; and
(ii) in sub-paragraph (b) the reference to the local authority proposing to make the order were a reference to the Commission, and the word "other" were omitted.]
Amendments (Textual)
F8. Para. 15. A inserted by Local Government Act 1985 (c. 51, SIF 81:1), s. 6, Sch. 2 para. 2. (4)

Operation of designation orders

16. (1)A designation order made by the Secretary of State shall not come into operation until the end of the period of six months beginning with the date on which it is made.
(2) A designation order made by a local authority and confirmed by the Secretary of State shall not come into operation until the end of the period of six months beginning with the date on which it is confirmed.

Variation and revocation of designation orders

17. (1)An order varying or revoking a designation order shall describe by reference to a map the area affected by the designation order and (in the case of an order varying a designation order) the reduction of that area made by the order.
(2) The map shall be to such a scale, and the order in such form, as the Secretary of State considers appropriate.
18. Before and on making an order varying or revoking a designation order the Secretary of State shall follow the procedure laid down for the making by him of a designation order, and paragraphs 2 to 7 above shall accordingly apply in any such case (taking references to the area affected as references to the area affected by the designation order).

Scotland

19. In relation to a designation order relating to an area in Scotland, references in this Schedule to the London Gazette shall be construed as references to the Edinburgh Gazette.

Interpretation

20. (1)In this Schedule "the area affected" means, in relation to a designation order, the area to which the order for the time being relates.
(2) For the purposes of this Schedule a local authority is a local authority concerned in relation to a designation order (or in relation to an order varying or revoking a designation order) if the area affected by the designation order, or any part of that area, is within the area of that local authority.

Schedule 4. Transitional Provisions

Section 64. (1).
1. (1)Where an interim preservation notice is in force with respect to any monument immediately before the commencement of this Act, sections 10. (3)(a) and (c) and 12. (1), (2)(b), (3)(b) and (4) of the M1. Historic Buildings and Ancient Monuments Act 1953 shall continue to apply to the notice and monument respectively as if this Act had not been passed, unless and until the monument is included in the Schedule under section 1. (3) of this Act.
(2) So long as by virtue of sub-paragraph (1) above section 12. (1) of the Historic Buildings and Ancient Monuments Act 1953 continues to apply after the commencement of this Act to any

monument which is under guardianship by virtue of this Act, section 28 of this Act shall have effect in relation to that monument as if for the reference in subsection (2) of that section to a scheduled monument consent there were substituted a reference to the consent of the Secretary of State under section 12. (1).
Marginal Citations
M11953 c. 49.

2. (1)Subject to sub-paragraph (2) below, where a guardianship order made under section 12. (5) of the M2. Historic Buildings and Ancient Monuments Act 1953 is in force immediately before the commencement of this Act that order shall continue in force notwithstanding the repeal by this Act of section 12. (5), and the provisions of this Act shall apply while the order is in force as if the Secretary of State had been constituted guardian of the monument by a deed not containing any restriction not contained in the order and executed by all the persons who, at the time when the order was made, were able by deed to constitute the Secretary of State guardian of the monument.
(2) A guardianship order continued in force by this paragraph may be revoked at any time by the Secretary of State.
Marginal Citations
M21953 c. 49.

3. (1)Where within the period of three months immediately preceding the commencement of this Act a person has given notice in accordance with section 6. (2) of the M3. Ancient Monuments Act 1931 of his intention to execute or permit to be executed any such work in relation to a monument as is there mentioned the notice shall have effect for the purposes of this Act as an application for scheduled monument consent for the execution of that work.
(2) Where—
(a) a monument becomes a scheduled monument under this Act; and
(b) before it is included in the Schedule any person has applied for the consent of the Secretary of State for the execution of any works affecting the monument which would otherwise be prohibited by section 12. (1) of the M4. Historic Buildings and Ancient Monuments Act 1953 (consent required for certain works in relation to a monument subject to an interim preservation notice or preservation order);
then, in a case where the Secretary of State's decision on the application has not been notified to the person in question before the monument is included in the Schedule, the application shall have effect for the purposes of this Act as an application for scheduled monument consent for the execution of those works.
(3) The Secretary of State shall consider and determine any application for scheduled monument consent which has effect as such by virtue of this paragraph notwithstanding that any requirements of regulations made by virtue of paragraph 1 or any requirements of paragraph 2 of Schedule 1 to this Act are not satisfied in relation to that application.
Marginal Citations
M31931 c. 16.
M41953 c. 49.

4. (1)Subject to the following provisions of this paragraph, where a person has given notice as mentioned in paragraph 3. (1) above with respect to any work more than three months before the commencement of this Act, the notice shall have effect for the purposes of this Act as if it were a scheduled monument consent for the execution of that work granted by the Secretary of State under section 2 of this Act on the date of the commencement of this Act (and it may be modified or revoked by the Secretary of State under section 4 of this Act accordingly).
(2) This paragraph does not apply in any case where an interim preservation notice or a preservation order is in force with respect to the monument in question immediately before the commencement of this Act.
(3) A scheduled monument consent which has effect as such by virtue of this paragraph shall not cease to have effect by virtue of section 4. (1) of this Act if any of the work to which it relates has been executed or started before the commencement of this Act.

5. (1)Subject to sub-paragraph (2) below, where—

(a) a monument becomes a scheduled monument under this Act; and
(b) before it is included in the Schedule the Secretary of State has granted consent for the execution of any works affecting the monument under section 12. (1) of the M5. Historic Buildings and Ancient Monuments Act 1953;
that consent shall have effect for the purposes of this Act as if it were a scheduled monument consent for the execution of those works granted by the Secretary of State under section 2 of this Act on the date when the monument became a scheduled monument (and it may be modified or revoked by the Secretary of State under section 4 of this Act accordingly).
(2) A scheduled monument consent which has effect as such by virtue of this paragraph shall not cease to have effect by virtue of section 4. (1) of this Act if any of the works to which it relates have been executed or started before the monument becomes a scheduled monument.
Marginal Citations
M51953 c. 49.
6. (1)[F1. Section 13. (2) of this Act shall not apply to any monument of which the Secretary of State or a local authority have been constituted guardians before the commencement of this Act, except where either—
(a) the guardianship deed provided for control and management of the monument by the guardians; or
(b) the persons for the time being immediately affected by the operation of the guardianship deed have consented to the exercise of control and management of the monument by the guardians.]
(2) Section 19. (1) of this Act shall not apply to any monument of which the M6. Secretary of State or a local authority had been constituted guardians before 15th August 1913 (being the date of commencement of the Ancient Monuments Consolidation and Amendment Act 1913), except where either—
(a) the guardianship deed provided for public access to the monument; or
(b) the persons for the time being immediately affected by the operation of the guardianship deed have consented to the public having access to the monument.
(3) Where any land adjoining or adjacent to a monument (in addition to its site) was acquired or taken into guardianship before the commencement of this Act under any enactment repealed by this Act, it shall be regarded for the purposes of this Act as having been acquired or taken into guardianship for a purpose relating to that monument by virtue of section 15 of this Act.
Amendments (Textual)
F1. Sch. 3 para. 6. (1) repealed (S.) (30.6.2011) by Historic Environment (Amendment) (Scotland) Act 2011 (asp 3), ss. 7. (5), 33. (2); S.S.I. 2011/174, art. 2, Sch.
Marginal Citations
M61913 c. 32.
7. Notwithstanding the repeal by this Act of the M7. Field Monuments Act 1972, the provisions of that Act shall continue to apply in relation to any acknowledgement payment agreement within the meaning of that Act which is in force immediately before the commencement of this Act.
Marginal Citations
M71972 c. 43.
8. Any reference in any document (including an enactment) to an enactment repealed by this Act shall be construed as or (as the case may be) as including a reference to the corresponding enactment in this Act.
9. Nothing in the preceding provisions of this Schedule shall be construed as prejudicing the effect of section 16 or 17 of the M8. Interpretation Act 1978 (effect of repeals).
Marginal Citations
M81978 c. 30.
10. In this Schedule—
"interim preservation notice" means a notice served under section 10. (1) of the M9. Historic Buildings and Ancient Monuments Act 1953; and
" preservation order" means an order made under section 11. (1) of that Act.
Marginal Citations

M9 1953 c. 49.

Schedule 5. Consequential amendments

Section 64. (2).
Editorial Information
X1. The text of Sch. 4 is in the form in which it was originally enacted: it was not reproduced in Statutes in Force and, except as specified, does not reflect any amendments or repeals which may have been made prior to 1.2.1991.
1. . . . . F1.
Amendments (Textual)
F1. Sch. 4 para. 1 repealed by Electricity Act 1989 (c. 29, SIF 44:1), s. 112. (3)(4), Sch. 17 para. 35. (1), Sch. 18
2. In section 47. (d) of the M1 Coast Protection Act 1949 (saving for law relating to ancient monuments), for the words "the Ancient Monuments Acts 1913 to 1931" there shall be substituted the words "the Ancient Monuments and Archaeological Areas Act 1979".
Marginal Citations
M1 1949 c. 74
3. (1)In sections 5. (2)(b) and 8. (1)(c) of the M2 Historic Buildings and Ancient Monuments Act 1953, for the words "the Ancient Monuments Consolidation and Amendment Act 1913" there shall be substituted the words "the Ancient Monuments and Archaeological Areas Act 1979".
(2) In section 8. (4) of that Act, for the words "the said Act of 1913" there shall be substituted the words "the said Act of 1979".
Marginal Citations
M2 1953 c. 49.
F2 4. . . . .
Amendments (Textual)
F2. Sch. 4 para. 4 repealed (30.11.1991) by Coal Mining Subsidence Act 1991 (c. 45, SIF 86), s. 53. (2), Sch.8 (with Sch. 7); S.I. 1991/2508, art.2
5. In section 6. (4)(b) of the M3. Land Powers (Defence) Act 1958 (restriction on use of land for training purposes)—
(a) for the words from "a list" to "1913" there shall be substituted the words "the Schedule compiled and maintained under section 1 of the Ancient Monuments and Archaeological Areas Act 1979"; and
(b) the words from "or which" to "1953" shall cease to have effect, except in relation to a monument to which paragraph 1. (1) of Schedule 3 to this Act applies.
Marginal Citations
M3 1958 c.30.
6[F3 In section 17. (2) of the M4 Building (Scotland) Act 1959 (requirements with respect to operations under that Act to be subject to special controls for ancient monuments and historic buildings)—
(a) for paragraph (a) there shall be substituted the following paragraph —
"(a)a building which is for the time being included in the Schedule of monuments compiled and maintained under section 1 of the Ancient Monuments and Archaeological Areas Act 1979";
(b) paragraph (d) and the words "or, as the case may be, the said Act of 1953" shall cease to have effect, except in relation to a monument to which paragraph 1. (1) of Schedule 3 to this Act applies ; and
(c) for the words "the said Act of 1931" there shall be substituted the words "the said Act of 1979 or".]
Amendments (Textual)
F3. Sch. 4 para. 6 repealed (S.) (1.5.2005) by Building (Scotland) Act 2003 (asp 8), s. 59. (1), Sch.

6 para. 13 (with s. 53); S.S.I. 2004/404, art. 2. (1)
Marginal Citations
M4 1959 c.24.
7. In section 3. (3)(a) of the M5. Flood Prevention (Scotland) Act 1961 (Act not to authorise contraventions of certain enactments), for the words "the Ancient Monuments Acts 1913 to 1953" there shall be substituted the words "the Ancient Monuments and Archaeological Areas Act 1979".
Marginal Citations
M5 1961 c.41.
8. In section 2. (5) of the M6. Faculty Jurisdiction Measure 1964 (limit on authority conferred by faculty for demolition of church), for the words "the Ancient Monuments Acts 1913 to 1953" there shall be substituted the words "the Ancient Monuments and Archaeological Areas Act 1979".
Marginal Citations
M6 1964 No. 5.
9. In section 7. (8) of the M7. Mines (Working Facilities and Support) Act 1966 (right to apply for restrictions on working minerals to secure support)—
(a) for the words "the Ancient Monuments Consolidation and Amendment Act 1913" there shall be substituted the words "the Ancient Monuments and Archaeological Areas Act 1979"; and.
(b) the words "or Part II of the Historic Buildings and Ancient Monuments Act 1953" shall be omitted.
Marginal Citations
M7 1966 c.4.
10. . . . . F4.
Amendments (Textual)
F4. Sch. 4 para. 10 repealed for financial years beginning in or after 1990 by Local Government Finance Act 1988 (c. 41, SIF 81:1), ss. 142, 149, Sch. 13 Pt. I (subject to any saving under s. 117. (8) of that 1988 Act)
11. . . . . F5.
Amendments (Textual)
F5. Sch. 4 para. 11 repealed by Planning (Consequential Provisions) Act 1990 (c. 11, SIF 123:1, 2), s. 3, Sch. 1
F6 12. . . . .
Amendments (Textual)
F6. Sch. 4 para. 12 repealed (27.5.1997) by 1997 c. 11, ss. 3, 6. (2), Sch. 1 Pt.I (with s. 5, Sch. 3)
13. In section 131. (2) of the M8 Local Government Act 1972 (general powers of local authority with respect to dealings in land not to affect certain enactments), for paragraph (f) there shall be substituted the following paragraph —
"(f)the Ancient Monuments and Archaeological Areas Act 1979".
Marginal Citations
M8 1972 c. 70.
14. In section 182. (1) of the M9. Local Government (Scotland) Act 1973 (functions of local authorities under the Ancient Monuments Acts to be district planning functions), for the words "the Ancient Monuments Acts 1913 and 1931" there shall be substituted the words "the Ancient Monuments and Archaeological Areas Act 1979".
Marginal Citations
M9 1973 c. 65.
15. . . . . F7.
Amendments (Textual)
F7. Sch. 4 para. 15 repealed by Capital Transfer Tax Act 1984 (c. 51, SIF 65), s. 277, Sch. 9
F8 16. In section 111 of the M10. Land Drainage Act 1976 (protection of ancient monuments), for the words "the Ancient Monuments Acts 1913 to 1972" there shall be substituted the words "the Ancient Monuments and Archaeological Areas Act 1979".S

Amendments (Textual)
F8. Sch. 4 para. 16 repealed (E.W.)(1.12.1991) by Water Consolidation (Consequential Provisions) Act 1991 (c. 60, SIF 130), ss. 3, 4. (2), Sch. 3 PartI (with Sch. 2 paras. 10, 14. (1), 15)
Marginal Citations
M101976 c. 70

Schedule 6. Enactments Repealed

Section 64. (3).
Editorial Information
X1. The text of Sch. 5 is in the form in which it was originally enacted: it was not reproduced in Statutes in Force and does not reflect any amendments or repeals which may have been made prior to 1.2.1991.

Open Government Licence v3.0

Contains public sector information licensed under the Open Government Licence v3.0.
The full licence if available at the following address:
http://www.nationalarchives.gov.uk/doc/open-government-licence/version/3/

Printed in Great Britain
by Amazon